PUT AWAY

BUT NOT DIVORCED

ROBERT WATERS

James Kay Publishing

Tulsa, Oklahoma

Put Away But Not Divorced
ISBN 978-1-943245-75-8

www.jameskaypublishing.com

e-mail: sales@jameskaypublishing.com

Original Published by Waters Publications
178 Madison 8657
Huntsville, AR 72740

Cover image "The Mariner's Wife"
© The Metropolitan Museum of Art
Image source: Art Resource, NY

Author Photo by Brandi Holt

FOREWORD

I first came face to face with the traditional theory on divorce and remarriage way back in 1960 when I was a young minister in the early part of my career. The doctrine brought trouble of an unusual kind into my ministry, forcing me to deal with it. It appeared that the theory had no Biblical foundation, but our brotherhood had accepted it everywhere I looked. It therefore became necessary to search out the facts.

But where could I begin my investigation? Almost no one had written on the subject, and most of the writings I did find supported the traditional view. I would have loved to have been able to get my hands on a book like this one by Robert Waters, which lays out just about every argument that has been put forth on the issue. But, as I said, we had no such material fifty years ago and I was alone to do my research.

I am glad that now the situation is better because many brethren are speaking out regarding divorce and subsequent marriage in books, articles, and sermons. That is where this book will be helpful. Robert and I have some differences on how to approach a point, but we do not differ on conclusions. We come out at the same place. We find that the traditional view is a human theory.

Near the end of the book Robert quotes Foy Wallace Jr., who rightly said that although Jesus condemned marriage breaking, He did NOT prescribe a "disciplinary procedure" and thus we cannot make one without human legislation. Robert and I both respect God's stated will that each person have a mate. Robert has experienced the frustration of trying to find the truth in the confused circumstances surrounding this subject. He has done a lot of research to get where he is, and he shares that in this book, cutting a wide swath so the reader will be able to look at good information and clear treatment of every point.

It is important that we survey the whole field and study this subject fully from the standpoint of what the Bible says about it. Many people are faced with decisions on this topic, and their conclusions have eternal consequences. They need some Bible answers. As Waters points out, God placed great importance on the role of marriage in preventing fornication. Forbidding marriage flies in the face of the need for everyone to have a mate. Those who insist on the breakup of marriages should especially stop and look this matter over again.

I welcome this book by Robert Waters. It is my prayer that God will bless the material that is put forth here to the intended purpose of God to give blessings to those who follow His will.

Olan Hicks

THE AUTHOR

What makes me uniquely qualified to write a book on divorce and remarriage—a very important, controversial, and complex subject? I am sixty-three years old and married to my first and only wife. I completed college with a degree in agricultural education. Other credits include one year at Florida College and three other colleges. I finished college in 1978 and immediately began preaching the gospel full-time. Divorce and remarriage was an immediate concern because I had been associated with brethren who taught the traditional position on divorce and remarriage (i.e., that divorced persons are not eligible for marriage). During my home study ministry, I occasionally taught people who were in second marriages. I did as a number of preachers do—I showed them Matthew 19:9 and let them decide whether they should break up their marriage. In most cases, they were unable to accept the "hard saying" or were unwilling to do as they were led to believe the text taught. This was very disturbing, and in the back of my mind, I knew something was not right about what I was teaching. I was not fully convinced of the truthfulness of this doctrine. Things just didn't add up. Even though I had been taught how to study and had access to many books and journals, the teaching I had heard on divorce and remarriage was not in harmony with God's character—particularly the teaching that those innocent of wrongdoing in a divorce must remain celibate if they did not instigate the divorce for fornication. For this reason, I continually put off preaching or writing on the issue. As a gospel preacher, I had been taught the responsibility to teach only the truth and I wanted to be sure I was right. After five years in the ministry, I decided to get out of full-time preaching. I continued to preach but was no longer dependent upon the church for my livelihood. This helped me to be more open-minded in my study. I could not only be more honest and open in my study but could also teach without fear of being fired and ostracized, which would bring hardships on my family if they had to move repeatedly from one place to another. In 1991, I was given some material that made more sense than anything I had seen. A woman gave me a video by Olan Hicks that was very helpful. But still cautious, I studied the subject diligently for about ten more years before preaching a sermon or writing a formal article. In the meantime, I got into numerous discussions on various Internet lists. These discussions helped me greatly in my effort to come to the knowledge of the truth and to be able to defend it. Olan's material helped me to learn the error of the traditional position and to have a grasp of the teaching of Paul; however, after a few years of seeking to defend Olan's position, with some difficulty, I learned of a position that made Jesus's teachings fully understandable, easy to teach, and easy to sustain in honorable debate. It was a position that made so much sense it caused defenders of the divorce and remarriage (MDR) tradition to scratch their heads as they sought to discredit me and my position. The title of this book, *Put Away but Not Divorced,* gives the reader a hint as to what I learned and the position I hold, which I have shared with thousands in this country and around the world through my website called **TotalHealth.bz** and through Facebook groups. I have fully tested the position I hold (though it is not new) and have found that very few defenders of tradition, including seasoned debaters, are willing to engage in honorable debate because the truth is so simple and so hard to defeat.

TABLE OF CONTENTS

A chapter by chapter study guide may be downloaded from www.TotalHealth.bz

CHAPTER 1:

PREPARING THE MIND TO COMBAT HUMAN TRADITION

Because of the ramifications, divorce and remarriage is one of the most hotly debated biblical issues in the church today. Many people find this issue to be a challenging subject. Preachers and dedicated Bible students have written numerous books and engaged in countless discussions seeking to answer the question of whether one who has been divorced, or has divorced, may marry again. Yet Christians are far from united on this issue. Many find it so difficult and troublesome to discern the truth that they refuse to even open their mind to an honest study of the subject. Others are so fully convinced they have the answer and that what they know is so vital to truth and morality, they will have no fellowship with those who differ with them.

Misleading teaching has led to needless guilt in the hearts of many people as they struggle to please God in regard to their marital status. Many homes have been destroyed and souls lost because of well-meaning, although misinformed, teachers who think they are merely teaching what Jesus taught.

A study of this subject will be unproductive if the desire is to prove tradition rather than find the truth. One's study will also be fruitless if he does not apply good hermeneutics. The following criteria are important:

1. one must seek a position that allows inspired writers to be in harmony;
2. key words must be properly defined (see the appendix);
3. the student must be willing to reject theories that have unacceptable problems or consequences; and
4. the student must be willing to accept what is most logical and reasonable. Such is often not easy for many because it is

difficult for them to accept what is logical and reasonable when it differs with what "scholars" and church leaders have taught, as these "great men" are highly respected and often blindly followed.

Seeing and standing for the truth is even more difficult for many because of the persecution they fear they will receive among their own party if they step out of line. Indeed, even a gospel preacher who regularly preaches as many as ten gospel meetings a year could envision having most of them canceled or even being fired from his located preaching position. On the other hand, faithful preachers who love truth and wish to put God above earthly pursuits will have little difficulty seeing the truth when it is ably presented to them and will then preach the truth and trust God for the outcome. Who knows whether a congregation will welcome the truth or become hostile until it is told to them? And woe to the preacher who holds back (Ezekiel 33:1–9). James gave a solemn warning to those who purport to be a watchman or preacher of the gospel. "Be not many [of you] teachers, my brethren, knowing that we shall receive heavier judgment" (3:1).

In this book, I make no effort to justify the ungodly actions of those who divorce their faithful spouse. To the contrary, I urge faithfulness in marriage and note biblical teaching that, if followed, prevents sin that often leads to divorce. It is my hope that this book will help to promote faithfulness in marriage, faithfulness to God, and unity in the church of the Lord.

"Study to shew thyself approved unto God, a workman that needeth not to be ashamed, rightly dividing the word of truth" (2 Timothy 2:15).

Prejudice and Tradition

When it comes to “divorce and remarriage,” prejudice and tradition form our beliefs far more often than most people realize. We may recognize their effect on others—keeping them from viewing the Bible the same way we do—but how many of us realize the strong impact prejudice and tradition have on each of us personally?

Consider a noted Bible character by the name of Saul, later known as the apostle Paul. How could Saul, a good and honest man, have taken so long to see and learn the truth about Jesus? After Christ’s ministry and even after the church was established, Saul was dragging Christians from their homes and casting them into prison (Acts 8:3). He also consented to the murder of Stephen, the first Christian martyr (Acts 8:1). It was not until he was on his way to Damascus to further persecute Christians that the Lord personally took action to change Paul’s thinking and behavior. Paul gives the account as recorded in Acts chapter 22. He said,

> I am verily a man which am a Jew, born in Tarsus, a city in Cilicia, yet brought up in this city at the feet of Gamaliel, and taught according to the perfect manner of the law of the fathers, and was zealous toward God, as ye all are this day. And I persecuted this way unto the death, binding and delivering into prisons both men and women. As also the high priest doth bear me witness, and all the estate of the elders: from whom also I received letters

> unto the brethren, and went to Damascus, to bring them which were there bound unto Jerusalem, for to be punished. And it came to pass, that, as I made my journey, and was come nigh unto Damascus about noon, suddenly there shone from heaven a great light round about me. And I fell unto the ground, and heard a voice saying unto me, Saul, Saul, why persecutest thou me? And I answered, Who art thou, Lord? And he said unto me, I am Jesus of Nazareth, whom thou persecutest.

Paul goes on to report specifically how he was converted, but that is another matter. I want us to note how much evidence it took before Paul was able to see the truth about Jesus. He had stood by and heard the words of Stephen who, having been filled with the Holy Spirit, spoke convincing words. No doubt Saul had seen miracles performed by the apostles, if not Jesus himself. And it is hard to believe that a man of his character and ability was not aware of the many prophecies that pointed not only to Jesus as the King and Savior but also explained the nature of his kingdom (Isaiah 2:1–4). Yet Paul was angry with those who opposed his religion—so angry that he was unable to see the truth and so angry that he sought to punish and destroy those who opposed his religious convictions.

Remember that Paul said to the Jewish Council: "I have lived in all good conscience before God until this day." Thus, his error was due to ignorance. He said, "I did it ignorantly in unbelief" (1 Timothy 1:13). This is not to say that he had not been presented with ample evidence to change his mind. No doubt he had. Saul had to have seen a mountain of evidence to support the fact that John the Baptist and Jesus were telling the truth, but he could not see because of tradition, which greatly influenced his thinking. It actually took a miracle to help him see! But being honest, when he did see the truth, he laid hold on it and defended it to the death.

In view of this perplexing fact regarding Saul, seriously consider the power of tradition and recognize that it could have such a hold on you that you could be wrong on some serious matters and not know it. Brethren today are, with good consciences, treating other Christians in a manner that is just as serious as the persecution Paul brought upon the Christians of his day.

Now, God is not going to come to you in a miraculous way to convince you of anything, but if you want the truth you will find it (John 8:32). The search for truth in the Bible requires that one follow certain rules of hermeneutics. Are you doing that or rejecting the rules that would require you to give up some belief and/or practice?

Whatever subject we are studying, we need to study with the idea that we may have learned or been taught error; however, I fear that many, like most of the Jews during Old Testament times, are not looking for truth but instead are merely studying, speaking, and acting in defense of tradition. The difference in Paul's not being able to recognize truth and people's failure to see the truth on various issues today is that Paul had been following the truth, but things suddenly changed. What is generally or traditionally taught on various subjects today never was factual. We need to put aside prejudice and human tradition and study God's Word with an open mind, having a willingness to change like Paul did when we see that we have been wrong.

> 5 Then the Pharisees and scribes asked him, Why walk not thy disciples according to the tradition of the elders, but eat bread with unwashen hands?
> 6 He answered and said unto them, Well hath Esaias prophesied of you hypocrites, as it is written, This people honoureth me with *their* lips, but their heart is far from me. 7 Howbeit in vain do they worship me, teaching *for* doctrines the commandments of men. 8 For laying aside the commandment of God, ye hold the tradition of men...Full well ye reject the commandment of God, that ye may keep your own tradition. 13 Making the word of God of none effect through your tradition, which ye have delivered: and many such like things do ye.
>
> Mark 7

When You Deal with a Bible Text Dishonestly…

- 1. You show your lack of concern for what God says.
- 2. You indicate you are willing to promote your own thoughts above the thoughts of God (Isiah. 55:9).
- 3. You choose to take a road that leads to destruction of your conscience and your soul.
- 4. You mislead others who may be lost eternally because of you.
- 5. You choose dishonesty over integrity (Rom. 12:17; Col. 3:9).
- 6. You destroy the influence you could have had with honest people.
- 7. Unless you repent you "make shipwreck" of your life and soul.

"Every act of dishonesty has at least two victims: the one we think of as the victim, and the perpetrator as well. Each little dishonesty makes a little rotten spot somewhere in the perpetrator's psyche."

"Handle aright the word of God" (2 Tim. 2:15 ASV)

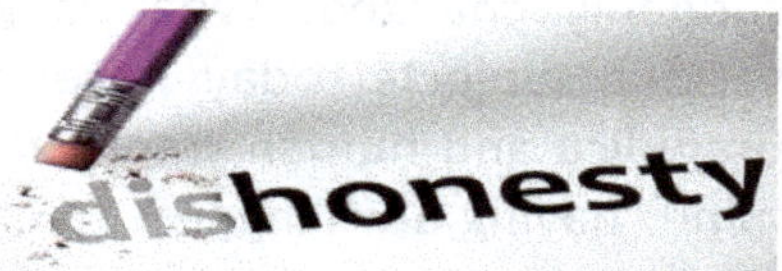

www.TotalHealth.bz

Are the Divorced Required to Live Celibate?

My friend, James Johnson, wrote an interesting piece (below) that is eye-opening on the matter of whether God ever requires celibacy.

"Just as you cannot wish away hunger, thirst, and fatigue and simply quit eating, drinking, and sleeping, neither can some people just wish away sexual desire. It will be satisfied in one way or another. I have a book called *A Secret World* by A. W. Richard Sipe, a Catholic priest. It presents a twenty-year study of sexuality among priests. When they become priests, they take a vow of no sex—no auto, no hetero, and no homo. In the study, less than three percent of all priests were completely faithful to their vows. They all found outlets for their sexuality in some way. Some with pornography and autoeroticism, some with prostitutes, some with other priests, some with parish boys, some with secret wives, and some with wives of members of the congregation. Sexuality has a way of coming out, even in people with the best of intentions.

"God knows what is best for man. He said it was better to marry than to burn. To condemn people to celibacy is doomed to failure and a recipe for sending people to hell. Paul permits every man to have his own wife to avoid this calamity. If a man does not have the gift of celibacy and is denied marriage, then he is trapped in a situation where he likely cannot avoid falling into sin. God says that he will always provide a way out (1 Corinthians 10:13). Marriage is the way (1 Corinthians 7:1, 2). A departing spouse cannot take away what God has granted as a means to avoid sin."

When you think about it you have to wonder if punishing by imposing celibacy is even practical.

The traditional position on divorce and marriage requires that the "guilty" party in a divorce be punished by not being allowed to marry. Many insist that even if one who is innocent is divorced he/she may not marry. Thus, innocent people are often victims of not only their spouse but teachers of religion who insist that they live celibate or be denied fellowship in the church.

I have had discussions with proponents of the traditional position who insist that celibacy is a consequence of sin. Let us test that assertion:

WordNet defines the word *consequence* as "A phenomenon that follows and is caused by some previous phenomenon."

A life of celibacy is not a phenomenon that follows due to having made a wrong choice in choosing a marriage partner. Celibacy is not even a consequence of divorcing or being divorced. It is a decree issued by church leaders that affects only those who are persuaded to believe it. Marriage is not a sacrament, as the Catholic Church teaches, and the Lord's church has no authority to regulate marriage or to impose celibacy on anyone.

An actual consequence of sin does not involve man's judgment, for men can avoid being caught. Many times, even when they are caught, they beat the rap due to a technicality or because of their skill at deception. Even the adulterer who divorces his faithful wife often avoids earthly "consequences" by simply ignoring traditional teachings and judgments that would require him to live a life of celibacy.

> God is practical. He says, ***"Come now, and let us reason together"*** (Isaiah 1:18). Therefore, why should we think He is not practical in dealing with the divorced?

The following is an example of a consequence of sin: a woman is promiscuous and does not practice "safe sex." She contracts a sexually transmitted disease or gets pregnant. In most such cases, people are aware of the possible consequences but act foolishly. But when it comes to marriage, often people do the best they can do and wind up being divorced. Then, some church leader tells them they are ineligible for marriage and may not marry and tries to justify it by saying, "It is a consequence of your sin."

In view of the fact that God is just and expects us to treat people justly and He has never given a law that requires innocent persons to be punished, shouldn't traditional MDR teachers have serious doubts about their belief and practice? How is requiring one who is innocent of marital sin to live a life of celibacy of benefit to anyone? This question poses such a problem for some traditional teachers that they have sought ways to get around this conundrum without totally giving up the basic traditional teaching that Jesus made things regarding marriage more strict. Some argue that since emphasis is not on the "legal process" but rather on the "cause" for the divorce, an innocent "put-away person" may then "mentally" "put away" the guilty one. Others use the term "cross-file." This is different because, when allowed, the innocent actually has evidence he/she divorced "for fornication." Though noble efforts to avoid punishing the innocent, these theories are a Band-Aid on a gangrenous limb that needs to be removed to save the life.

Another problem with the traditional view that many question is the practicality of punishing people who "unscripturally" divorced their spouse, or were divorced, and married another when they were aliens from God's grace. Chances are, even after hearing and believing the gospel, those who are told they must break up their happy home and live celibate are going to have grave concerns about the ingenuousness of the traditional teaching. Many, especially among the young and sexually active, who are deceived into accepting that Jesus requires this punishment, do not have the "gift" of celibacy— they "cannot contain" (1 Corinthians 7:7, 9), and therefore, will not become a member of the evangelist's church as long as his stipulations remain. They need marriage to "avoid fornication" (1 Corinthians 7:1, 2). When marriage is taken away by church leaders, fornication often results.

Imposing celibacy on a woman who is divorced is about as practical as the Jewish men's practice of putting a wife out of the house and not giving her a certificate of divorcement so she may marry. In both cases, the woman has no man to care for her and meet her needs. But in one case, her situation is caused by the man who "owned" her like a slave but committed adultery against her by sending her out and marrying another to replace her. Jesus said such action is "adultery against her" and that it causes "her to commit adultery" (Matthew 5:32; Mark 10:11). In the other case, the woman's predicament is due to the teachings of uninformed men who are seeking her best interest.

> **Censure pardons the ravens but rebukes the doves. [The innocent are punished and the wicked escape.]**
>
> JUVENAL

A woman with children may have a very difficult time making ends meet. It is easy for preachers to sit in their homes with their wives and get their needs met while they tell other people that they have to live like monks and nuns. Jesus said, "My burden is light," but they make it heavy. Yet they never seriously consider that they might have misunderstood the Bible's teaching on the matter—until they get divorced.

Think about the fact that those who are not interested in spiritual matters are not affected by church decrees and directives. This being true, the only people the traditional MDR doctrine will even be able to truly punish are the ones who want to repent and serve God. Yet the very punishment that is exacted often causes them to turn away. Often their lives are made miserable. Thus, we have to question not the wisdom of God but the scripturalness of the doctrine of men that insists that putting away (separation) is divorce. This "wisdom of men" changes the teaching of Jesus from being something good to being something evil—so evil that God called it "forbidding to marry" and put it into the catalog of "doctrines of devils" (1 Timothy 4:1–3).

God is a wise and "practical" God. He says, "Come now, and let us reason together" (Isa. 1:18). The law he has given us is for our good and it is reasonable, sensible, and practical. It is not reasonable, sensible, and practical to blindly follow tradition that has God making requirements of his servants that go against his nature and serve no practical purpose.

Jewish Women in Chains

In discussion with brethren on an e-mail discussion group regarding my stating that the Jewish men were "putting away" their wives and not divorcing them (as per Deuteronomy 24:1–4), the reply was that what I said was untrue. It was truly amazing how the participants on the list took up for the Jews. In doing some Internet surfing, I ran across an article, *"Jewish Women in Chains,"* (Jewish Federation of Palm Springs and Desert Area, that indicates that what I was pointing out is still being practiced today. The following is copied by permission:

> Jewish divorce, like any other, can be simple or complicated; a release or a tragedy; straightforward or a swindle. It can set people free to resume or reinvent their lives or it can embroil individuals and families in a never-ending cycle of abuse. The intent of rabbinic Judaism was to ensure a tolerable disengagement. Regrettably, the current implementation of the halakhic (Jewish legal) system does not meet that minimal standard.
>
> Many individuals, women and men, rabbis and volunteers, have labored to maintain a fair practice. And in some cases, it does work.
>
> However, the biblical account of divorce found in Deuteronomy, while accepting marital breakups, establishes a procedure that is at the heart of the problem.

> When a man has taken a wife, and married her, and it comes to pass that she finds no favor in his eyes, because he has found some unseemliness in her: then let him write her a bill of divorce, and give it in her hand, and send her out of his house. And when she is departed out of his house, she may go and be another man's wife.
>
> Deuteronomy 24: 1–2

Clearly, the man is the initiator, the actor. And while rabbinic law established that there need be no grounds for divorce other than mutual consent, it enforced the structured order of the verse: the male is the active legal principle. He must initiate, author, and give the document to her. She receives it, and only then, is free to resume control.

While in most cases Judaism's tolerant acceptance of divorce enables a decent split, in too many situations this male prerogative becomes the means for extortion, vengeance, and affliction—certainly not a biblical ideal. Thus, although her consent to the divorce is necessary, the woman is still at the mercy of the man. In the course of the development of Jewish law, many improvements have been incorporated into the system in an attempt to limit the man's unilateral power and prevent the misery. The rabbis were aware of and sensitive to women's vulnerability. But a Jewish divorce requires a get, a document that a man freely gives to his wife, and she must voluntarily accept. Without this document, neither partner may remarry according to Jewish law. Today, this affects Conservative, Orthodox, and all Israeli Jews. The Reform movement often relies on local civil divorce courts, and the Conservative movement has empowered its central court to intervene and act unilaterally to affect a divorce when there are insurmountable problems.

But throughout Israel and in the Orthodox community outside of Israel, the pattern of insisting on the biblical directive has left too many women *agunot*. An *agunah* is a woman who cannot remarry because her husband is unable or unwilling to give her a get. The term literally means "anchored" or "tied down" and is first found in verb form in the biblical story of Ruth (1:13). The original *talmudic* use of the word was limited to cases in which the man had disappeared and literally could not act as a legal instrument in the Jewish divorce proceedings. Recently, popular usage has expanded the term to apply to all cases of women who are unable to remarry because their husbands will not acquiesce and give the divorce document.

The problems for women within this system are obvious. Procedurally dependent on her husband and on a rabbinic court, her future children also become pawns in this tug of war. If a woman without a *get* gives birth, her newborn children will be considered the product of an adulterous union, and hence, be categorized as *mamzerim*, Jews who are not allowed to marry other Jews. There is no remedy. To be sure, both a man and a woman can be found guilty of adultery, but the category depends on the marital status of the woman only. The applicable result is that the woman suffers the most from an incomplete divorce: not only from the possible consequences for future children but in being chained to a marriage that has for all intents and purposes ended.

The irony is that if the Jewish process of divorce was established to set one free, even to encourage remarriage, the current reality is one in which the process itself has created a group of people who are not free. And the numbers and problems are increasing— but the numerical dimensions of this issue should not become the primary consideration. Our social activism should not become a matter of counting heads. Where there is injustice, we are commanded to pursue justice. I personally know many silenced women suffering the fate of an anchored life. Their stories, not their numbers, are our call to action.

For Jewish society today, for all of us, divorce constitutes a major moral problem. Not because of the increase in numbers or because of the guilt of either party but because of the inequities of the process and the indifference of the larger community. People no longer married, no longer living together, are still tied to each other—bound together and abandoned. The credibility, viability, and continuity of Judaism are on the line.

The proliferation of unsettled cases has convinced many individuals and organizations to come forward. There are solutions and vehicles for action. Social awareness and education are the first steps. In the necessarily incomplete list that follows, there are numerous groups and resources available. Some organizations have taken on the task of working with individual cases, others have promoted educational formats. Working within both the secular and Jewish systems, activists have initiated both civil and *halakhic* remedies.

The Mosaic Law never allowed the practice of putting away and not divorcing, although it was suffered or tolerated. But India law actually, at least at one time, allowed it. And it is interesting that these people clearly understood the difference in being divorced and put away.

A wife who is barren may be "put away" but not divorced, and then another wife may be taken without fault... Separate residence merely affords a presumption, which however may be rebutted that such a woman is a concubine and not a wife.

The All India Digest Section II (Civil) 1811–1911 by T.V. Sanjivi Row

CHAPTER 2:

IT JUST DOES NOT ADD UP

God says, "For my thoughts are not your thoughts, neither are your ways my ways, saith the LORD. For as the heavens are higher than the earth, so are my ways higher than your ways, and my thoughts than your thoughts" (Isaiah 55:8-9). Therefore, our search is not for a pleasant sounding theory. It is a search for what God said.

How many times have you heard someone who is in doubt about the validity, authenticity, or truthfulness of something say, "It just does not add up"? Well, that was my feeling after reading articles on the subject of "divorce and remarriage" in various journals.

I am not proficient in math; nevertheless, I am familiar with the simplest of equations and formulas for arriving at a determination or conclusion of fact based upon the variables provided and available data. I want to present a lesson here that, if applied, will aid you in discovering the truth on this important subject that does "add up."

John's dad gave him three baseball cards, and John acquired two more from his uncle. He shows these cards to his friend, George, saying, "Look, I have six baseball cards."

"Where did you get them?" George asks.

"I got three from my dad and two from my uncle," John replies. George thinks for a moment and says, "That does not add up. You are telling me you now have six cards—three from your dad and two from your uncle. That, my friend, adds up to five. You are mistaken about having six cards."

Looking a little embarrassed, John says, "Oh, yeah, you're right—three plus two equals five."

Regarding the scenario above:

Three plus two does not equal six. The statement or figure is incorrect. The figures do not add up. Instead, three plus two equals five. This is correct. It adds up. It is the truth.

We can all understand the above, and if we make a mistake, like John with the cards, we immediately see that things do not add up and correct our mistake when someone draws our attention to the error. We would not close our minds to truth and argue against reason, logic, and the obvious facts—because we do not want to be seen as close-minded and we want to be right.

A preacher, Bob, reads that Jesus teaches that a man commits adultery if he puts away his wife and marries another, and so does any person who marries either of them. Bob believes (based on what he has heard from others) that "put away" (*apoluo*) means "divorced" and that a person whose spouse has divorced him may not marry. Further, Bob believes that those who have been divorced and remarry are living in adultery.

Bob ponders this for a while and says to himself, "This just does not add up. What about a common case where a man divorces his faithful wife, and she remarries? My current beliefs would forbid such a divorced woman from remarrying. If she did remarry, I would have to tell her that she must divorce again to get her life right in God's sight! This would mean that this innocent wife would, in essence, be punished when she has done no wrong. The husband who sinned would remarry, but she could not remarry because of what *he* did. She wants and needs a husband, for God has said, 'It is not good that man should be alone,' and Paul said to let her marry (1 Corinthians 7:1, 2; 8, 9; 27, 28). How, then, can my current beliefs possibly be true?"

Deeply concerned, Bob turns to the scriptures for some clear answers. He reads 1 Timothy 4:1–3, that says "forbidding to marry" is a doctrine of demons. He realizes that the woman has no spouse, and the only evidence he has to uphold the traditional view that says she may not remarry is his assumption of what Jesus is teaching. Bob turns to 1 Corinthians 7 verses two, eight, and nine, where he reads that all are to be allowed to have a spouse and that the *unmarried* are to be allowed to marry. This makes him think. *Could my assumption of what Jesus teaches be wrong? Things are not adding up here.* Bob is then determined to get to the truth on this matter. *This is a serious matter. I cannot teach others what I have assumed to be true. What if I am wrong? Think of all the people I would be leading astray and advising them to do something that may be wrong in itself, and possibly even cause someone to reject the Lord.* Bob turns again to Matthew 19:3–9. After much studying, Bob realizes that Jesus was responding to the Pharisees who were trying to entrap Him with their questions. They wanted Jesus to say something they could use against Him in order to accuse Him of breaking the law. Their question pertained to the teachings of Moses concerning the practice of husbands' putting away their wives in order to marry another woman.

Bob finds the Old Testament reference (Deuteronomy 24:1–4) and discovers that the problem Moses dealt with was men's putting away their wives and marrying another, which would (did) leave the women without means of taking care of themselves or the right to marry another. If the "put-away" women were found with a man or married another, they would be committing adultery, which required the death penalty. Thus, Moses commanded a man to give his wife a "bill of divorcement," which released her from the marriage.

Bob considers what was in the mind of the Pharisees (their plan to destroy Jesus) and what would have been the wisest response from Jesus. He looks at various translations and sees that they are not consistent in translating the terms "put away" and "divorce." So he consults a lexicon and learns that *apoluo* is the word that is translated "put away," but that there is another word for *divorce* and that it takes *both* to actually be a divorce. Things begin to come together when Bob realizes that Jesus's response was in reference to husbands who were putting away their wives without any evidence that a legal/scriptural divorce had taken place. And it was this very thing that prompted God to instruct Moses to command that a "bill of divorce" be given to the woman if the man was determined to *put her away*. Jesus was saying that when a woman is *put away* (*apoluo*) without the bill of divorce (*apostasion*), then anyone who marries the "put-away" person is committing adultery. That is really very simple, isn't it?

Bob considers the common teaching that a divorced person may rightly marry only the person that divorced him but he sees that Moses's Law (which was in effect at the time of Jesus's teachings) forbad the husband from taking back his wife after she had been with another man (Deuteronomy 24:4).

Bob considers the common teaching that a divorced person may rightly marry only the person that divorced him but he sees that Moses's Law (which was in effect at the time of Jesus's teachings) forbad the husband from taking back his wife after she had been with another man (Deuteronomy 24:4).

Bob realizes that with this understanding, things do indeed "add up." When he thinks about the fact that his first conclusion could have been true only if Jesus had taught something contrary to Moses (the law under which He lived) Bob wonders how he could have ever come to the conclusion he did regarding Jesus's teachings. Then he remembers the sermons he had heard, the articles he had read, and the actions of the church, that everyone had assumed were supported by the "clear teachings of Jesus." He thinks, *I had a lot of help in misunderstanding this matter.* He then sets out to do his best to help others see the truth. He realizes that he is not dealing with a simple math problem and that he must help people to learn and change their position and teaching on a very important doctrinal matter. So, he diligently prays and prepares and determines to teach with love and patience.

CHAPTER 3:

THE CONSTANT AND ONGOING WAR

SPIRITUAL WARFARE
Ephesians 6:12-17

> "All scripture is given by inspiration of God, and is profitable for doctrine, for reproof, for correction, for instruction in righteousness: That the man of God may be perfect, throughly furnished unto all good works" (2 Tim. 3:15-17).

One prescribed use of the scriptures is to make corrections in our viewpoint.

The people of God have been engaged in controversy over divorce and remarriage since the days of Moses. Although divorce is usually not a good thing, it was many years after the death of Christ that men got the idea that a person who had been divorced was no longer eligible to have a spouse. Of course, God foresaw the damage this evil idea could do to his people and inspired men to deal with the matter. Though it is likely that in 1 Timothy 4:1–4 Paul had in mind a sect or religion, who can deny that his condemnation of the practice of "forbidding to marry" was to be applied to any who would do the same in principle? Also, the apostle Paul wrote a rather lengthy chapter that was evidently designed to deal with questions from Christians (to include us today) who wanted guidance regarding God's will in the matter of divorce and remarriage.

The Christian is referred to in the scriptures as a "soldier of Jesus Christ" (2 Timothy 2:2). Even a popular song exhorts, "Soldiers of Christ arise and put your armor on." Many have put on their armor and are engaged in the war currently called MDR (marriage, divorce, and remarriage). When there is a war, there are sides, rules of engagement, rules of ethics, tactics, abilities, confrontations, hostilities, lies, fighting, battles, ploys for peace, cries for division, mercies, judgments, atrocities, hatred, friendships, allies, cronies, enemies, casualties, victims, punishing, captives, executions, suffering, champions, spectators, photographers, winners, and losers. In a war, people take sides, and we have rules. The winners in the MDR war will be those who learn, accept, practice, and teach the truth.

Our effort to capture the minds of the sincere on the MDR issue is truly a war, and each aspect of the study between those who are ostensibly set in their beliefs and ways is a fierce battle. It is inconceivable that a Christian would not want to get involved in learning God's will about MDR. Satan uses many devices to shield the multitudes from the truth. Considering that MDR is undoubtedly the most conflict-ridden, divisive, and troublesome Bible subject, it surely would help if we could back off and look at this war as a neutral or unbiased party might view it.

Observations Regarding the Participants Involved in the MDR War:

Many and varied Christians engage in the MDR war. Those who are honest and dishonest, honorable and dishonorable, and prejudiced and open-minded all come together to battle it out. Some engage in the battles because they like to fight or want to defend or maintain tradition, whereas others do so because they are compelled to defend the truth (as did the apostle Paul—1 Corinthians 9:16). Many believe in their cause, while others are fighting "just because." Some are at war because they hate the enemy. Unfortunately, quite a few are confused as to who the enemy is. But a great many are at war because they love truth and all people and want to assure that God's way of avoiding fornication is available to all (1 Corinthians 7:2).

Most who discuss MDR are in a battle for the minds. Some are smart and know how to persuade; others have no clue about what evidence is necessary to make their position appear believable. Some use noble means to persuade. Others seem to be even willing to sacrifice themselves to destroy those they perceive to be the enemy; and, because of their imprudence truth suffers and the Lord's church is shamed.

Methods and Tactics:

When it comes to methods and tactics in battle, some think it necessary or helpful to call names such as "liberal," "false teacher," "errorist," etc. they make unjustifiable, false, and slanderous charges and judgmental accusations regarding motives and eternal destiny, using sophistry, confusion, innuendo, equivocation, and other measures designed to prevent honorable and productive exchange of thoughts and ideas, or building straw men, erecting decoys, and blowing smoke. Others refuse to employ such devices and endeavor to fight using principled rules and stay with the issues, trying to be brotherly and leaving the judging to God.

The Issues:

The issues in the MDR war are neither clear to all nor settled in the mind of most. Some who engage in the battle believe the real issue is about divorce, whereas others say it is about marriage. A few think it is about treachery—putting away without releasing by giving a bill of divorcement. This is what the author understands Jesus to have condemned.

Some contend that the issue is about avoiding adultery, whereas others say it is about avoiding fornication, maintaining that marriage—a tool from God—is for all so they can avoid sexual sins (1 Corinthians 7:1, 2).

Some say marriage is not good (and is even sinful) for certain persons even though God says, "It is not good that man should be alone" (Genesis 2:18). Others believe the church must not fellowship those who have been divorced if they insist on getting married or staying married. Some believers contend that all sins are forgivable (following repentance) and that marriage must be allowed in order to avoid a number of problems:

1. Outright disobedience to God (1 Timothy 4:1–3);
2. Causing division;
3. More divorce (covenant-breaking) and causing those depressed because of divorce to be further traumatized; and
4. Placing on the divorced a burden hard to bear, which usually results in their rejecting or turning from Christ.

The following list of contradictory positions can be found among Christians all professing to follow the Bible:

1a. Adultery is committed by having sex in a second marriage.

1b. A man cannot commit adultery with his own spouse. A man commits adultery "against her" (his wife—Mark 10:11) if he "puts her away" and marries another. This makes sense because if "put away" was all he did, he would still be married to her.

2a. "Put away" means legal/scriptural *divorce*.

2b. It is possible to be "put away" but not legally/scripturally divorced, which, if true, proves that "put away" is *not* the same as divorce.

3a. Divorce is sinful and those divorced cannot marry without committing adultery.

3b. Divorce ends a marriage and all "unmarried" (1 Corinthians 7:2; 8, 9) persons have a right to a spouse.

4a. The meaning of *adultery* is to be determined by lexicons written by men.

4b. Meanings of words are best determined by how they are used in context.

5a. We must know some Greek to fully understand MDR.

5b. We can get the facts if we look to the most trusted, accurate, and reliable translations.

6a. The Gospels, which record Jesus's teachings to the Jews on MDR, are part of the Old Testament.

6b. The Gospels are New Testament law.

6c. It doesn't matter because God's law pertaining to divorce has not changed, and in Jesus's teaching we must consider who is addressed and what the circumstances were.

7a. Jesus was teaching "new law," which was not applicable to the Jews but would become effective at Jesus's death.

7b. What Jesus taught must have been applicable at the time Jesus spoke and to His then-present audience—else he did not tell them the truth.

8a. *Adultery* is committed when one divorces his/her spouse, marries, and has sex.

8b. Adultery is committed when a man "puts away" his wife who marries another (as the text says) because "putting away" is not a complete legal divorce, which means the marriage still legally/scripturally exists.

9a. "Adultery" in certain passages is metaphoric or spiritual and such passages are not helpful in defining *adultery*.

9b. "Adultery" is adultery regardless of where it is found in the Bible. 10a. One can "put away" for any cause.

10b. One may divorce his spouse only for *adultery*. This actually encourages divorce, making it a race to the courthouse.

10c. "Put away" comes from a word that does not mean divorce and "putting away" without giving the "bill of divorcement" is what God *hates* (Malachi 2:16).

11a. The definition of "adultery" is "sexual intercourse," which is only an act that is committed with someone outside the marriage.

11b. The real sin is much more than the sexual act itself—it is the betrayal, disloyalty, and treachery, which often result in heartache, splitting of families, and, during the time of Jesus, women being left destitute to care for themselves.

Some students of the Bible argue that the New Testament epistles containing instructions to Christians (which include sex, divorce, and marriage) should be the first place to start in building a foundation for knowledge. Yet others look first to the teachings of Jesus to the Jews and then seek to harmonize the teachings in the epistles (written to Christians) with their understanding of the teachings of Jesus to Jews regarding an issue that was mostly unique to them. Strangely enough, the latter are willing to accept the fact that Jesus could not and did not transgress the Law but refuse to apply this fact in the case of MDR, which would destroy their idea that a divorced person commits adultery if he remarries. Divorced women (and the men who divorced them) were allowed to marry under the Law if the Law was followed (Deuteronomy 24:1–4; Jerimiah 3:8).

The proper hermeneutic involved in the issues is to consider the audience, the immediate circumstances (including the practices of those asking the questions of Jesus), the Law under which the teachings of Jesus were given, and the consequences of any given position. It is not good exegesis of the written word to be content with proof texts while ignoring sound hermeneutics.

Some defenders of tradition accuse the author of teaching that "anyone may marry anyone." What member of the Lord's church believes that? The real issue is whether an unmarried man or woman (which includes one divorced) may marry another person of the opposite sex who is also unmarried and not close kin?

Arguments:

Some people argue that only God can *unite* a couple and only God can *end* a marriage. Others assert that a marriage is a covenant between a man and woman with God as witness. They use Malachi 2:14 to show that the covenant is between the man and the woman, and God witnesses it. Some argue that it is indeed true that only God can divorce, but man can accomplish it by following God's command for how it is to be done (Deuteronomy 24:1–4; Jeramiah 3:8).

Some disciples contend that when God said, "Let not man put asunder," he meant that it was not *possible* for man to so do; whereas others believe that "let not" does not mean *cannot*.

At least one defender of tradition has declared that when men under the Law were *putting away* their wives and Moses commanded to give them a "bill of divorcement" (Deuteronomy 24:1–4), it was for no practical reason. Others contend that, although Moses was not sanctioning divorce, the paper was for the benefit of the woman so she "may go be another man's wife."

Many insist that Jesus could not have gone against Moses's Law because the Jews viewed Him as a man and would have charged him with sin. Others declare that Jesus, because he was God, could and did change the Law, yet they have no plausible explanation as to why the Jews did not charge Him with sin in allegedly contradicting Moses, which would have been a sinful act worthy of death.

Some Christians (dissenting from tradition a bit) state that when one is unjustly divorced, the divorced one may then *mentally* put his/ her spouse away "for fornication" and be free to marry. Steadfast traditionalists staunchly maintain that the original divorce must be initiated by the innocent spouse "for fornication" if there is to be "eligibility" for marriage. Yet others maintain that "unmarried" persons have a right, given from God, to marry (Genesis 2:18; 1 Corinthians 7:8, 9; 27, 28).

Many loyal traditionalists insist that the only ones who are qualified or eligible for marriage are:

1. "Those never married";
2. "Those who have divorced their spouse for fornication"; and
3. "Those whose spouse has died."

These words are often said or written as if the words themselves are authority from God and settle the matter. (See Mark 7:5-13)

Other disciples have observed that the qualifications for marriage are clearly set forth by an inspired apostle: 1) the male must be a "man" (1 Corinthians 7:36); the female must be old enough or have reached "the flower of her age" (1 Corinthians 7:36); and 2) to be a candidate for marriage one must be "*unmarried*" (1 Corinthians 7:8, 9), which by definition includes the never married, the divorced, and the widowed.

Catholics, and others who have been influenced by their teachings, contend that the divorced are still married. Others say that such is contrary to the Law, the New Testament, reason, and scripture; and further contend that if one is "still married" to a previous spouse when he marries another, then those who would disallow it should first prove their assertion and then charge him with *bigamy*.

Some Christians believe that the "divorced and remarried" are not truly married "in God's eyes." Others allow that they are truly married, in the second marriage, but commit adultery (when they have sex) just because "Jesus said so." Yet others accept that a couple is truly married when they have covenanted with each other according to the applicable law of the land in which they abide.

Many traditionalists encourage the breakup of marriages (where one has been divorced) and demand that one or both live a celibate life. Others baptize all believers, including those who have been divorced, and show them *both sides* of the arguments on MDR and let them decide what to do.

Some preachers feel obligated and duty-bound by scripture to refuse to baptize one who is married but has been previously divorced unless he shows "repentance" by agreeing to break up the marriage and live celibate. Others consider such to be tantamount to "forbidding to marry," which is described by Paul as "doctrines of devils" (1 Timothy 4:1–3); they point to 1 Corinthians 7:2, 8, 9 as authorization for having a spouse.

Some Christians (including the author) contend that it is unjust, unreasonable, and unscriptural to punish people with celibacy for the sins of another, such as when one has been a faithful spouse but was divorced by an unfaithful spouse. Others state that Jesus taught celibacy in Matthew 5:32 and that such is God's will. They argue that "the way of the transgressor is hard" but fail to show how an innocent one who was divorced by his/her spouse has transgressed or how punishing an innocent one does any good. Neither can they show how punishing the innocent fits in with God's grace and justice. Some believe that Jesus taught "celibacy" in his statement to those who said (in view of what he had taught), "If the case of the man be so with his wife, it is not good to marry" (Matthew 19:10). Others insist that the disciples were agreeing that one should not marry someone if it would result in fornication such as in the examples of incest in the New Testament (1 Corinthians 5:1; Mark 6:18): "Jesus answered saying, 'All men cannot receive this saying, save they to whom it is given.'" Jesus was not talking about celibacy.

He was talking about marrying someone you should not marry because of legal matters. Those who were Christians and intent on following the teaching of God could hear it.

Traditional teachers advocate that Paul taught celibacy in 1 Corinthians 7:10, 11. Non-traditional teachers (and some scholars) observe the context and see that the case Paul discussed is to be considered only when a divorce has not yet occurred and in view of "the present distress" (1 Corinthians 7:26–28).

Some maintain that Romans 7:2–3 teaches that one who is divorced may not marry another as long as the divorcing spouse lives. Others contend that one should consider the context (verses 1-4) and observe that Paul said "them that know the law" (Israel, whom God divorced) actually might now be married to Christ.

All would, or should, agree that God's laws contain no loopholes. Yet those who would tell a divorced person that he may not marry as long as the spouse to whom he is still "bound" lives realize and admit that the divorced spouse could murder his previous spouse and scripturally remarry. It has been pointed out that one could kill the spouse that divorced him, and thereby be free to marry, and that this admitted fact proves the divorced may marry unless God's law does indeed contain a loophole. Since God's law provides no loopholes, it becomes obvious that a major principle or belief among Christians is based upon an invalid premise, which violates sound hermeneutics.

All would, or should, agree that God's laws contain no loopholes. Yet those who would tell a divorced person that he may not marry as long as the spouse to whom he is still "bound" lives realize and admit that the divorced spouse could murder his previous spouse and scripturally remarry. It has been pointed out that one could kill the spouse that divorced him, and thereby be free to marry, and that this admitted fact proves the divorced may marry unless God's law does indeed contain a loophole. Since God's law provides no loopholes, it becomes obvious that a major principle or belief among Christians is based upon an invalid premise, which violates sound hermeneutics.

Observant disciples have noted that no command or example in the entire Bible forbids an unmarried person from marrying. Defenders of tradition argue that we don't have to have an example.

"Just believe what Jesus said," they say, but of course the differences are over what He actually said.

Some guardians of traditional MDR teachings assert that the teachings of Jesus are "plain and emphatic." Others remind them that the same argument is made by advocates of "faith only" pertaining to their proof texts and emphasize the need to observe proper hermeneutics, which requires that one consider all that is said on the matter of salvation and then draw a conclusion that is logical.

Some teach that when a man divorces his wife "for fornication" and marries another, the divorced one is still "bound" and is not eligible for marriage. Others wonder how one person in a marriage can be free (after a legal divorce) from the covenant and not the other. It is a conundrum.

The phrase "let them marry" is found twice in the New Testament (1 Corinthians 7:8–9, 36). Some contend that these passages are talking about only those who are "eligible" to marry and state that divorce makes them ineligible. Others contend that the context indicates that the "unmarried" and "any man" (to include the divorced) have a right to marry.

Bible teachers sometimes assert that the divorced have no right to a marriage. Others point out that "any man" (according to Paul) may have a marriage without sin ("he sinneth not"), and any who would object, must "let them marry" (1 Corinthians 7:36).

It is a real challenge for one to restudy divorce and remarriage like it was for the first time, free of preconceived ideas. Yet a person must do so and with an intense determination to learn the truth. But before that will happen, he must have resolved in his mind that he is going to find the truth and will teach it and practice it regardless of whether others like it or not.

Fight the good fight of faith, lay hold on eternal life, whereunto thou art also called, and hast professed a good profession before many witnesses (1 Timothy 6:12).

CHAPTER 4:

HANDLING ARIGHT THE WORD OF GOD INVOLVES HANDLING THE EVIDENCE

The apostle Paul wrote to the young evangelist, Timothy, and told him to "handle aright the Word of God" (2 Timothy 2:15, ASV). This must be applied to anyone who studies the Bible with the idea of teaching it to others. Failure to apply this teaching will result in departure from God's Word. This text is generally used to apply to the need to understand the difference between the Old Testament and the New Testament; however, it certainly is not limited to that. It requires making judgments based upon available evidence.

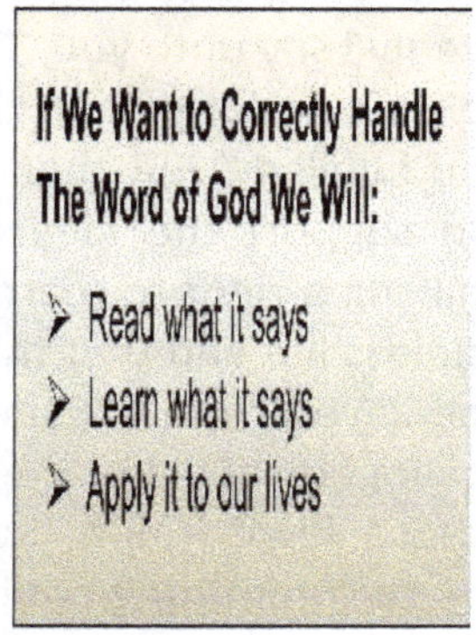

If We Want to Correctly Handle
The Word of God We Will:
➢ Read what it says
➢ Learn what it says
➢ Apply it to our lives

It is detrimental to one's spiritual wellbeing to haphazardly approach an important Bible topic, especially one that has been complicated and twisted by human thinking. Such folly is well illustrated by the story of the man who boasted of how he was prepared to do what the scriptures say. He then flipped open his Bible and began reading. He read where Judas "went away and hanged himself" (Matthew 27:5). He closed the Bible and opened it again. He read, "Go, and do thou likewise" (Luke 10:37). This is the way that many people "handle" the Word of God, and it explains why so much error is taught in the religious world. We must apply good hermeneutics in our study of the Bible if we expect to obtain the truth.

"Don't lie, because the same people who believe your lies are also the ones who believe in you."

When it comes to studying various Bible subjects, particularly on divorce and marriage, many completely ignore serious problems.

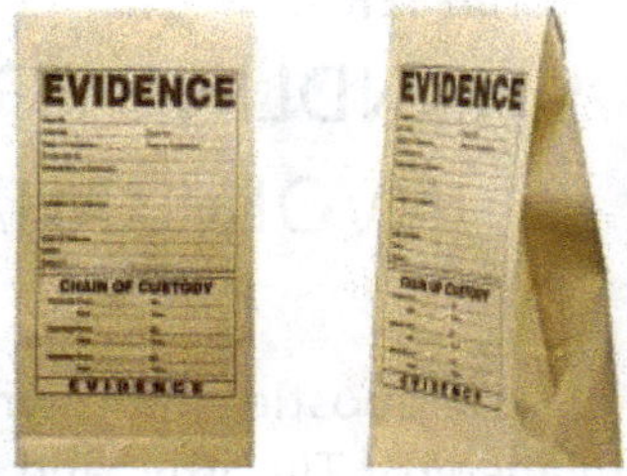

For example, people read that Jesus said to the Jews (Matthew 5:18): "For verily I say unto you, Till heaven and earth pass, one jot or one tittle shall in no wise pass from the law, till all be fulfilled." But then they use verse thirty-two of the same chapter to support the idea that Jesus changed the Law regarding one's having a right to marry if divorced. They also read that Jesus lived a sinless life and that this sinless life made it possible for every man to be saved from his sins; however, they fail to consider that if Jesus changed the Law, He not only transgressed it but also lied. He told those Jewish men that they (not people in the next dispensation) were committing adultery by putting away their wives and marrying another. Thus, when one concludes that Jesus was teaching contrary to Moses, which makes Jesus a transgressor of the Law, he is not "handling aright" the Word of God and is not using good hermeneutics.

We must find a better explanation for the teaching of Jesus in Matthew 5:32 than the one that is generally or traditionally taught. We must reject what we know cannot be true and seek to interpret Matthew 5:32 in a way that will allow harmony of the Scriptures.

One of the greatest factors contributing to the misunderstanding of the Bible's teachings on divorce and marriage is the improper translation of the Greek word *apoluo*. In the passages relating to marriage, *apoluo* is translated *divorce* in many of the new versions. Its basic meaning, as used in the New Testament, is to "dismiss, put away, send away, repudiate." In the "divorce and remarriage" texts found in the gospels, *apoluo* is commonly translated "put away." The idea of "putting away" can come to mean *divorce*, if it is used incorrectly long enough. But a divorce (as defined by God) in the day of Moses's Law (which Jesus lived and died under) required three things: 1) the writing of divorcement papers; 2) putting it into the hands of the spouse; and 3) sending her away. This is what the text says (Deuteronomy 24:1–4). Did the Jews use *apoluo* to refer to legal divorce, which would have been incorrect in the absence of a bill of divorce? Did Jesus use the word incorrectly?

One who wishes to "handle aright" the Word of God will not ignore these observations. If "put away" is part of the divorce procedure, and it obviously is, how can it be *the* divorce procedure? Also, if one can be "put away" but not divorced (and it is obvious this is true), is it not then evident that "put away" does not mean divorce?

The reason for the command to give the "bill of divorcement" was because men were putting away their wives (sending them out of the house), and God considered this to be unfair treatment because the women could not marry or be with another man. The divorce procedure released a woman to "go be another man's wife." But today, some preachers are emphatically declaring that *"put away"* means *divorce*. They use the words interchangeably (at least in their writings) and insist that when Jesus said a *put-away* woman commits adultery when she remarries, He meant that a *divorced* person commits adultery when he/she remarries.

Is this the correct way to handle the Word of God? Are you going to believe the preacher who tells you something that cannot be reasonably accepted without first disregarding some important fact or truth?

One more piece of evidence: Paul said to let every man and every woman have a spouse, and he gave the reason for his command. It was so they could "avoid fornication" (1 Corinthians 7:1, 2). When speaking about the "unmarried," he said, in case some might be otherwise inclined, "It is good for them if they abide even as I. But if they cannot contain, let them marry: for it is better to marry than to burn" (1 Corinthians 7:8–9).

Many preachers seem to be willing to jump through hoops to keep others from seeing what Paul clearly taught. I'm not saying they are dishonest; they may just be unable to see that Jesus did not say what they think He said. Therefore, they feel compelled to explain Paul's teachings to harmonize with what they believe Jesus taught. Nevertheless, in their efforts and (regardless of noble intentions), they have Paul contradicting himself. In view of the fact that Jesus could not have changed the Law, which indicates that the traditional or common interpretation of what He said is error, it is imprudent, to say the least, to try to make Paul's teaching harmonize with the idea that Jesus changed the Law regarding divorce.

Is it not now becoming apparent to you that we do not have to twist Paul's clear teachings to conform to the idea that Jesus said divorced persons have no right to marry? This is good news to those wanting unity on this subject; it is good news to those whose lives have been turned upside down because of misunderstanding of God's Word; and it is encouraging to evangelists who can now know that those to whom they teach the gospel can be forgiven of all sins and they do not need to break up legal marriages and impose celibacy.

> The true follower of Christ will not ask, "If I embrace this truth, what will it cost me?" Rather he will say, "This is true. God help me to walk in it, let come what may!"
>
> A.W. Tozer

CHAPTER 5:

PUT AWAY FOR FORNICATION

We often hear teachers explain Jesus's teaching as being that those "put away (meaning divorced) for fornication" have no right to marry? Furthermore, they insist that only the one who "puts away his spouse for fornication" may marry another. We hear it often, but is the statement in harmony with the Scriptures? If disciples of Jesus would just step back and take a look at the big picture, they could see the problems inherent in this position. In this chapter, I propose to note a few of those problems.

> **There was no such thing as "divorce for fornication" under the Old Testament Law. *"If a man be found lying with a woman married to an husband, then they shall both of them die, both the man that lay with the woman, and the woman: so shalt thou put away evil from Israel"* (Deut. 22:22).**

First, it must be acknowledged that Jesus's teachings had to be in harmony with the law under which He lived. Otherwise, He would have transgressed that law, and therefore, would have sinned and could not be the sinless Savior. This reasoning is sound, and the argument is irefutable. That Jesus did not transgress the Law is as fundamental to unity on divorce and marriage as "inspiration of the scriptures" is to all believers.

Second, it must be acknowledged that the Law allowed divorced women to "go and be another man's wife." The fact the divorce procedure was given (Deuteronomy 24:1–4) is proof that, because of the fact men had hardened hearts, divorce was authorized of God. Thus, one's exegesis of texts like Matthew 5:32 and 19:9 must harmonize with the known facts, as noted above.

Third, under the Law, there was no "putting away for fornication" (adultery) as the term is used by brethren today. What is meant when the phrase is used is that "remarriage" is allowed only if one divorces his spouse for adultery. If we are really interested in the facts of the matter, we must acknowledge that the Law did not allow divorce for adultery—it stated that adulterers were to be stoned.

Though the Romans did not allow the Jews to execute capital punishment, Jesus certainly did not teach contrary to that decree.

Fourth, the teaching of our day is that if a divorce was not for fornication, the person is not permitted a spouse unless he goes back to his former spouse. Thus, even if both parties have married another, divorce is encouraged so that the original marriage might be reinstated. This is contrary to the teaching of the Law. The Law stated it was an *abomination* for a man to take back his wife after she had married another. To him she was defiled (Deuteronomy 24:4) and to take her back would "cause the land to sin." Has God changed his thinking about this? Whether God has or has not changed his thinking, the practice noted above is not justified by Jesus's teachings because Jesus did not contradict the Law on divorce. He only rebuked the Jews for their misconception of what the Law actually said, as well as for their practice of "putting away" instead of divorcing, which was contrary to the law for divorce, as it demanded a divorce procedure.

The fifth problem with the common usage of the phrase "put away fornicator" is that the exception clause is completely misunderstood. If one is able to see and acknowledge the problems noted above, he should then be able to see what I'm going to say next. The phrase "put away" comes from the Greek word *apoluo*. It simply means "to send away, repudiate, or put away," and the best translators *never* translate it as *divorce*. The Jewish men would have had to give back the dowry they received from the woman's father if they actually divorced according to Deuteronomy 24:1–4. Thus, they continued the evil practice of "putting away" and not releasing by giving a full legal divorce, even after Moses authorized the divorce procedure, which would free the woman.

Finally, the exception clause applied only to cases in which the marriage itself was fornication. The problem here is that most are programmed to see this "fornication" as a willful sexual act committed against the spouse with another person. This was not the situation to which the exception clause applied. The application was to an illicit or unlawful "marriage." Please note the response by the disciples to Jesus's comment involving the "exception": "His disciples say unto him, 'If the case of the man be so with his wife, it is not good to marry'" (Matthew 19:10). Their reasoning was, if the marriage is not legal and would result in "fornication," it would be better not to marry the woman. Remember, in the Greek language, which is the original language of the New Testament, the word *gune* is translated as both "woman" and "wife." Thus, Jesus's disciples were reasoning that one should not marry his woman or fiancée if it is contrary to the Law. Here are some scriptural examples: Mark 6:18; Leviticus 20:21; 1 Corinthians 5:1.

Does this not make much more sense than the idea that the disciples took issue with God, who said, "It is not good that man should be alone," or the idea that Jesus changed the Law of Moses and now declares that all who are divorced must remain celibate and the "remarried" must divorce? The entire "divorce and remarriage text" makes complete sense when we see that what Jesus said is true: that adultery is committed when one merely "puts away" and marries another. Why? The answer is because the man dealt treacherously with his wife to whom he is still legally married. He "committeth adultery against her" (Mark 10:11).

If the problems with the traditional position that I have listed above are not enough to cause one to do some rethinking, consider that any view not in harmony with the nature of God simply must be wrong. It is not God's nature to punish innocent people with celibacy when they are unwillingly divorced. Thus, it is time for the masses to rethink their position on divorce and remarriage.

The following links pertain to Jewish dowry:

http://www.jewishvirtuallibrary.org/dowry

http://archive.jta.org/1933/05/21/archive/no-dowry-no-bride-jewish-court-rules-adding-cohen-comes-first

CHAPTER 6:

MUSINGS ON "PUT AWAY"

The phrase "put away" is translated from the Greek word *apoluo*. Thayer defines the "luo" part as "1) *to loose any person (or thing) tied or fastened.*" He says the prefix "apo" means "*1. of local separation, after verbs of motion from a place (of departing, fleeing, removing, expelling, throwing, etc.*" Joining these two together makes "apoluo," which means to "release and send away." This could be accomplished by simply saying, "Get your things, leave and don't come back." *Divorce* is a different word—*apostasion*, which is an essential part of divorce as God defined it and as we commonly understand it (Deut. 24:1, 3; Jer. 3:8).

Some argue that the word *apoluo*, as used in Matthew 5:32, 19:9, must refer to divorce. Although they admit that the word itself actually means to "send away," "repudiate," or "put away," they claim that it was used during Christ's lifetime to refer to the whole process of divorce that included a "writ of divorcement." This assertion, that *apoluo* refers to divorce (even though the most reliable versions do not so translate it), is commonly made by preachers in their effort to defend what we call, for lack of a better term, the traditional marriage, divorce, and remarriage (MDR) doctrine.

We all have to admit that people sometimes do not really say what they mean. For example, a man comes into my office, hands me a piece of paper, and says, "Will you Xerox this for me?" He used the noun "Xerox" as a verb. Thus, those who do not know that Xerox was the first (or one of the first) copy machines might not even know what the man was talking about.

After years of being puzzled as to what is truth on the "divorce and remarriage" issue, I finally came to the conclusion that the subject is really very simple. A divorce, as defined by Moses (Deuteronomy 24:1–4), ends the marriage and frees the parties to marry another.

Thus, divorce does what it was designed by God to do. Nevertheless, it is no secret that the majority of Bible students believe that we are to look to Jesus's teaching to the Jews and make the teachings applicable to people of a different dispensation. But what if Jesus is misunderstood, and doctrine He never intended is attributed to him? No one argues against the idea that *apoluo* means "put away" or "send away," yet it is insisted by many that because unbelievers and people who did not know or respect the Law define divorce as mere separation, then it is proper to translate *apoluo* as divorce. And this is supposed to prove that Jesus was teaching that the divorced may not marry unless they divorced their spouse for the cause of fornication. Well, regardless of what the Pharisees (who questioned Jesus) *meant*, Jesus dealt with what they *said* when they asked Him about "putting away."

When one uses the phrase "put away" when referring to the marital relationship, he does not fully communicate that he is talking about anything more than a permanent *separation*. A *separation* is not a divorce, as defined by Moses, although some gospel preachers, to the detriment of their integrity, are saying *divorce* and *separation* are the same thing and that Deuteronomy 24:1–4 has no bearing on the divorce issue.

It is important that we understand what a divorce is and what it is not. See the definitions from *Random House Dictionary* in the "summary" chapter.

It is irresponsible to argue that a divorce and a separation are the same thing because both are involved in the definition of divorce as given to us from God. (Why, even a "judicial separation" is not a divorce.) And one can separate from his wife yet not be divorced, which is evident from the fact that no divorce decree has been written or given and that the couple can get back together without having to marry again. This was the situation of which Paul spoke in 1 Corinthians 7:10-11.

How did the Jews know Jesus was responding to what they said rather than what is asserted that they *meant*? Evidently, they did understand Jesus to have responded to what they first said (or asked) because they never charged Jesus with teaching contrary to the Law that allowed the divorced to marry. Also, we must remember what Jesus said, recorded in Matthew 5:17–19, before he ever uttered a word that related to the MDR issue. Jesus, in the words of the text noted above, made it clear that he was not intending to change the Law of Moses by saying what He was to immediately thereafter say—verses thirty-one through thirty-two of the same chapter—which is the misunderstood teaching on which the traditional MDR doctrine is based. This is a major point that must not be ignored or overlooked.

Jesus used the word *apoluo*, which means "put away," when he was talking about a practice that results in adultery. If He meant something other than a legal divorce that ends the marriage, could He have made that clear to his listeners? Yes, with non-verbal communication, if even needed, He could have clearly communicated that He was talking only about separation. Let me give you an example: the place where I work is rented. I'm responsible to assure that the facility meets the needs of the agency for which I work. This requires that I consult with the landlord from time to time regarding repairs that need to be made. Usually, when the landlord sees me coming, he knows it is going to cost him some money; thus, he does not like me to bring up these matters. At any rate, I once went to the landlord, and as I was explaining the problem we had, he gestured with his foot—a kicking motion. I immediately took it that he was talking about kicking our agency out of the house— "putting away" if you will, even though not a single "word" was even used to convey that idea. He was talking about sending us out on the street.

Often, especially in some languages, gestures, facial expressions, and intonations are helpful and sometimes essential to communicate effectively. Thus, it is reasonable to conclude that those who saw and heard Jesus speak the words recorded in Matthew chapters 5 and 19 understood Him to have meant nothing more than what He actually said when he used the word *apoluo* (put away), even though the word may have been commonly used (among unbelievers) for an actual legal divorce. For instance, Jesus might have said, "Whoever *puts away* his wife… " And he may have looked around at those who were guilty of sending away their wives without a divorce decree, letting them know that He was aware of their treacherous behavior. We cannot know because we were not there, but the language itself literally means *to send away*; and when we look at the rest of the scriptures and harmonize them with Jesus's words and God's character and also realize that to believe that Jesus taught new doctrine contrary to the Law is totally unacceptable, we can know that Jesus did indeed mean simply "put away."

The point of all of this is to rebut the argument that *apoluo* must mean divorce because most scholars say that is what it means based on how the word may have been used, to some degree, at the time in the context of marriage. Nevertheless, when all things are considered, we have to understand that the Jews did not perceive Jesus to be contradicting Moses, regarding divorced persons having the right to marry again, but they instead perceived him to be rebuking them for "putting away"; thus, making a very difficult situation for their women—a situation described as *adultery* and *treachery* against the women (Mark 10:11; Malachi 2:15).

CHAPTER 7:

SCRIPTURES IN CONFLICT

Believing in the inspiration of the Scriptures is fundamental for the Christian. We just cannot believe in God if the Scriptures are not inspired of Him. The Bible tells us about Him and when we learn of His characteristics, we know He not only is capable of inspiring His message to us, but that it is in His nature.

Most preachers of the gospel agree to the above, but many seem not to be at all disturbed that there is very clear language that conflicts with their view regarding divorce and marriage. For example, Matthew 19:9 is often set forth as THE teaching regarding whether a divorced person may marry. Here is the text most often quoted:

> I tell you that anyone who divorces his wife, except for sexual immorality, and marries another woman commits adultery (NIV).

Below is a text from the apostle Paul (rarely quoted) who answered questions regarding marriage and divorce asked by Christians:

> Art thou bound unto a wife? seek not to be loosed. Art thou loosed from a wife? seek not a wife. But and if thou marry, thou hast not sinned (1 Cor. 7:27, 28).

Do the two passages noted above contradict—one teaching that a divorced person will sin by marrying while the other teaches that he will not sin? The answer is too simple for many people. The former text mistranslates the Greek word *apoluo* as divorce. It means "put away" and is so translated in virtually all the older trusted versions. One does not have to be a scholar to know that to "put away" is only part of the divorce process that Moses, through inspiration of God, defined (Deut. 24:1,2; Jer. 3:8). And, does it just make sense that one merely put out of the house but not divorced would commit adultery if she marries? Also, think about the fact that translating *apoluo* as divorce has Jesus contradicting Moses' Law that said the divorced woman "may go and be another man's wife". Add to that the fact that Jesus, before saying anything about divorce and marriage said this:

> Think not that I am come to destroy the law, or the prophets: I am not come to destroy, but to fulfil. For verily I say unto you, Till heaven and earth pass, one jot or one tittle shall in no wise pass from the law, till all be fulfilled. Whosoever therefore shall break one of these least commandments, and shall teach men so, he shall be called the least in the kingdom of heaven: but whosoever shall do and teach them, the same shall be called great in the kingdom of heaven (Matthew 5:17-19).

Did Jesus say that and then immediately contradict Moses' teaching? If you think so, why did the Pharisees who sought to find reason to kill Jesus not think He contradicted Moses?

That there is confusion in religion—particular on divorce and marriage is not disputed. But God is not responsible. The Bible is inspired and has no contradictions when translated properly (1 Cor. 14:33).

CHAPTER 8:

DISSENTING SCHOLARS

When I first began to publicly teach the position on MDR that I now hold, some said that no scholars support the idea that the *apoluo*-ing (putting away) Jesus condemned (Matthew 19:9) was *not* legal divorce, but a non-legal permanent *separation*. At that time, about all I had to present that showed otherwise was a list of New Testament versions that never translated apoluo as divorce. Since then, I have found several statements from scholars that lend support to the position set forth in this book. Admittedly, few of them had a good understanding of the "divorce and remarriage" (MDR) issue. Yet their observations of particular truths revealed in various passages contribute significantly to our efforts to put the pieces of the puzzle together so we can see and understand the truth and have the evidence needed to convince others. Though they may not have known it or admitted it, the scholars noted below were "dissenting" from the traditional teaching. (See the appendix for a more complete study of pertinent words used in this book.)

Our effort to document scholars that dissent from the traditional view (at least by differing on specific points) is a continual process. I'm encouraged by the number of disciples throughout the world that know the truth and are teaching it in books, tracts, videos, sermons, written and oral debates, and Internet lists and websites.

Authorities on the Meaning of *Apoluo*

Wuest (Word Studies):

> Mark 10:11— "The words 'to put away' are apoluo, literally, 'to release.' When used in connection with divorce, it means 'to repudiate.'"

Wuest Translation:

> And having come to Him, Pharisees kept on asking Him whether it is lawful for a man to repudiate a wife, putting Him to the test. Matthew 5:32: Whoever marries her who has been dismissed commits adultery.

Thayer says *apoluo* means "to dismiss from the house, to repudiate." (*Thayer's Greek-English Lexicon of the New Testament*, p. 66).

Later in the definition "divorce" is noted, but that definition is apparently included because some think the context of Matthew 1:19 indicates that Joseph was "of a mind to" *divorce* his spouse. Actually, they were not yet married, and therefore, the example of Joseph in no way justifies including "divorce" in the meaning of this text. So by just looking at the definition, the reader is left to wonder if Mr. Thayer was not confused. He correctly defines the word but then states that it is "used of divorce." But note what he said: "The wife of a Greek or Roman may divorce her husband." The Greeks and Romans, who had little knowledge of God's teachings on divorce, may well have used *apoluo* (put away) when speaking of divorce, but that is not the primary biblical meaning, according to Thayer. Jesus would understand and use the phrase "put away" as not being a scriptural divorce. This is evident from the question he asked those who sought to entrap him: "What did Moses command you?"

Bagster's Analytical Lexicon:

> *Apoluo*. Put away: to let go; to let loose; to send away.
> [This definition was taken from an article published in *Truth Magazine*. Some have noted that their version of Bagster's work includes divorce.]

George Lamsa's Translation of the New Testament:

> It has been said that whoever divorces his wife, must give her the divorce papers. But I say to you, that whoever divorces his wife, except for fornication, causes her to commit adultery; and whoever marries a woman who is separated but not divorced, commits adultery.
>
> Matthew 5:31

Mr. Lamsa is not completely consistent in his thinking because he translated *apoluo* as divorce twice in this verse and only once translated it correctly as *separated*; however, he makes it quite clear that the meaning, according to the context, is that marrying a woman that has been *separated* from her husband but has not received the "bill of divorcement" results in adultery, which I believe is correct.

The three versions below miss it on the meaning of *apoluo* but correctly explain the exception that Jesus gave:

New Jerusalem New Testament:

> But I say this to you, everyone who divorces his wife, except for the case of an illicit marriage [emphasis added], makes her an adulteress; and anyone who marries a divorced woman commits adultery.
>
> Matthew 5:32

New American with Apocrypha:

> But I say to you, whoever divorces his wife (unless the marriage is unlawful) causes her to commit adultery, and whoever marries a divorced woman commits adultery.
>
> Matthew 5:32

Holman Christian Standard:

> It was also said, Whoever divorces his wife must give her a written notice of divorce. But I tell you, everyone who divorces his wife, except in a case of sexual immorality, fornication, or *possibly a violation of Jewish marriage laws* [emphasis added] causes her to commit adultery. And whoever marries a divorced woman commits adultery.
>
> Matthew 5:31–32

Authorities on the Meaning of *Schalach*

LSJ Gloss: κβλλω to throw

Dodson: κβλλωI throw (cast, put) out; I banish; I bring forth, produce.

Strong's: κβάλλω to eject (literally or figuratively)
Derivation: from G1537 and G906;

KJV Usage: bring forth, cast (forth, out), drive (out), expel, leave, pluck (pull, take, thrust) out, put forth (out), send away (forth, out). G1537 G906

Thayer:

1) to cast out, drive out, to send out
  1a) with notion of violence
    1a1) to drive out (cast out) 1a2) to cast out
    1a2a) of the world, i.e. be deprived of the power and influence he exercises in the world
    1a2b) a thing: excrement from the belly into the sin

Vine's Expository Dictionary of New Testament Words:

Bring, Bringing, Brought, Cast, Drive, Driven, Drave, Drove, Leave, Left, Put, Send, Take, Thrust
κβλλω
ekballō
ek-bal'-lo
From G1537 and G906; to *eject* (literally or figuratively)

Note: the Hebrew word "*schalach*" (used to indicate the action of sending out of the house AFTER giving a "bill of divorcement," Deut. 24:2 KJV) corresponds to the Greek word "put away" and thus means the same thing in the context of divorce and marriage.

Authorities on the Meaning of the English Words *Put Away*

When I did the web search for the phrase "put away" in June of 2010, I did not find a single authority that even mentioned divorce. This is significant because all agree that *apoluo* is properly translated "put away," and in the English language, "put away" does not mean divorce. This means that the "exception clause" found in Matthew 5:32 and 19:9 does not forbid the "divorced" to marry, but only the "put away"—those who are merely separated, and thus, still married.

How can traditional MDR teachers expect to be taken seriously when they expect everyone to accept that *put away* means *divorce* when we read it in the Bible even though it does not mean divorce in our own language?

Authorities on the Meaning of Divorce

Strong:

> *Apostasion,* properly translated "divorce" or "divorcement." [Grk. 647] apostasion (ap-os-tas'-ee-on) "neuter of a (presumed) adjective from a derivative of 868; properly, something separative, i.e. (specially) divorce:—(writing of) divorcement.

Smith's Bible Dictionary defines divorce as, "A legal dissolution of the marriage relation." It is true that several translations have translated *apoluo* as *divorce* and even the KJV does so in Matthew 5:32. I could only speculate why the KJV translators were inconsistent here. Some argue they did it because "divorce" and "put away" mean the same thing. First, that is not true. Second, it does not explain the inconsistency. Previous to the KJV was the Wycliffe version (WYC) and it did not translate *apoluo* as divorce.

Note the following (emphasis added):

> Whosoever *putteth awaye* his *wyfe* and maryeth another, breaketh wedlock to herward. And if a woman *forsake* her husband and be maryed to another, she committeth advoutry also.
>
> Mark 10:11

> But I say to you, that every man that leaveth his wife [that every man that shall leave his wife], except (for) [the] cause of fornication, maketh her to do lechery, and he that weddeth the forsaken wife, doeth adultery.
>
> Matthew 5:32

A margin note in *The Geneva Bible*, translated from the Textus Receptus in 1599 (years before the KJV), concerning the term "put away" said, *"that is, was not lawfully divorced."*

Why is this worthy of note? It gives support to the idea that Jesus was talking about men merely *putting away* their wives and not divorcing them lawfully.

Below we have two scholars indicating one may be *put away* but not divorced. Jamison Fausset Brown quotes Horsley.

Jamison Fausset Brown:

> [Isaiah 50:1] Horsey best explains (as the antithesis between "I" and "yourselves' shows, though Lowth translates, "Ye are sold") I have never given your mother a regular bill of divorcement; I have merely "put her away" for a time, and can, therefore, by right as her husband still take her back on her submission; I have not made you, the children, over to any "creditor" to satisfy a debt; I therefore still have the right of a father over you, and can take you back on repentance, though as rebellious children

you have sold yourselves to sin and its penalty (1 Kings 21:25).

Authorities That Deal with the Woman That Departs (1 Corinthians 7:10–11)

Below are six versions that lend support to the explanation this author uses to refute a "proof text" that traditional teachers use to support their position:

> *(Waymouth)* Or if she has already left him, let her either remain as she is [separated] or be reconciled to him; and that a husband is not to send away his wife.
>
> *(Montgomery)* (Or if she has already left him let her either remain as she is, or be reconciled to him), and also that a husband is not to put away his wife.
>
> *(New Life Bible)* But if she does leave him, she should not get married to another man. It would be better for her to go back to her husband. The husband should not divorce his wife. [Instead, he is married to her and should seek to get her back]
>
> *(GOD'S WORD Translation)* If she does, she should stay single or make up with her husband. Likewise, a husband should not divorce his wife.
>
> *(NLV)* but if she does leave him, she should not get married to another man. It would be better for her to go back to her husband. The husband should not divorce his wife.
>
> *(OJB)* But, if indeed she is separated, let her remain so, or be reconciled to her *basherter*; and a *ba'al should not leave his isha.*

Albert Barnes New Testament Commentary:

> *But and if she depart:* if she have withdrawn by a rash and foolish act; if she has attempted to dissolve the marriage vow, she is to remain unmarried, or be reconciled. She is not at liberty to marry another. This may refer, I suppose, to instances where wives, ignorant of the rule of Christ, and supposing that they had a right to separate themselves from their husbands, had rashly left them, and had supposed that the marriage contract was dissolved. Paul tells them that this was impossible; and that if they had so separated from their husbands, the pure laws of Christianity, did not recognize this right, and they must either be reconciled to their husbands, or remain alone. The marriage tie was so sacred that it could not be dissolved by the will of either party.
>
> *Let her remain unmarried: that is, let her not marry another.*
>
> *Or be reconciled to her husband:* let this be done, if possible. If it cannot be, let her remain unmarried. It was a duty to be reconciled if it was possible. If not, she should not violate her vows to her husband so far as to marry another. It is evident that this rule is still binding, and that no one who has separated from her husband, whatever be the cause, unless there be a regular divorce, according to the law of Christ (Matthew 5:32), can be at liberty to marry again.

Note: It is clear that Albert Barnes understood the context to be about *separation* rather than divorce and that a divorce would give liberty to marry again.

Jamieson, Fausset and Brown Commentary:

> But and if she depart: or "be separated." If the sin of separation has been committed, that of a new marriage is not to be added (Matthew 5:32).

Strong (quoted from SwordSearcher):

> [Grk. 5563] *chorizo* (*kho-rid'-zo*) from 5561; to place room between, i.e. part; reflexively, to go away:— depart, put asunder, separate.

Below is a comment from Robertson that clearly shows he thought Paul was talking about *separation* when he spoke of departing:

Robertson's Word Pictures:

> But and if she depart... if, in spite of Christ's clear prohibition, she get separated...
>
> 1 Corinthians 7:11

> Matthew 5:31: A writing of divorcement (*apostasion*), "a divorce certificate" (Moffatt), "a written notice of divorce" (Weymouth). The Greek is an abbreviation of *biblion apostasiou* (Matthew 19:7; Mark 10:4). Vulgate has here *libellum repudii*. The papyri use *suggraphe apostasiou* in commercial transactions as "a bond of release" (see Moulton and Milligan's *Vocabulary*, etc). The written notice (*biblion*) was a protection to the wife against an angry whim of the husband who might send her away with no paper to show for it.

Another highly respected scholar speaks about the language and the context regarding the phrase "let her remain unmarried":

Bloomfield [*The Greek New Testament*]

> From the use of καταλλ [reconcile] and the air of the context it is plain that the apostle is not speaking of formal divorces, affected by law, but separations whether agreed on or not, arising from misunderstandings or otherwise.

New Testament Translations

The strongest evidence of a proper translation of a word is the meaning rendered by respected translators. The ASV is considered by many to be the most respected for accuracy and reliability. Also, a few of the other versions noted below are highly respected and quoted from often. It is primarily the new versions that are known for unfaithfulness to the original language, that in some instances render *apoluo* as divorce.

Below are 24 versions that do not translate *apoluo* as *divorce* in Matthew 5:32 (emphasis added):

> (An Attempt toward Revising our English Translation of the Greek Scriptures, or the New Covenant of Jesus Christ) But I say unto you, that whosoever shall put away his wife, except on account of whoredom, causeth her to commit adultery: and whosoever shall marry her that is put away, committeth adultery.

> *(AKJV)* but I say unto you, That whosoever shall put away his wife, saving for the cause of fornication, causeth her to commit adultery: and whosoever shall marry her that is divorced committeth adultery.

> (*ASV*) But I say unto you, that every one that *putteth away* his wife, saving for the cause of fornication, maketh her an adulteress: and whosoever shall marry her when she is *put away* committeth adultery.

> (*Bible in Basic English*) But I say to you that everyone

who *puts away* his wife for any other cause but the loss of her virtue, makes her false to her husband; and whoever takes her as his wife after she is *put away* is no true husband to her.

(DLNT) But I say *to* you that everyone sending-away his wife except for *a* matter *of* sexual-immorality is causing her to commit-adultery. And whoever marries *a woman* having been sent-away [from her husband] is committing adultery.

(DRA) But I say to you, that whosoever shall put away his wife, excepting for the cause of fornication, maketh her to commit adultery: and he that shall marry her that is put away, committeth adultery.

(BRG) But I say unto you, That whosoever shall put away his wife, saving for the cause of fornication, causeth her to commit adultery: and whosoever shall marry her that is divorced committeth adultery.

(*Confraternity Version --- Holy Bible, New American Catholic Edition*) But I say unto you that everyone who puts away his wife, save on the account of immorality, causes her to commit adultery; and he who marries a woman who has been put away commits adultery.

(*Darby*) But I say unto you, that whosoever shall *put away* his wife, except for cause of fornication, makes her commit adultery, and whosoever marries one that is *put away* commits adultery.

(DRB) But I say to you, that whosoever shall put away his wife, excepting the cause of fornication, maketh her to commit adultery: and he that shall marry her that is put away, committeth adultery.

(*Disciple Literal New Testament*) But I say *to* you that everyone *sending-away* his wife except for *a* matter *of* sexual-immorality is causing her to commit-adultery. And whoever marries *a woman* having been *sent-away* [from her husband] is committing-adultery.

(English Revised Version) But I say unto you, that every one that putteth away his wife, saving for the cause of fornication, maketh her an adulteress: and whosoever shall marry her when she is put away committeth adultery.

(*Geneva Bible*) But I say unto you, whosoever shall put away his wife (except it be for fornication) causeth her to commit adultery: and whosoever shall marry her that is divorced, committeth adultery.

(GNV) But I say unto you, whosoever shall put away his wife (except it be for fornication) causeth her to commit adultery: and whosoever shall marry her that is divorced, committeth adultery.

(JUB) but I say unto you, That whosoever shall put away his wife, except for the cause of fornication, causes her to commit adultery; and whosoever shall marry her that is divorced commits adultery.

(*KJ3 Literal Translation Bible*) But I say to you, Whoever *puts away* his wife, apart from a matter of fornication, causes her to commit adultery. And whoever shall marry the one *put away* commits adultery.

(*LITV*) But I say to you, Whoever *puts away* his wife, apart from a matter of fornication, causes her to commit adultery. And whoever shall marry the one *put away* commits adultery.

(*Living Oracles New Testament*) --- Campbell) But I say unto you, whosoever shall dismiss his wife, except for whoredom, is the occasion of becoming an adulterous; and whosoever marries her that is dismissed, commits adultery.

(*MKJV*) But I say to you that whoever shall *put away* his wife, except for the cause of fornication, causes her to commit adultery. And whoever shall marry her who is *put away* commits adultery.

(The Holy Bible Contain the Old and New Testaments) But I say to you, that every one who puts away his wife, except for the cause of fornication, maketh her an adulteress; and whosoever marries her when [so] put away, commits adultery.

(The Holy Bible: Containing the Old and New Testaments; Translated Literally from the Original Tongues) But I say to you, That whosoever shall let go his wife, except for the reason of adultery, makes her to commit adultery; and whosoever should marry her having been loosed, commits adultery.

(*The New Testament by John Wesley*) But I say unto you, Whosoever shall put away his wife, save for the cause of whoredom, causeth her to commit adultery: and whosoever shall marry her that is put away committeth adultery: and whosoever shall marry her that is put away committeth adultery.

(WEB) but I tell you that whoever puts away his wife, except for the cause of sexual immorality, makes her an adulteress; and whoever marries her when she is put away commits adultery.

(Worldwide English) But I tell you, no man may *send away* his wife unless she has committed adultery. If he does *send her away,* he is making her commit adultery. And if a man marries a woman who has been *sent away* from her husband, he commits adultery.

(*World English Bible*) But I tell you that whoever *puts away his wife, except for the cause of sexual immorality,* makes her an adulteress; and whoever marries her when she is *put away* commits adultery.

(*WTNT*) But I say unto you: whosoever put away his wife, (except it be for fornication) causeth her to break matrimony. And whosoever marrieth her that is divorced, breaketh wedlock.

(*Wuest*) But, as for myself, I am saying to you, Everyone who dismisses his wife except in a case of unchastity, causes her to commit adultery, and whoever marries her who has been dismissed, commits adultery.

(*WYC*) But I say to you, that every man that *leaveth* his wife [that every man that shall *leave* his wife], except (for) [the] cause of fornication, maketh her to do lechery, and he that weddeth the *forsaken* wife, doeth adultery.

(*Young's Literal Translation*) But I—I say to you, that whoever may *put away* his wife, save for the matter of whoredom, doth make her to commit adultery; and whoever may marry her who hath been *put away* doth commit adultery.

Foy Wallace Jr. on "The Pauline Privilege" or "Doctrine of Abandonment"

Wallace was a respected scholar because of his great speaking ability and his written works on various important issues. He taught ideas that are helpful to understanding MDR. He clearly and forcefully taught against what I refer to as the "traditional view" on MDR, which maintains that persons who have divorced are to be disciplined; yet in his time, he was considered a scholar and faithful gospel preacher. I believe Foy Wallace Jr. misunderstood some truths regarding MDR; nevertheless, again, he wrote some helpful things.

> Verses fifteen and sixteen of 1 Corinthians 7, in the case of the abandonment of the believer by the unbeliever, whereby the believer is "not under bondage" and is therefore set free. If the bondage here does not refer to the marriage bond, then the believer would still be in the bondage of it. To advocate, as some do, that the passage means the believer is not bound to live or remain with the departing unbeliever would be a truism, for it is set forth as a case of abandonment and the abandoned one obviously could not abide with the one who had departed. It appears evident that when the unbeliever so departs it presupposes a state of adultery which exists in the principle previously discussed, and here the apostle's inspired teaching is again projected beyond the Lord's own strictures and declares the abandoned believer "not under bondage." If that does not mean that the believer in these circumstances is free to marry, then it cannot mean anything, for if the one involved is not altogether free the bondage would still exist. *The Sermon on the Mount and the Civil State*, p. 45.

The word adultery in New Testament usage does not necessarily refer to the sinful physical [sexual] act, it is not restricted to the one way of violating the bond. In the four passages in Matthew, Mark, and Luke, the term *adultery* is given the sense of ignoring the bond, of which a man is guilty who formally puts away his wife unjustifiably and regards himself unhitched. These passages in Matthew 19, Mark 10, and Luke 16 discuss hypothetically the man who manifests this view by marrying again. His sin of adultery consisted in treating the original contract as null and void when it was not. The phrase "put away" in the verses means to formally divorce, not merely to "send away," or separate, and he thereby assumed the bond to be wholly dissolved.

The Sermon on the Mount and the Civil State, p. 42.

> With no course of action legislated, revealed, or prescribed, we cannot make one without human legislation. The course of some preachers in demanding separations and the breaking up of family

relations and the refusal to even baptize certain ones whose marriage status does not measure up to his standard of approval is a presumptuous procedure. It reveals the tendency to displace God as the judge of us all, and a preacher ascends to the bench. More than teaching the moral principles involved, the preacher has no course of action revealed, and to establish one would result in human legislation, more far reaching in evil consequences than the moral effects of divorcement limited to the persons involved. There are some things that are not subject to the law of restitution, things done in certain circumstances which cannot in later circumstances be undone, which remain as matters between God and the individual, and therefore, reserved for the judgment. It is certain, however, that if the Lord Jesus Christ had intended a course of action in these cases, he would not have left it for preachers to prescribe but would have himself legislated it.

The Sermon on the Mount and the Civil State, p. 41.

CHAPTER 9:

WHO MAY MARRY?

Divorce and remarriage, in the last few decades, has been a hot issue in the church. Unfortunately, often the focal point for concern has been in the direction of who may NOT marry rather than who MAY marry. The issue is not "whom one may marry" for there certainly are some people, such as all those of the same sex, for which it would be forbidden to marry. The issue is whether one may have a marriage at all.

Each individual must look only to the Bible, the inspired word of God, for authority essential to arrive at a truthful answer to our question. No magazine or book authored by men has any biblical authority whatsoever. Lectures and sermons are beneficial only to the extent that truth is taught.

It will be impossible to understand what Jesus meant in his teaching on this issue if we fail to use good hermeneutics, which include the following rules:

1. Use common sense in studying the Bible, just as we would in studying any book.

2. Consider who is being addressed and all surrounding circumstances, such as the intentions of the querist and the dispensation or law in effect at the time.

3. Do not interpret one statement in a manner that contradicts another statement in the Bible.

4. A correct understanding takes into account the context of the statement and all of the related material in the rest of the Bible.

5. Obscure passages may be understood in light of clearer passages on the same subject.

6. A correct understanding is what a passage says, not what someone else says it says.

7. A correct and authoritative understanding will provide sufficient evidence to be clearly understood by the honest person.

8. When two differing interpretations of a passage are presented, they cannot both be correct. One or the other is wrong and both may be wrong. An incorrect understanding will have always violated the rules.

9. A correct understanding of the passage will violate no logical hermeneutical rules and will be in harmony with all truth.

10. Have a love for truth and a determination to find it regardless of what others may think and say.

While the New Testament is the "law of Christ" (Gal. 6:2) and the creed for the church, the Old Testament contains teaching pertaining to our subject that is not found in the New Testament. We must therefore start our search there.

The teaching of the Law was the focal point of various discussions Jesus had with Jews who were looking for any reason to kill him. Only in the Old Testament writings can we find the definition of divorce. First, Moses actually gave a command to the Jewish men informing them as to how to do divorce in a manner that would free the woman to "go be another man's wife" (Deut. 24:-1-2; Mark 10:3). Second, we see, in the book of Joshua, God's own divorce described in detail, to include confirmation of Moses' teaching to be from the Lord. God's personal example of how a divorce is to be done (Josh. 8:3, 14) is in contrast to a man's putting asunder (Matt 19:6) or attempting to dissolve a marriage his own way.

It is commonly taught that adultery breaks the marriage bond. That idea is not in harmony with the texts noted above. While adultery is contrary to the covenant known as marriage, the bond is intact until the divorce decree is written and presented, at which time the putting away should occur. From God's own example he teaches the spouse to be willing to forgive and to patiently wait for repentance. Only when it becomes apparent that repentance is not going to occur should one proceed with the divorce. Thus, by falsely asserting that adultery breaks the marriage bond, one is actually encouraging divorce.

Many tools are available to help us comprehend Jesus' teachings. Let us consider a couple of ideas that will aid us in understanding. First, in view of the fact that Jesus was known to have kept the Law perfectly, it is not possible that he could contradict an established law, such as the instruction Moses gave regarding divorce. Second, before Jesus made any recorded statement that might be construed as referring to divorce, he made a point to be clear that what he was about to say was not to be taken as teaching contrary to the Law (see Matt. 5:17-32).

Since we know the Law taught that a divorced woman "may go be another man's wife" and that Jesus did not contradict the Law, how do we explain passages like Matthew 19:9 that say that if a man divorces his wife, except for fornication, he commits adultery? First, the older and best versions, like the ASV, never use the word "divorce" in translating the Greek word *apoluo*. This original Greek word is used 67 times in the New Testament and is usually translated to mean "put away, repudiate, send away," etc. Therefore, should we not question whether it is correct to force this word to mean divorce in Matthew 19:9? After all, if it does mean divorce then Jesus contradicted the Law and broke his promise not to do so. Is this a consequence we are willing to accept? Should we just ignore these facts and follow tradition? We should not if we want the truth. Truth is not established in our heart in this way. Truth is established by study while using good hermeneutics.

What then did Jesus say if he was not talking about divorce when he condemned the man for putting away his wife and marrying another, and at the same time noted that the one "put away" commits adultery if she marries another? We have already noted that Moses gave the definition of divorce and God confirmed it with his own personal example. The actions involved in a divorce were as follows: 1) Write a bill of divorcement; 2) put it into her hand; and 3) send her away (Deut. 24:1-2). Doesn't this last part sound like what Jesus was talking about? Let's test the idea from several angles.

First, when we look at what Jesus actually said, does it not appear to be the same thing as the last part of the definition of divorce (sending away), which must mean he was not talking about divorce that ends a marriage? The Hebrew word for "send away," found in Deuteronomy 24:2, is *shalach.* The corresponding Greek word, apoluo, has basically the same meaning. Unfortunately, some scholars have concluded that apoluo means divorce based on the context of how it was used in one instance, Matthew 1:19, where it is said to be "used of divorce." The text speaks of Joseph's thinking of *apoluo-ing,* if you will, his woman because he thought she was with child by another man. Some say he was thinking of divorcing her. But no divorce is needed when no legal/scriptural marriage has occurred, and Mary and Joseph had yet to marry. All that was necessary was to end the relationship by repudiating or sending away. This is all Jesus had in mind when he noted the exception, or when sending away would not be "adultery against her" (Mark 10:11).

Second, we can go to other passages to get clarification for what a difficult passage actually means. Let's look more closely at Mark 10:11. In Mark's account it is clear that the adultery the man committed was not with someone in a subsequent marriage, but rather "against her" - the one that he sent away. Why was it adultery against her? It was adultery because he violated the covenant and sent her away, making it impossible for her to carry out her duties as wife. Now, this isn't to say he DISSOLVED the covenant or broke the bond. That can be done only by death or divorce.

The word "adultery" does not always have a sexual connotation. We know that Israel committed adultery against God with "stones and stocks" (Jer. 3:9). Thus, the word "adultery" is not used only with regard to sexual practices.

It is commonly taught, using Matthew 19:9, that if a man divorces his wife, unless she committed adultery, he must remain celibate. This conclusion was reached and the doctrine advanced without using good hermeneutics. Under the Old Testament, where Jesus lived and died, a man could have more than one wife. This fact is impossible to harmonize with the idea that Jesus taught that a divorced man must live celibate. And if Jesus was not saying this of a divorced MAN, then is it not reasonable to doubt whether he was teaching that a divorced WOMAN may not marry?

Some assert that Jesus did not mean for his teaching to apply at the time he spoke but that it became law after the cross. But when we look at the context very carefully it becomes apparent that he meant what he said TO those to whom he spoke. If it did not apply to them then he lied to them. If it did apply and he was speaking to the "divorced," rather than a woman "sent away," he contradicted the Law and broke his promise not to do so. In view of the fact that Jesus spoke of the act he referred to as being "adultery against her," it becomes apparent that Jesus was talking about the Jewish men's merely "putting away" rather than freeing their wives with divorce papers in accordance with the Law.

The phrase "except it be for fornication" must be studied in light of what we now know is true, and it is really very simple. The man who ends a relationship with a woman he married illegally (and is thus committing fornication in this illegal marriage) does not commit adultery against her. In fact, he is doing the right thing by "putting away" or calling it quits. We have two examples in the New Testament of an illegal marriage [Matt. 14:4; (see also Lev. 18:16; 20:21); 1 Cor. 5:1]. Because these marriages were not legal, fornication was involved. Thus, a "putting away" was necessary and it would not be "adultery against her" nor would she commit adultery if she married another.

The apostle Paul presented some very clear teaching that should cause us to at least wonder if what we have heard and been taught is the truth. Now that we know what Jesus did not say and what he actually meant, we can become even more confident that we have the truth regarding the question "Who may marry?" when we look at what the apostle Paul taught.

First, he prophesied of some who would be guilty of what he called "forbidding to marry," which he classified as a sinful practice when he put it in the category of "doctrines of devils" (1 Tim. 4:13). Bible students offer various explanations; but any way we slice it, a person who forbids an unmarried adult to marry is guilty of this sin. The above should serve as forewarning and put fear in the hearts of anyone who might be inclined to follow tradition and twist Paul's instruction to harmonize with traditional teaching that breaks up legal marriages and imposes celibacy.

Second, the bulk of Paul's teaching on marriage is in 1 Corinthians 7. He began by noting that he was answering questions that had been asked. We don't have the questions but we could surmise the basic content based on his answers. In giving his answers his main concern appears to have been the same as he had when he spoke of "forbidding to marry" as being contrary to God's will (1 Tim. 4:1-3). Twice he used the phrase "let them marry" (vs. 9, 36) and assured that if one who is "loosed" does marry it is not a sin ("thou hast not sinned," v 28).

Paul evidently received a question that indicated some were thinking marriage itself was not good. This he set straight in the very beginning (see verses 1-2). This is in harmony with the statement "it is not good that the man should be alone" (Gen. 2:18).

Another apparent question asked of Paul was whether one who had been married, but was currently "unmarried," might marry. Naturally, Paul's answer was in line with God's universal teaching on divorce, as found in the Law (Deut. 24:1, 2; Jer. 3:8). Paul wrote, "I say therefore to the unmarried and widows, It is good for them if they abide even as I. But if they cannot contain, let them marry: for it is better to marry than to burn" (1 Cor. 7:8, 9). Paul's answer was that the "unmarried" (which by definition includes the divorced) may marry. The command to "let them marry" is directed to any who might be otherwise inclined, whether due to false religion or some human tradition among those professing Christianity. To help assure his instructions were understood, Paul used a different approach:

"Art thou bound unto a wife? seek not to be loosed. Art thou loosed from a wife? seek not a wife. But and if thou marry, thou hast not sinned ... " (1 Cor. 7:27, 28).

Here Paul made the contrast between "bound" and "loosed" with the implication that one must first be bound (married) in order to be loosed (divorced). If marriage is not what does the binding, what does? If divorce does not result in being "loosed" then divorce does not do what God intended it to do. Paul also contrasted a "loosed" man with a virgin, but he said both may marry without sin. That the "bound" are married and the "loosed" divorced is evident from the context. Nowhere in any of Paul's teaching can we find so much as a hint that a divorce is not a divorce unless it is for some particular reason.

God was married to Israel (Jer. 3:14), but he divorced her for unfaithfulness and unwillingness to repent. Yet she could marry another even though her husband (God) was still living. If what Paul said, recorded in Romans 7:1-4, teaches what some insist, then these Hebrews who had married Christ would be in an adulterous union with Christ. But the passage teaches the opposite-it teaches that these divorced Hebrews could "be married to another, even to him who is raised from the dead." So God's previous wife, Israel, who was divorced for unfaithfulness, was later given as a bride to another-Jesus Christ. Teachers who do not see and believe that a divorce (as defined by Moses) does what God intended it to do, are forced to view the above situation as the Jews' (God's wife) having two husbands--both the Father and the Son--and therefore practicing bigamy. But Paul said, "For I have espoused you to one husband, that I may present you as a chaste virgin to Christ" (2 Cor 11:2b). This applied to all, including Hebrews who had been married to God but were divorced.

In the text under study, Paul's intention was to get the Hebrews to come out from under the Law of Moses and to be married to Christ or come under the law of Christ. This is the same principle involved in Paul's charge to let the "unmarried" marry found in various places in 1 Corinthians 7. Those who could be married to Christ included the divorced that were unfaithful under the previous covenant. To this day, the Jews must come to Christ if they seek to "bring forth fruit unto God."

The question "Who may marry?" is one of extreme importance because of the destructive effects forbidding someone to have a spouse may have on his or her life and family, not to mention what adverse effects this error can have on the evangelist, the church, and our own souls. To take away marriage is to take away God's tool to help one "avoid fornication" (1 Cor. 7:1, 2). Paul's negative comments, as to who has a scriptural right to marry, are limited to the following: 1) The female must have reached the "flower of her age"; 2) The male must be a "man" (1 Cor.7:36); and 3) the widow must marry "only in the Lord" (1 Cor. 7:39). Additional restrictions (other than bigamy laws) are supported only by the traditions and doctrines of men (Matt. 15:9).

If you would like to see more material from this author on this subject, including tracts, articles, audios, videos, and several written debates, visit www.TotalHealth.bz.

CHAPTER 10:

FOUR NEEDED CORNERSTONES: ALL LACKING

> **And every one that heareth these sayings of mine, and doeth them not, shall be likened unto a foolish man, which built his house upon the sand: 27 And the rain descended, and the floods came, and the winds blew, and beat upon that house; and it fell: and great was the fall of it (Matthew 7:26-27).**

When a building or a theory is brought into existence, it will withstand the tests of the circumstances and conditions that will ultimately face it only if it has a solid foundation. Many passages in the Bible teach the importance of a solid foundation and many passages talk about "cornerstones" as being an essential part of a building (Isaiah 28:16; Psalms 144:12; Luke 6:48, 49). This chapter is about the "cornerstones" that are thought to support the traditional divorce and remarriage point of view.

The following are four "cornerstones" that are needed to support the traditional position on divorce and remarriage. If only one of the stones is proven to be lacking, then the traditional position is lacking in foundation.

Cornerstone 1: only God joins and only God un-joins marriages.

Cornerstone 2: Jesus taught new law, which contradicted the Law of Moses.

Cornerstone 3: the Greek word *apoluo*, often translated "put away," means *divorce*, and Jesus, therefore, condemned those who are divorced to a life of celibacy (Matthew 19:9).

Cornerstone 4: in the exception clause found in Matthew 19:9, "except it be for fornication," Jesus taught that unless adultery is the reason for the divorce, adultery is committed by both parties when they marry again.

Cornerstone 1: Only God Joins and Only God Un-joins Marriages

The idea that "only God joins and only God un-joins" is a popular argument among those who teach the traditional position on MDR. It is indispensable that they establish this point. Failure to so do would result in them not being believed when they preach that certain people may not marry and that others must break up their marriages because, as alleged, they are still married or "bound" to someone else. Thus, it is clear that without this *cornerstone*, the traditional position will be seen to be merely an unjust, harsh, destructive, and unscriptural opinion of men.

The defenders of the traditional MDR doctrine quote Jesus who said, "What God has joined together let not man put asunder." The problem here is that the passage simply does not say what they need it to say—that man *cannot* "put asunder." Yet based upon this passage they argue that "in the eyes of God" one is still married unless God sanctioned (or approved of) the divorce. While it is true that a divorce must follow the procedure as defined in Deuteronomy 24:1, 2 (the three parts), the passage does not say man "cannot put asunder"; therefore, no scriptural foundation supports their conclusion and assumption. It is found to be nothing more than a false assertion. For the traditional position to have a foundation, it is essential that this idea (i.e., cornerstone) that man cannot divorce without God's approval, be proven true. Seeing that scriptural support for this particular "cornerstone" is lacking, the whole traditional MDR doctrine is found to be error.

Cornerstone 2: Jesus Taught New Law, Which Contradicted the Law of Moses

Traditional teachers on MDR maintain that the teachings of Christ on MDR are no different from what God's Word has taught "from the beginning." They quote Jesus who said, regarding the Jews' practice of divorcing and remarrying, "From the beginning it was not so." It is interesting to note that they emphatically declare that Jesus taught that any divorced person must remain celibate; however, this interpretation of what Jesus said is contrary to the clear teachings of Moses, and this presents an enormous problem.

> When a man hath taken a wife, and married her, and it come to pass that she find no favor in his eyes, because he hath found some uncleanness in her: then let him write her a bill of divorcement, and give [it] in her hand, and send her out of his house. And when she is departed out of his house, she may go and be another man's [wife].
>
> Deuteronomy 24:1, 2

In view of what the above passage says, in order for the traditional position to have a foundation, its advocates *must* be able to show that Jesus taught *new* law—that He in fact flatly contradicted Moses. This puts them in a real predicament. You see, the Jews looked upon Jesus as a man. They did not like Him and sought to charge Him with crimes worthy of death. Had Jesus taught anything contrary to Moses, they would have caught it and have used it against Him. Jesus was God, but the Jews did not accept that fact, and had He sinned in contradicting the Law of Moses, they would certainly have dealt with Him as a man who taught heresy. Now, why would Jesus want to teach contrary to the Law only a short time before it was to be abrogated? It would make no sense, especially in view of the fact that His inspired apostles would do the teaching that would make up doctrine in the new Covenant (Jeramiah 29-31) made with God's people.

The traditional position desperately needs Jesus to have contradicted Moses, but he could not have done so and be the Savior. Proponents of this doctrine have assumed that Jesus's teachings forbad a divorced person from marrying another, yet the Law he taught under allowed a divorced person to marry another.

Since Jesus could not have contradicted Moses and be the sinless Savior, this cornerstone, which is so desperately needed by those who would defend the traditional position, is lacking.

Cornerstone 3: The Greek Word *Apoluo*, Often Translated "Put Away," Means Divorce, and Jesus (Matthew 19:9) Therefore Condemned Those Who Are Divorced to a Life of Celibacy

That several versions, especially the new ones, translate *apoluo* as divorce is admitted. However, it is significant that several versions known for their accuracy, including the *American Standard Version, Young's Literal Translation, Darby*, and others, do not translate *apoluo* as *divorce*—not once.

Lexicographers often include *divorce* in their definition of *apoluo*. They may say, "used of divorce in Matthew 1:19," where Joseph had a mind to *apoluo* Mary privately. Many conclude that Joseph and Mary were, in fact, married because the text, as often translated into English, indicates that they were husband and wife; however, the word from which "husband" is translated can also mean "man." Thus, Joseph was her "man," which would certainly be true in the situation of being betrothed; or, to use our word, "engaged." The same was true with the word for "wife." Nevertheless, many have concluded that Joseph and Mary were married at the time this passage was written, and therefore, *apoluo*, as used in the text, means "divorce." But this is obviously a false conclusion because Joseph and Mary were merely *espoused* at the time and actually married *later*. In the situation with reference to marriage, *apoluo* is usually translated into English by respected scholars as "put away," which is a phrase that does not constitute a complete divorce. Does merely putting away, letting go, or sending away constitute "a legal dissolution of the marriage"?

In addition to Deuteronomy 24:1–4, Jeremiah 3:8 indicate that "put away" is not a divorce but only part of the process:

> And I saw, when for all the causes whereby backsliding Israel committed adultery I had put her away (*shalach* H7971), and given her a bill of divorce (*kerıythû th* H3748): yet her treacherous sister Judah feared not, but went and played the harlot also.

If one asserts that "put away" and "divorce" are used interchangeably and mean the same, then they have God saying, "I *divorced* her and gave her a *divorce*." Without solid evidence that *apoluo* means *divorce*, as used in the text, the common teaching that divorced persons commit adultery if they marry is apparently based upon a false assumption that a legal/scriptural divorce was under consideration when Jesus and the Pharisees conversed. Evidently, Jesus was dealing with a common practice of the Jews—the treacherous act of "putting away" and not releasing or freeing the wife by giving the bill of divorcement, as was commanded by Moses (Deuteronomy 24:1–4; Mark 10:3). Thus, another needed corner-stone for the "traditional" MDR position is lacking.

Cornerstone 4: In the Exception Clause Found in Matthew 19:9, "Except It Be for Fornication," Jesus Taught that Unless Adultery Is the Reason for the Divorce, Adultery Is Committed by Either Party When He/She Marries

An alarming number of Bible teachers contend that a divorce does not take place "in the eyes of God" unless the reason for the divorce is adultery on the part of the one being divorced. The result of this mindset is that people who have been married before and who want to become a Christian are given a litmus test: "Did your spouse commit adultery?" or "Did you divorce your spouse because of adultery?" If they answer "yes," they are invited to be baptized and are accepted into fellowship in the church. If they answer "no," they are told that repentance is a prerequisite to baptism and repentance requires that they divorce their present spouse and avow never to marry.

Actually, the word *porneia*, in the exception clause, does not refer specifically to adultery (*moichao*) as is commonly thought. It does include "incest" or unions that are not legal because of close kin (1 Corinthians 5:1; John 14:4; Leviticus 20:21; Genesis 28:1); or, as was the case with the Israelites, unions with foreign women. If a Jew married someone he was forbidden to marry, he could *apoluo* her (put her away) and marry another and he would not be guilty of adultery against her (Mark 10:11). It would, in fact, be right to "put away" or separate to stop the fornication in such cases.

The traditional explanation of Jesus's phrase "except it be for fornication," regarding which MDR traditional defenders say refers to unfaithfulness (sexual adultery on the part of the spouse), is yet another needed cornerstone to support the practice of breaking up legal marriages and imposing celibacy.

We have looked at four points that are needed as cornerstones for the traditional doctrine that requires celibacy for those who have been divorced. If only one of these cornerstones is lacking, the foundation cannot be sound, and the doctrine is seen to be error. We have shown that not just one but *all* the needed cornerstones are lacking. Thus, the traditional position on divorce and remarriage lacks foundation. It is based entirely upon false assumptions and human tradition.

CHAPTER 11:

THE TRADITIONAL ARGUMENT: MATTHEW 19:9 IS "PLAIN AND EMPHATIC"

Sometimes it is imperative that we take a closer look.

From time to time, I read where traditional MDR teachers assert that Matthew 19:9 is "plain and emphatic." These teachers acknowledge that their interpretation and application of this passage is problematic and unpopular, but they dismiss the hermeneutical problems because they view the passage as clearly supporting their view. While it is nice to be able to base a doctrine on scripture that has plain, clear language, it is reckless to do so based only on one passage that may, because of hermeneutical concerns, be obscure. (See chapter 22, Understanding the "Exception Clause" --- Ten Rules to Observe.)

Traditional teachers do seek to apply other scriptures to support their theory as to what Matthew 19:9 teaches, such as Proverbs 13:15 which says, "Good understanding giveth favour: but the way of transgressor is hard." But before we can accept that this text gives any support to the traditional doctrine we have to assume that all those who have divorced, or been divorced, have actually transgressed. The Jewish men were guilty of sending their wives out of the house without legally divorcing them, and it is happening to this day. What sin did the women commit? In our day numerous individuals, both men and women, have been faithful to their spouse but are divorced. What transgression did they commit for which punishment of a life of celibacy is deserved? Obviously, this is a huge problem for the traditional MDR teachers. The passage has reference to such matters as stealing, lying, murder, and promiscuity. Those who do such things will, unless they repent, have a difficult and unhappy life; i.e., it will be "hard." This text does not lend support to the idea that one must be punished with celibacy because he/she is divorced, which is tantamount to teaching that those divorced have no right to a marriage. Such must be the case because an inspired apostle tells us that "forbidding to marry" is a doctrine of devils (1 Timothy 4:1–3), that all men and women are permitted to have a spouse "to avoid fornication" (1 Corinthians 7:2), and that those who would object to the "unmarried" (divorced) marrying are to "let them marry" for it is not a sin for them to so do (1 Corinthians 7:8, 9; 27, 28; 36). Particularly note verse 28 that pertains to the "loosed" (divorced): "But and if thou marry, thou hast not sinned..."

Whether a doctrine is popular or unpopular should not be a consideration. What is true, factual, and right is all that should concern disciples of Christ. What Matthew 19:9 says is indeed plain if one understands the surrounding circumstances and the terms used in it. The real challenge is for disciples to restudy divorce and remarriage as if it were for the first time and to do so with an intense determination to learn the truth. But before that will happen, one must have resolved in his mind that he is going to find the truth and will teach it and practice it regardless of whether other preachers like it or not.

CHAPTER 12:

"THE CODE OF HAMMURABI"

"What did Moses command you?" (Mark 10:3).

A phrase commonly used to defend the traditional belief that divorced persons may not marry again is Jesus's statement: "Let not man put asunder." The thinking apparently is that man *cannot* put asunder; however, that is not what the text says. We want to look closely at this text to determine just what Jesus had in mind. Let us look at the preceding verses to get the context.

> The Pharisees also came unto him, tempting him, and saying unto him, Is it lawful for a man to put away his wife for every cause? And he answered and said unto them, Have ye not read, that he which made them at the beginning made them male and female, And said, For this cause shall a man leave father and mother, and shall cleave to his wife: and they twain shall be one flesh? Wherefore they are no more twain, but one flesh. What therefore God hath joined together, let not man put asunder.
>
> Matthew 19:3–6

It is important to note that the Pharisees first asked about "putting away," which is only one part of the divorce process (prescribed by Moses, Deuteronomy 24:1, 2), and which, obviously, would not end a marriage. The Lord's response was designed to teach that when a man and woman marry they become "one flesh" and that man must not put asunder.

A common statement made by traditionalists is that "only God can join and only God can un-join." (This statement contains some truth, as we shall see, but it does not help the traditional position, which forbids legally divorced persons to marry.) Furthermore, it is argued that the un-joining is done only when the divorce is "for fornication" and only for the one doing the divorcing, the other is still "bound," which some argue is to be distinguished from being married.

(This theory is dealt with in chapters 17 and 25.) God instituted *marriage* and he instituted *divorce*. But from the beginning of mankind, to this day, man has sought to establish his own set of rules; and during biblical times, such was true regarding divorce and marriage. The Code of Hammurabi is an example that illustrates *man's* putting asunder as opposed to doing a divorce God's way.

Under the Code of Hammurabi, the divorce procedure was different in two very important areas from that given by God: 1) God's law did not demand any written document to indicate a marriage, whereas Hammurabi did. 2) God's law demanded a written document, the "bill of divorcement," if a marriage was to be ended, but under the Code of Hammurabi, divorces were verbal. This was bound to cause problems in many cases, so God sought to head off the problem among His people by commanding that divorces be written. When we consider the teachings of man, as noted above, it is apparent that when God said, "Let not man put asunder," he was talking about the unscriptural procedure, which was to merely "put away" (*apoluo*), as opposed to doing it *God's* way. A divorce ends a marriage, as God intended, *if* it is done *His* way. While it is true that God can put asunder (when man follows *H*is law), it remains true that we should "let not *man* put asunder." This is the Jewish practice that Jesus condemned. It was an evil practice of the men that was a sin against the woman. Jesus said they "committeth adultery against her" (Mark 10:11).

CHAPTER 13:

ADULTERY: THE BIBLICAL DEFINITION

In presenting any subject for discussion, it is essential that pertinent words be accurately defined. It has been said that if one is allowed to define or redefine words he will be able to "prove" anything. Thus, in the present discussion it is crucial that the term *adultery* is accurately defined and that it is comprehensible.

First, we must establish how we are going to arrive at a definition. Are we going to allow men who purport to be scholars to define *adultery* or should we look to the scriptures? Not everyone agrees that using scripture, rather than scholars, to define a word is a preferable method. Those disagreeing with this approach will, no doubt, go with the "believe the scholars" philosophy when seeking for a definition of *adultery*; however, those who seek the truth soon realize that the influence tradition has had on scholars has tainted the view of some as they attempt to define the term.

The Bible is not a dictionary; thus, we should not expect it to define a word in the same manner as would a dictionary. The Bible is the Word of God composed of various books and letters. In defining adultery, we must study and compare various passages of scripture to see how the word is used in various contexts. This is the only way to ensure an accurate, scriptural definition.

As is often the case, a word may have more than one definition. Some, for example, would say that adultery is nothing more than "the act of sex a married person has with the spouse of another." To believe this, one would have to be ignorant of or deliberately ignore a number of scriptures that contradict such a definition. The Scriptures reveal that adultery is used to describe different actions committed by an individual or group. But the result is always an action contrary and detrimental to the covenant known as marriage.

The narrow definition of the word that some espouse is merely an effort to defend traditional error.

In defining adultery, consider the following scriptures:

> And it came to pass through the lightness of her whoredom, that she defiled the land, and committed adultery with stones and with stocks.
>
> Jeremiah 3:9, KJV

This passage tells us that "she" (God's people) committed adultery with *stones* and *stocks*. These things were party to the sin. When we understand the sin, we will understand *adultery* as it relates to the present marriage, divorce, and marriage controversy.

A covenant was made between the nation of Israel and God. Israel agreed to abide by the terms of the covenant, and God promised to bless them. The *stones* and *stocks* were the objects to which God's wife (Israel) gave its affections. The foreign object that adulterated the relationship served to replace God. God divorced Israel, and the relationship He had with them ceased to exist. No sex involved, yet adultery was committed! Therefore, if anyone tells you that "adultery is nothing but a sex act," you may want to refer him or her to the scripture noted above.

Some, in an attempt to defend the traditional definition, may argue that adultery in the passage under study is *spiritual adultery*. But the sin in view here is *marital adultery* (Jeremiah 3:14), a sin that was an act of unfaithfulness to the marital vows, even though sex was not involved.

Today, a person can commit adultery against his spouse in exactly the same way without sex being involved. Virtually all admit that adultery is committed by "putting away" and marrying another (Matthew 19:9). Even those who are not capable of having sex are able to commit adultery in various ways, namely by simply being unfaithful to their spouse—acting as if the marriage does not exist and taking up with another.

> And He saith unto them, Whosoever shall put away his wife, and marry another, committeth adultery against her."
>
> Mark 10:11

This scripture does not agree with the traditional definition of adultery. Jesus says that adultery is committed against the *previous* spouse rather than WITH the *second* woman a man marries! We are compelled, therefore, to reject the *traditional* definition in favor of the *biblical* definition. This scripture makes it clear that adultery includes the idea of the breaking of a covenant. But do not confuse the word *breaking* with the word *destruction*. One may break the terms of a covenant; yet, if repentance and forgiveness follow, the covenant remains intact. A marriage is ended, destroyed, or over only when one dies or one or both parties have legally declared the marriage to be over. The Jewish Law and U.S. law require a "bill of divorcement" or divorce certificate, as is the case in most places in the world. When one who is divorced, and therefore "unmarried," is unable to resist sexual temptations, he may marry another (1 Corinthians 7:8, 9, 28).

Referring to the definition of adultery, Foy Wallace Jr. wrote:

> The word adultery in New Testament usage does not necessarily refer to the sinful physical [sexual] act, it is not restricted to the one way of violating the bond. In the four passages in Matthew, Mark, and Luke, the term adultery is given the sense of ignoring the bond, of which a man is guilty who formally puts away his wife unjustifiably and regards himself unhitched.
>
> *The Sermon on the Mount and the Civil State*, p. 42.

> They say unto him, Master, this woman was taken in adultery, in the very act.
>
> John 8:4

For many, the above passage confirms the traditional definition of adultery. It appears that this woman was caught having sex with a married man or, more likely, she was married to another. This scripture further defines adultery. The idea that having sex with someone who is not your spouse is an adulterous act has merit. Indeed, when a married woman cheats on her husband, she is committing adultery, i.e., she is breaking the vows she has made to her husband (Ezekiel 16:38).

Those who are reluctant to put their trust entirely in a dictionary, commentary, or lexicon might find what I'm about to say to be convincing. The only human authority that one could consider as being more credible than a dictionary, lexicon, or commentary would be not one person but a group of unbiased qualified men who have put together a version of the Bible. Admittedly, all versions are not credible. Some, such as *New World Translation*, put out by Jehovah's Witnesses, are designed to defend and promote their own denominational faith. But many translations are credible. Now, what if some credible translators translate a word as "adultery" while others translate the same word as "break wedlock" and yet others translate the same word as "unfaithfulness" and "untrue to"? Such would indicate they saw more in the word they were translating than mere sex, wouldn't it?

Note the following versions:

American Standard Version:

> And I will judge thee, as women that break wedlock and shed blood are judged; and I will bring upon thee the blood of wrath and jealousy.
>
> Ezekiel 16:38

Bible in Basic English:

> And you will be judged by me as women are judged who have been untrue to their husbands and have taken life; and I will let loose against you passion and bitter feeling.
>
> Ezekiel 16:38

CEV:

> I will find you guilty of being an unfaithful wife and a murderer, and in my fierce anger I will sentence you to death!
>
> Ezekiel 16:38

Adultery is:

1. A sexual act committed outside of a marriage relationship and against the marriage (John 8:4).
2. The act of "putting away" and marrying another (Matthew 19:9).
3. A sin against one's spouse, which is contrary to the marital vows (Mark 10:11).
4. Within the scope of marriage—the display of improper affection for another (Jeremiah 3:9).
5. Ignoring the bond and considering oneself unmarried (1 Corinthians 7:15).

Scholars who define adultery as "sexual relations outside of marriage" are not in error; however, if or when a "scholar" (or any teacher) limits adultery to a sexual matter or says sex is *always* involved, he is mistaken.

Those who reject the biblical definition of adultery (whether ignorantly or defiantly) and engage in the practice of breaking up marriages and "forbidding to marry" (1 Timothy 4:1–3) are on dangerous ground. This ungodly and destructive practice is based on the assumption that adultery is nothing more than sex in a second marriage since the second marriage presumably does not exist in God's eyes and that the adultery continues. This is not true because a state of adultery exists even if the physical act is never committed. In Mark 10:11, we see that the man commits adultery against the woman who is "put away." He is obviously done with her. This makes it apparent that *adultery* can be something other than a sex act.

If you have been faithful to your spouse, but he/she divorces you, for whatever reason that might be noted, what sin would you have committed? None! Any conclusion that has God punishing innocent people for the sins of another cannot be scriptural. God has never established a decree that calls for the innocent to be punished.

Many passages warn against punishing innocent people. Consider the following examples:

> Thus saith the Lord; Execute ye judgment and righteousness, and deliver the spoiled out of the hand of the oppressor: and do no wrong, do no violence to the stranger, the fatherless, nor the widow, neither shed innocent blood in this place.
>
> Jeremiah 22:3

> Remember, I pray thee, who ever perished, being innocent? or where were the righteous cut off?
>
> Job 4:7

> Judge not according to the appearance, but judge righteous judgment.
>
> John 7:24

> "But go ye and learn what this meaneth, 'I desire mercy, and not sacrifice, for I came not to call the righteous, but sinners.'"
>
> Matthew 9:13

> "But if ye had known what this meaneth, 'I desire mercy, and not sacrifice, ye would not have condemned the guiltless.'"
>
> Matthew 12:7

It is not righteous judgment to punish a person not charged with sin. Don't cut off the righteous by insisting they must remain celibate because of something their spouse has done.

When desertion, separation, or a "putting away" occurs, and at least one person marries another without first completing a legal divorce (composed of three parts according to Deuteronomy 24:1–2), adultery is committed by at least one of the parties in the original marriage.

Innocent individuals who are legally divorced by their spouse do not sin by marrying (1 Corinthians 7:8–9; 27, 28, 36).

We have no scriptural support for breaking up legal marriages between men and women or for the idea that certain people have no right to marry. It is against justice to suggest that innocent persons must be punished for the sins of another. It is against reason to conclude that someone is still married and/or "bound" or in some way martially obligated to a person who has a legal divorce. It is against scripture to argue that one is not eligible to marry in cases where he obviously is not married (1 Corinthians 7:2; 8, 9, 27, 28). It is against a direct command of God to "forbid" marriage (1 Timothy 4:1–3) for those who are "unmarried" or have no marriage because the apostle Paul said, "Let them marry." It is against proper hermeneutics to construe what Jesus taught to mean something that is against what is elsewhere taught in various ways and in numerous passages throughout the Bible.

> If one is allowed to change the meaning of words he will then be able to "prove" just about anything. Bible words are best defined by the Scriptures.

CHAPTER 14:

DOES DIVORCE END A MARRIAGE?

One of the most basic concepts in a civilized society is the fact that divorce ends marriage. Nevertheless, many preachers preach something different because they do not view the issue as being this simple. That is because of their misinterpretation of certain New Testament passages, which I shall show to be in harmony with the idea that divorce does indeed end a marriage.

Some say "only death ends a marriage," but this denies the purpose of divorce. God does not act, nor require others to act, in ways that serve no good purpose. The main objection to the concept that divorce ends a marriage is the thinking that Jesus said a divorce had to be for "cause" for God to recognize it, and adultery is usually noted as being the required cause. To complicate matters further, some insist that only the person who actually initiates the divorce proceeding for the specific cause of adultery is divorced "in God's eyes." Of course, this requires investigation, prosecution and judging to determine WHO God sees as "innocent," and therefore the one He considers to be "eligible" to marry. If a divorce was not initiated for adultery, these preachers argue that the other spouse is still "bound" (married) and this is the reason he/she cannot marry another. But if you read 1 Corinthians 7:27, 28, you will see that the word "bound" is in contrast to "married" and that the word "loosed" is in contrast to "divorced." This seems evident since the text states that the "loosed" do not sin if they marry. "Art thou loosed from a wife? seek not a wife. But and if thou marry, thou hast not sinned."

Problems with the Traditional View

We can easily see numerous obvious problems with the view that only the one who initiates a divorce for adultery may marry:

First, it can't be from God because it is not even wise. Instead of seeking repentance and forgiveness, in the case wherein both husband and wife have been guilty of adultery, the theory encourages a race to the courthouse to be the one to file for divorce. Also, people who do not believe in God may choose to avoid marriage altogether and just "shack up." Or, they may get married only because the other party wants to, or perhaps to gain tax benefits. Therefore, the doctrine that the divorced are not really divorced, and therefore commit adultery if they marry, has no affect on them at all. It affects only (and always adversely) those who are inclined to follow what they think is God's will. The result (from such teaching) is that people who need both God and a spouse (see 1 Cor. 7:1, 2) are often driven away from Christ, and evangelists are greatly discouraged. Is there any wonder why God chose to call this "forbidding to marry" theory "doctrines of devils" (1 Tim. 4:1-3)? Instead of allowing themselves to be misled by well-meaning preachers, people should do their own research and study and come to their own conclusion.

Second, if the theory noted above is true, we must come to grips with the idea that God told Moses to write something He did not like (in defining divorce and giving the command; Deut. 24:1-2, Mark 10:3) and that Jesus, at a point when His enemies were seeking some reason to kill him, decided to contradict the Law that allowed the divorced to marry.

Third, the Bible simply does not support the theory. How can one person be free from a marriage, after divorce, while the other is not? This false notion is based on what is thought to be Jesus' teaching to Jewish men; but Paul, who answered questions from Christians, gave answers that conflict with this incorrect premise. Regarding the "unmarried" (divorced) Paul commanded any who might think it necessary to impose celibacy to "let them marry" (1 Cor. 7:8-9). He previously (verses 1 and 2 of the same chapter) had given the reason for the command to allow those who have no spouse (both men and women) to marry. It was so they might "avoid fornication." (For more thorough study of 1 Corinthians 7, follow the links at the end of this article.)

The Definition of Divorce

One should begin his study of the question "Who has a right to marry?" by learning the definition of divorce. Note the definition below:

"A divorce is a formal ending of a marriage. It's more permanent than a separation and involves a legal process. If you get a divorce, that means the marriage is officially over. Divorce has both a noun and a verb form. The noun describes the thing you get — you are getting a divorce." ------ www.vocabulary.com

Sometimes the "world's" definition of a word is contradicted by the Bible, but is this the case regarding divorce? Is the idea that a legal divorce is not recognized by God, unless it was done because of adultery, taught in the Bible? We have looked at the world's definition of divorce; now let's see how the Bible defines it. The definition is found only in the Old Testament, which means it is intended to be a universal command for all people in all times. Here is the command that God inspired Moses to write:

> When a man hath taken a wife, and married her, and it come to pass that she find no favour in his eyes, because he hath found some uncleanness in her: then let him write her a bill of divorcement, and give it in her hand, and send her out of his house. And when she is departed out of his house, she may go and be another man's wife (Deut. 24:1, 2).

Some seek to pervert the above text because it does not support their theory, or tradition, regarding what Jesus taught. They realize that if this passage means what it says (as translated in the KJV) then Jesus contradicted it; and this is not something honest defenders of the Bible are willing to accept. This is because they understand that Jesus was obligated to follow the Law and that contradicting it would have given his enemies justifiable reason to kill Him. The best commentaries explain that Jesus did not take issue with the teachings of Moses, but rather with the false notions of the Jews who, at the time, were "teaching for doctrines the commandments of men." The command Moses gave Jewish men regarding divorce is of utmost importance in our study regarding divorce and marriage because it not only gives us God's definition, but also was the focal point of the discussion that Jesus had with Jewish men (enemies) who were seeking to entrap Him in His words. It is almost impossible to get away with perverting God's definition of divorce, and deceiving others, because God confirmed the truth of what Moses wrote when He told us about his OWN divorce of Israel.

> And I saw, when for all the causes whereby backsliding Israel committed adultery I had put her away, and given her a bill of divorce; yet her treacherous sister Judah feared not, but went and played the harlot also.
>
> Jer. 3:8

The above text confirms Moses' definition of divorce that requires THREE parts, not just ONE (separation or sending away). This passage, along with revelation from the apostle Paul, confirms (using a divine personal example) that a woman who is divorced (according to the instruction the man was given) "may go and be another man's wife." God divorced Israel, not just by putting away (which does not meet the definition of divorce) but also by giving her a bill or certificate of divorce. This ended the marriage and freed Israel to marry another. To marry a false god was out of the question because such is contrary to God's will. There was a divorce and Israel was freed to marry, but whom would Israel marry? God never ceased his pleading for Israel to repent. He had a plan for her restoration and it unfolded as the church (bride of Christ, Rev. 21:2, 9; 22:17) came into existence. A passage in the 7th chapter of Romans has often been misused to teach that the divorced may not marry, which, if true, would include Israel. But many are seeing the true light of the teaching therein. Verse one identifies to whom the passage is addressed: "Them that know the Law" (Israel). Then, verse 4 (which has generally been left out of the discussion completely) identifies the Israelites who had become dead to the Law (not God) by MARRYING Christ.

> Know ye not, brethren, (for I speak to them that know the law,) how that the law hath dominion over a man as long as he liveth? Wherefore, my brethren, ye also are become dead to the law by the body of Christ; that ye should be married to another, even to him who is raised from the dead, that we should bring forth fruit unto God.
>
> Rom. 7:1-4.

Some object to what the above text clearly teaches—that Israel married Christ and is therefore His bride. This is because when the light is shined on these passages the props are knocked out from under the traditional teaching that forbids marriage (1 Tim. 4:1-3). Thus, tradition is held in higher esteem than the Bible. In view of Jesus' comment (Matt. 15:9), the seriousness of such evil cannot be overemphasized. He said, "But in vain they do worship me, teaching for doctrines the commandments of men."

What Did Jesus Really Teach?

Now that you have an understanding of the basics regarding divorce, you are in position to benefit even more by learning what Jesus really said, which most misunderstand. The Jewish men had somehow managed to change the dowry custom. Instead of the prospective husband's bringing the dowry to the woman's father, the father paid a dowry to the husband, which would be returned to the woman if her husband divorced her. This, then, became a clear motive not to divorce a woman, but merely to send her away, if the husband should come to hate her or become tired of her and want to marry another. Of course, a man could have as many wives as he wanted, according to the Law; so whether he divorced or merely put away the woman did not affect his next marriage in any way. Yes, some insist such a man commits adultery WITH the woman he marries, unless he divorced his previous wife for adultery, but we should look to what Jesus said and be willing to accept it. He said the man "committeth adultery against her" (the wife he sent away, Mark 10:11). So the teaching of celibacy that is enforced in many churches today by preachers and elders is being forced to apply to *men* contrary to these preachers' and elders' own proof text.

The problem of both *women* and *men* being forced to live celibate after divorce, even in cases wherein they did not sin and are divorced against their will, is a concern to all. Some try to get around this conundrum using an idea called "mental divorce." This is basically the belief that if you get divorced by an unfaithful spouse you can then, in your own mind, divorce that person for his or her unfaithfulness. Inventors of this doctrine see the unjustness in the traditional teaching. But not knowing the truth about what Jesus was dealing with, they seek to harmonize His teaching with passages that portray Him as just, fair and reasonable. The truth they need to see is that Jesus' condemnation of these evil Jewish men was based upon their practice of sending away but not divorcing according to God's definition. When Jesus said, "What therefore God hath joined together, let not man put asunder" (Mark

10:9) He was not saying divorce does not end a marriage. He was saying man should not attempt to do a divorce his own way. (To do so would not be recognized as divorce.) In the last couple of decades more and more preachers are taking the position that divorce and separation are the same thing. They need this to be true to force the Greek word *apoluo* to mean divorce. But when they do this they unwittingly are guilty of teaching a way of putting asunder (divorcing) that is not taught in the word of God. Sending away, putting away, departing, etc., is common, but it is NOT divorce. For example, Joe's young wife, Sue, gets angry and departs—goes back to her parents. Then after a week of wise counsel she returns and there is reconciliation, but since there was no divorce there is no need for marriage.

Let's turn the above example around and seek to illustrate the meaning of *apoluo* in a different way: Joe caught Sue (his wife) in what appeared to be inappropriate relations with another man. Being angry Joe told her to *leave* and not to come back. He was so angry he would not listen to a single word she said. After a period of time, Joe learned that the man his wife was hugging was an old friend who had just lost his only son in a car accident. Joe apologized to Sue and they were reconciled. Those who hold the view that *separation* and *divorce* are the same are forced to say Joe and Sue, in the above example, were divorced. This would require *marriage* rather than mere *reconciliation*. In 1 Corinthians 7:10-11, we have the same circumstance. The woman whom Paul speaks of as having departed (left) is said, by MDR tradition teachers, to be *divorced,* which changes the entire situation.

Conclusion

The truth that divorce ends a marriage was evident when God gave the law (in the Old Testament) for the purpose of freeing the woman, and it is evident today. Human tradition is powerful, but it does not compare to the truth, the word of God. The Hebrew writer wrote:

> For the word of God is quick, and powerful, and sharper than any twoedged sword, piercing even to the dividing asunder of soul and spirit, and of the joints and marrow, and is a discerner of the thoughts and intents of the heart.
>
> Heb. 4:12

In commenting on the power of the word, as noted in the above passage, *Albert Barnes* wrote the following:

> And powerful --- Mighty. Its power is seen in awakening the conscience; alarming the fears; laying bare the secret feelings of the heart, and causing the sinner to tremble with the apprehension of the coming judgment. All the great changes in the moral world for the better, have been caused by the power of truth. They are such as the truth in its own nature is suited to effect, and if we may judge of its power by the greatness of the revolutions produced, no words can over-estimate the might of the truth which God has revealed.

CHAPTER 15:

DID JESUS MARRY ISRAEL? IF SO, WHAT DOES THIS PROVE? ROMANS 7:1-4

> **AND AS MANY AS WALK ACCORDING TO THIS RULE, PEACE BE ON THEM, AND MERCY, AND UPON THE ISRAEL OF GOD.**
> (Galatians 6:16)

If it can be established that Jesus married Israel it could be very insightful for those seeking the truth regarding whether or not the Bible teaches that the divorced must remain celibate. If Christ married Israel, whom God married but divorced (Jer. 3:8, 14), then this divine example teaches us that a divorced person is not required to remain celibate.

The Text

> Know ye not, brethren, (for I speak to them that know the law,) how that the law hath dominion over a man as long as he liveth? 2 For the woman which hath an husband is bound by the law to her husband so long as he liveth; but if the husband be dead, she is loosed from the law of her husband. 3 So then if, while her husband liveth, she be married to another man, she shall be called an adulteress: but if her husband be dead, she is free from that law; so that she is no adulteress, though she be married to another man. 4 Wherefore, my brethren, ye also are become dead to the law by the body of Christ; that ye should be married to another, even to him who is raised from the dead, that we should bring forth fruit unto God.
>
> Romans 7:1-4

While it is true that the word "Israel" is not found in the above text, when we consider what the text does say, along with other teachings in both the Old and New Testaments, we find abundant reason to conclude that Jesus did indeed marry Israel. Actually, that Christ married Israel is a well-established fact, one that virtually no one would seek to deny in formal debate. Unfortunately, many are not able to accept it and this is to their own hurt as well as those they influence. No matter how clearly a thing may be stated, or how much evidence supports a doctrine, in order for us to see it we have to be able to see beyond our preconceptions and look at the evidence with open eyes and ears. But seeing the truth is not the end of the battle; we must apply the truth regardless of feared earthly consequences.

What the Text Does Not Say

Before we discuss what the text says let us observe some ideas it does not convey: 1) It does not say divorce does not end a marriage—divorce ended God's marriage with Israel, therefore it is imprudent to conclude that Paul now teaches a different doctrine; 2) it does not declare that a divorced person must remain celibate; 3) it does not express anything contrary to God's definition of divorce (Deuteronomy 24:1,2; Jeramiah 3:8); and 4) it does not state that only death ends a marriage. Those who would like to use this text to support their teaching that the divorced may not marry are hit with the reality that it teaches too much. If the text teaches that only death ends a marriage it excludes divorce even in the case of adultery that is asserted to be essential before God will recognize it as valid.

In view of the fact that the first three verses of the passage under study (Romans 7:1-3) has often been used in an effort to teach that the divorced may not marry, it may be surprising to the reader that the same text, when verse 4 is included in context, actually teaches the opposite. Indeed, verse 4 is very plain language teaching, by divine example, that a divorced person may marry another. What could be more authoritative and clear teaching than for God to use Himself and His Own wife, by way of divine example, to teach us that divorce ends a marriage and the divorced may marry?

What the Text Says

Let's now take a close look at the text (Romans 7:1-4). Numerous times I've seen brethren use verses 1-3 to support their belief and practice on MDR, but to determine truth we must consider context. Stopping at verse 3 and ignoring verse 4 is not good hermeneutics. It is not even honest. If verse 4 actually teaches what it appears to say then it soundly defeats the traditional position that the divorced must remain celibate.

Beginning in verse one, Paul clarifies whom he is addressing: "those who know the law." This would be the Israelites whom the Scriptures speak of as being the wife of God, but whom He divorced (Jeramiah 3:8, 14) and whom are now married to Christ. This is very important because of what is said in verse 4 of the passage. Now, God was not married to the people as individuals; as individuals they were spiritually married to God. We might say He was married to them as a corporate entity. This is the same group who may become the bride of Christ ("married to another").

Notice verse 2a:

> "For the woman which hath an husband is bound by
> the law to her husband so long as he liveth;..."

As long as a woman is married to a man she is *bound* to him, but if she is divorced from him she does not have "an husband," which means she is no longer *bound* to him. He has "loosed" her already. (On the word "loosed" see 1 Cor. 7:27, 28). Otherwise, she is bound to him until death. Death *looses* her from him. To insist that verse 2b teaches that only death ends a marriage is to deny that divorce does what God intended it to do, no matter what the circumstances.

Verse 2b:

> "...but if the husband be dead, she is loosed from the
> law of her husband."

There is nothing here that anyone denies. But the contention that only death ends a marriage is very much in dispute as it denies that divorce does what God intended it to do. We must not read into this passage something that is not there.

Verse 3:

> "So then if, while her husband liveth, she be married to another man, she shall be called an adulteress: but if her husband be dead, she is free from that law; so that she is no adulteress, though she be married to another man."

If while married to one man a woman marries another man she "shall be called an adulteress." (This is what would take place if a man sent a woman away—refusing to give her a certificate of divorce. The man who married her would also commit adultery. See Matt. 5:31, 32.) We have observed in comments on verse two that if divorced she is not married; thus if a divorced woman marries another the above condemnation would not be applicable. It is only applicable if she is married. Nevertheless, if married to a man who dies death does free her, according to Paul. (Some cultures have buried a man's wives with him.) Upon Christ's death the Jews were then freed from the Law to marry another—Christ.

Some have asserted that my usage of Jeremiah 3:8, 14 and Romans 7:4 is a misuse of scripture and that I have taken it out of context. Both charges are obviously false. In Jeremiah 3:8 and 14 the application is marriage–the marriage between God and Israel. This established to whom Israel was married. In Romans 7:4, marriage is the application but it is to another person in the godhead–Jesus. While it is true that the context involves law and covenant relations this does not discount the fact of the marriage of God and Israel. Isn't it strange that over the years some brethren have used verses 1-3 of Romans 7 to make an argument about MDR while ignoring the context, which is Israel's now being allowed to marry Christ, but I am accused of misapplying verse 4 when I use it in its proper context?

Dealing with Responses

The most common response to the teachings presented above is to merely ignore verse 4 and put emphasis on verse 2b. But, as in algebra, if you leave out part of the equation you will not get the correct answer.

Some deemphasize to whom the text is addressed. For example, it might be said "WE are allowed to be married to another because the Old Law is now dead to us." But instead of it being dead to us it is us that are dead to it. Barclay (Romans, p. 95) said,

> "Paul could still have put the thing quite simply. He could have said that we were married to the law; that the law was killed by the work of Christ; and that now we are free to be married to God. But, quite suddenly, he puts it the other way, and, in his suddenly changed picture, it is we who die to the law."

With emphasis on the word "we" it becomes about "us" gentiles whom were not previously married to Christ. Again, I remind the reader whom Paul addressed: "those who know the law" (Israelites). Gentiles never were under the Law or married to God. Paul is teaching that those who were under the Law (those who knew the Law) are allowed to be married to "another." This context clearly indicates there was a "previous" marriage. That this marriage was between Israel and God is undeniable. Yet it is true that both Jew and gentile are baptized into one body—the body of Christ (1 Cor. 12:13) and make up the bride of Christ, the Israel of God, the church.

It is argued that "The church is 'spiritual' Israel." Well, call it what you like, it is still Israel—the true children of God. Since all the spiritual promises to Israel are realized in the church the church is the new Israel that was previously married to God but after divorced married to Jesus.

Supporting Passages

Galatians 6:16

> "And as many as walk according to this rule, peace be on them, and mercy, and upon the Israel of God."

Barnes comments: "And upon the Israel of God. The true church of God; all who are his true worshippers. See [Ro 2:28]; See [Ro 2:29]; See [Ro 9:6]."

Hebrews 8:10

> "For this is the covenant that I will make with the house of Israel..."

Gill comments: "That is, this is the sum and substance of the covenant, which God promised to make with, or to make manifest and known to his chosen people, the true Israelites, under the Gospel dispensation;"

God made a new covenant with Israel. This covenant is without question the New Testament that governs the church. Thus, the church and Israel, about which the Hebrew writer speaks, are the same—the bride of Christ.

Revelation 21:2

> "And I John saw the holy city, new Jerusalem, coming down from God out of heaven, prepared as a bride adorned for her husband."

Jerusalem was the holy city of Israel, God's wife. In this text is depicted the "bride" (the church), the new Israel, and Christ the husband. National Israel typified and foreshadowed the spiritual Israel of God that was to become the eternal bride of Christ.

Galatians 3:26-29

> "For ye are all the children of God by faith in Christ Jesus. For as many of you as have been baptized into Christ have put on Christ. There is neither Jew nor Greek, there is neither bond nor free, there is neither male nor female: for ye are all one in Christ Jesus. And if ye be Christ's, then are ye Abraham's seed, and heirs according to the promise."

We, both Jew and Gentile, are of Abraham's seed that make up the church. Israelites (Abraham's seed) were previously married to God. Now, these same people are married to Jesus when "baptized into Christ."

Below are Some Comments from Respected Scholars that Relate to Romans 7:4:

Hank Hanegraaff's Comments

"The faithful remnant of Old Testament Israel and New Testament Christianity are together the one genuine seed of Abraham and thus heirs according to the promise. This remnant is not chosen on the basis of religion or race but rather on the basis of relationship to the resurrected Redeemer."

"Finally, the one chosen people, who form one covenant community, are beautifully symbolized in the book of Romans as one cultivated olive tree (see Romans 11:11–24). The tree symbolizes Israel; its branches symbolize those who believe; and its root symbolizes Jesus—the root and the offspring of David (Revelation 22:16). Natural branches broken off represent Jews who reject Jesus. Wild branches grafted in represent Gentiles who receive Jesus. Thus says Paul, "Not all who are descended from Israel are Israel. Nor because they are his descendants are they all Abraham's children....In other words, it is not the natural children who are God's children, but it is the children of the promise who are regarded as Abraham's offspring" (Romans 9:6–8). Jesus is the one genuine seed of Abraham! And all clothed in Christ constitute one congruent chosen covenant community connected by the cross."

Hank Hanegraaff, Christian Research Institute.
http://www.equip.org/articles/does-the-bible-make-a-distinction-between-israel-and-the-church/

Joseph Benson's Commentary on the Old and New Testament

That ye should be married to another — (2 Corinthians 11:2;) so that you must now give up yourselves to Christ, as your second husband, that you may be justified by faith in him. The apostle speaks of Christ as the husband of the believing Jews, because he was now become their Lord and head; and he calls him *another husband,* because they had been formerly, as it were, married to the Mosaic law, and relied on that alone for salvation.

Bryan Vinson, SR. (p. 128)

We become dead to the law by reason of it abrogation, that is, the Jews did, for they only were ever subject it, married to it and thus bound by it.

(I do not agree with Vinson that Israel was married to the Law. They were married to God. Jeramiah 3:14, R.W.)

Coffman Commentaries on the Bible

For Jewish Christians, Christ died to annul their old contract with God; thus they were free to be united with Christ as a portion of his bride the church, this being the import of the words, "that ye should be joined to another."

Geneva Bible Footnotes

2. An application of the similitude of marriage. "So", he says, "it is the same with us: for now we are joined to the Spirit, as it were to the second husband, by whom we must bring forth new children: we are dead with regard to the first husband, but with regard to the latter, we are as it were raised from the dead."

Romans: Verse by Verse (Newell)

To the Jewish believer, then, the announcement is now directly made that he was made dead to the Law through the body of Christ, in order to be to Another, to the risen Christ, thus to bring forth fruit to God; and that he has been [verse 6] discharged from the Law [literally, an- nulled with respect to the Law], thus bringing him out into service in newness of spirit.(1) This was the startling announcement made to those who, for 1500 years had known nothing but the Law: they had died to it all; the Law knew them no more.

Justin Edwards' Family Bible N.T.

By the body of Christ; by his crucified body making expiation for your sins. Thus ye are released from the law as a means of justification before God, so that ye are no longer in this respect bound to it, any more than a woman is bound to her husband after he is dead. Thus the way is prepared that ye should be married to another, even Christ; in other words, should come into a state of justification by virtue of your union with Christ through faith.

John Gill

they are loosed from it, and may be, and are lawfully married to Christ,

People's New Testament Commentary

Wherefore, my brethren, ye also are dead to the law. This principle, under the figure of marriage, is applied to those church members who were once under the law of Moses. They were then related to it as a wife to a husband. But in the chapter VI, it has been shown that all disciples of Christ had died, been buried, and risen with him (Ro 6:2-5); hence, having died, they had been released from the law. As new creatures, they could, as those freed from the marriage to law, be espoused to another, even Christ. Christians are so united to Christ, living by vital union with him, being found in him, that whatever was done to him is said to have been done to them in his person, or through his body. The church is spiritually the Body of Christ [1Co 12:27].

Conclusion

In view of the apparent fact that God's wife (that became unfaithful and whom God therefore divorced) was allowed to marry, who can argue against the idea that we are taught through divine example to allow the divorced to marry? Add this teaching to what Paul says regarding the "unmarried" (that includes those divorced) — "LET THEM MARRY" — and we have a solid reason to reject the idea that Jesus was talking about legal divorce when He said a woman "put away" (but not divorced) commits adultery in marrying another. Apparently, He was talking about permanent separations (wherein the woman was not given a certificate of divorce, as Moses commanded, Deuteronomy 24:1-4; Mark 10:3) that logically would result in sin should the woman marry another. If the traditional teaching that "put away" means legal divorce is true then we are left to conclude that Jesus did not even deal with the more evil issue of men (who could have more than one wife) sending away a wife but not giving her a certificate of divorce "so she may go and be another man's wife." Actually, in Marks account it is made clear that the adultery committed in "putting away" was a nonsexual act—it was "against her" rather than "with" a new wife (Mark 10:11).

The first three verses of Romans 7 state what the married woman's situation was under the law. She was bound to her husband by that law until he died—at least as long as she was married to him. Verse 4 states what the situation of New Testament Israel is after the cross. This also is specifically stated in the text. They are dead to that law, free from it, in order that they might be married to another, specifically Christ. Words could not say this any more plainly.

The bottom line is that if the traditional theory (from Catholicism that does not accept that divorce ends marriage) is correct then the Jews who obey the gospel are living in spiritual adultery with Christ.

Israel and the Church

1. Saints (Num. 16:3; Deut. 33:3)	1. Saints (Eph. 1:1; Rom. 1:7)
2. Elect (Deut. 7:6,7; 14:2)	2. Elect (Col. 3:12; Titus 1:1)
3. Beloved (Deut. 7:7; 4:37)	3. Beloved (Col. 3:12; 1 Thess. 1:4)
4. Called (Isa. 41:9; 43:1)	4. Called (Rom. 1:6,7; 1 Cor. 1:2)
5. Church (Ps. 89:5; Mic. 2:5	5. Church Eph 1:1; Acts 20:28
6. Flock (Ezek. 34: Ps. 77:20)	6. Flock (Luke 2:32; 1 Pet. 5:2)
7. Holy Nation (Exod. 19:5,6)	7. Holy Nation (1 Pet. 2:9)
8. Kingdom of Priests (Exod. 19:5,6)	8. Kingdom of Priests (1 Pet. 2:9)
9. Peculiar Treasure (Exod. 19:5,6)	9. Peculiar Treasure (1 Pet. 2:9)
10. God's People (Hos. 1:9, 10)	10. God's People (1 Pet. 2:10)
11. Holy People (Deut. 7:5)	11. Holy People (1 Pet. 1:15,16)
12. People of Inheritance (Deut. 4:20)	12. People of Inheritance (Eph 1:18)
13. God's Tabernacle in Israel (Lev. 26:11)	13. God's Tabernacle in Church (Jn 1:14)
14. God walks among them (Lev. 2:12)	14. God walk among them (2 Cor. 6:16-18)
15. Twelve Patriarchs	15. Twelve Apostles
16. God married to them (Isa. 54:5; Jer. 3:14; Hos. 2;19; Jer. 6:2;	16. Christ married to them (Eph. 5:22, 23; 2 Cor. 11:2; Rom. 7:1,4) 31:32)

CHAPTER 16:

THE UNMARRIED (AGAMOS): WHO ARE THEY?

(Text: 1 Corinthians 7:8, 9, and 11)

The apostle Paul, who answered questions from Christians pertaining to divorce and marriage (1 Cor. 7:1, 2), is the only New Testament writer that used the word *agamos*. He employed it four times and all are found in one chapter (1 Cor. 7:8, 11, 32, and 34). This is the chapter where he sought to settle an issue that was plaguing (and continues to plague) preachers and church leaders in their pursuit of an answer to the question "Who may marry?" (which clearly is the gist of the chapter). The apostle set forth some straightforward answers. Some are given in the form of direct commands; but, unfortunately, there remains disagreement as to whom the "unmarried" refers. I set forth two relevant questions at the outset of this study: 1) "Would it be reasonable to conclude that the divorced, during the time of Paul's writing, did not consider themselves as being "unmarried"? 2) Did the apostle write anything that would suggest that the divorced, regardless of the reason, were not to be included in his instructions as to how to deal with the unmarried, i.e., to "let them marry"?

Strong's Concordance

***agamos*: unmarried**
Original Word: ἄγαμος, οῦ, ὁ, ἡ
Part of Speech: Noun, Feminine; Noun, Masculine
Transliteration: agamos
Phonetic Spelling: (ag'-am-os)
Definition: unmarried
Usage: unmarried, of a person not in a state of wedlock, whether he or she has formerly been married or not.

A very common tradition in many Christian-based religious circles is that the divorced commit continuous adultery by marrying and must therefore remain celibate. Those who believe, teach, and promote this position understand that their view has Paul teaching contrary to their idea of what Jesus taught if it can be shown that the "unmarried," in verse 8, includes the divorced. ("I say therefore to the **unmarried** and widows, It is good for them if they abide even as I.") This is because in the next verse Paul emphatically states, "But if they cannot contain let them marry." These teachers contend that the context, where *agamos* is used, indicates that Paul has reference to virgins and/or widows—except in verse 11, where they need the same word to refer to the divorced.

To understand the context, one must back up to the beginning of the chapter. Here Paul commands to "Let every man have his own wife, and let every woman have her own husband." The fact that he uses the word "EVERY" indicates that he has in mind the common need of man for marriage "to avoid fornication." This would logically include those divorced because people who have been married are generally more prone to the temptation to commit fornication than one who has not previously had a spouse.

The renowned scholar **Albert Barnes**, a proponent of the traditional MDR position, wrote comments pertaining to 1 Corinthians 7:8, 9. Regarding the "unmarried" he said:

> **"To the unmarried.** The word unmarried (~agamoiv~) may refer either to those who had never been married, or to widowers. It here means simply those who were at that time unmarried, and his reasoning applies to both classes."

Yes, "It here means simply those who were at that time unmarried."

In view of the absence of context that indicates the above passage applies ONLY to those who have never married or who are widows, the natural interpretation is that the "unmarried" includes those divorced. God authorized divorce (a timeless law) under the Law of Moses. It was designed to end a marriage, which would allow the woman to marry another. (Divorce was a non-issue for the man because he could have more than one wife.) Before God instituted this law, when a man ended his relationship with a wife she was still married to him and could not marry another man. This is the reason God commanded men to give the woman a certificate of divorcement (Deut. 24:1, 2) —that she might "go and be another man's wife." We know for certain that this was not a man-made law because Moses was inspired by God to write the law (John 5:45-47). Furthermore, God used the very same law in divorcing His wife, Israel (Jer. 3:8), which tells us He approved of the divorce law.

Barnes Verse 9:

> "**But if they cannot contain**. If they have not the gift of continence; if they cannot be secure against temptation; if they have not strength of virtue enough to preserve them from the danger of sin, and of bringing reproach and scandal on the church.
>
> **"It is better.** It is to be preferred.
>
> **"Than to burn.** The passion here referred to is often compared to a fire. See Virg. AEn. iv. 68. It is better to marry, even with all the inconveniences attending the marriage life in a time of distress and persecution in the church, #1Co 7:26, than to be the prey of raging, consuming, and exciting passions."

In view of the NEED for marriage, which was ably and ardently articulated by Mr. Barnes, and Paul's classifying "forbidding to marry" as "doctrines of devils" (1 Tim. 4:1-3), the idea that Paul failed to authorize the divorced to marry would seem to be imprudent and irresponsible.

The substance of the chapter, which includes verses 27 and 28 (that we will address later), supports the view that the "divorced" are "unmarried." Thus, the emphatic command in verse 9 to "let them marry" (directed to any who might object due to human tradition handed down through sermons and magazine articles) applies to those who have been divorced.

Verses 10, 11:

> "And unto the married I command, yet not I, but the Lord, Let not the wife depart from her husband: But and if she depart, let her remain unmarried, or be reconciled to her husband: and let not the husband put away his wife."

Admittedly, this passage presents some difficulty in under-standing the apostle's message regarding divorce and marriage, but the difficulty is not limited to one position. If *agamos* means divorce, as God defined it (Deut. 24:1, 2), in the above passage, then it must also mean divorce in verse 9, which, if proven true, is devastating to the positon that the divorced may not marry. Since it has been established that *agamos* refers to the divorced in verse 9 what are we going to do with the seeming notion that Paul contradicted himself by first teaching that the divorced may marry and then later saying they must not? Perhaps there is some logical explanation that allows these two passages to be in harmony.

A word may have a different meaning in a different context. This is apparently the case with Paul's use of *agamos* in verse 11—it does not mean the same thing as it does in verse 9. In verse 11, **the context is not divorce** but simply a case in which a married woman "departs" or "leaves" (*aphieami).* That some use this passage in an attempt to make it appear that Paul is teaching celibacy—right in the middle of a chapter where he has taught the opposite, commanded Christians to allow the unmarried to marry, and asserted that "they do not sin" —shows total lack of respect for context. Let's take an honest look at this often abused text:

Three things must be considered in trying to determine the meaning of "unmarried" in the above passage: 1) it has been established that Paul commanded to allow the "unmarried" to marry; 2) the "unmarried" includes the divorced; and 3) the context supports the notion that the woman merely *departed* or *left* and that she was NOT divorced. Thus, "unmarried," in this context, must have a somewhat different meaning than it does in verse 9.

First, the passage is addressed to "the married." This suggests that the context is not about divorce. The woman is currently married and the Lord's instruction is that she not "depart" or "leave" her husband. Paul provides no instructions here as to what a "divorced" person may or may not do, nor does he so much as give a hint (anywhere in his writings) that a divorce must be initiated for adultery and that only the innocent party may marry. Had this been Paul's understanding he surely would have addressed it. But, again, he did not even hint in that direction. To the contrary, he gave every indication that the "unmarried" (the divorced, for whatever reason) are to be allowed to marry.

Scholars do not think the context of verse 11 is about divorce. Let's note some comments:

STRONG (as quoted from *SwordSearcher*):

> [Grk. 5563] *chorizo* (kho-rid'-zo) from 5561; to place room between, i.e. part; reflexively, to go away: --depart, put asunder, separate.

Below is a comment from Robertson that makes it clear that he thought Paul was talking about "separation" when he spoke of *departing*:

***Robertson's Word Pictures*:**

> "But and if she depart....If, in spite of Christ's clear prohibition, she get separated...."

Another highly respected scholar, below, speaks about the language and the context regarding the phrase "let her remain unmarried":

Bloomfield [*The Greek New Testament*]:

> From the use of καταλλ [reconcile] and the air of the context it is plain that the apostle is not speaking of formal divorces, affected by law, but separations whether agreed on or not, arising from misunderstandings or otherwise.

JFB:

> **But and if she depart** — or 'be separated.' If the sin of separation has been committed, that of a new marriage is not to be added. (Mt 5:32).

Pulpit Commentary:

> **If she depart.** The reference throughout the verse is to separation due to incompatibility of temper, etc.; not to legal divorce.

Weymouth Translation:

> Or if she has already left him, let her either remain as she is or be reconciled to him; and that a husband is not to send away his wife.

Montgomery Translation:

> Or if she has already left him let her either remain as she is, or be reconciled to him), and also that a husband is not to put away his wife.

Robertson's Word Studies (1 Cor. 7:8):

> *Agamos* is an old word and in N.T. occurs only in this passage. In 1Co 7:11, 1Co 7:34 it is used of women where the old Greeks would have used *anandros*, without a husband.

Robertson suggests that the word in verse 8 is not the same word as that found in verse 11. If this is true then the idea that our usual English translation "unmarried" has a different meaning in verse 11 than the meaning in verse 8 would follow. Whether Robertson is correct or not the following definitions of "unmarried" do no injustice to the word translated "unmarried" in verse 11:

> *1. not married. 2. a person who lives celibate. 3. a person living solo after a past relationship failed. 4. a person who chooses to live single.*

Verses 27, 28:

While this passage does not contain the word "unmarried" it would be irresponsible not to consider it in seeking to understand the meaning of Paul's teaching in the chapter regarding the "unmarried."

> Art thou bound unto a wife? seek not to be loosed. Art thou loosed from a wife? seek not a wife. But and if thou marry, thou hast not sinned; and if a virgin marry, she hath not sinned. Nevertheless, such shall have trouble in the flesh: but I spare you.

It is clear that Paul addressed "virgins" in verse 25, but he now addresses those who are married or have been married. He encourages those who are married not to seek divorce and advises those who are already divorced, and perhaps also those whose spouse has died, not to seek a wife. But since he later addresses widows specifically (verse 39) this text may not have been applicable to them. He follows with a statement intended to be pertinent to the "loosed" as well as those who had never married.

Since Paul's command was directed to a woman who is, or would be, separated, rather than divorced, it is irresponsible to try to force 1 Corinthians 7:11 to support the assumption that Paul taught celibacy. That concept is contrary to everything recorded in the chapter relating to marriage. It is not consistent with the context or the language nor is it consistent with the gist of Paul's teaching. He was totally against requiring celibacy and classified it as "doctrines of devils" (1 Tim. 4:1-3).

If one contends that the word "unmarried," in verse 11, means "divorced," to be consistent he must apply that same meaning to the same word where it is found in verses 8 and 9, which would prove too much. Here the apostle writes: **"I say therefore to the unmarried and widows, it is good for them if they abide even as I. But if they cannot contain, let them marry: for it is better to marry than to burn."** Why would the apostle Paul command to let the unmarried marry in one passage and then immediately turn around and say the opposite, using the same word? Of course, he wouldn't and he didn't. In verses 8 and 9, the teaching is that those who do not have a marriage are to be allowed to marry, whereas verses 10 and 11 teach that the "married" are to remain in that state, even if separated, due to the "present distress."

One important rule of hermeneutics is "do not construe one passage so as to contradict another." Since there is no getting around the fact that verses 8 and 9 refer to the divorced and that in verse 11 the context is not about divorce, the latter passage must be the one with the word that has the alternate meaning.

If the wife has "departed" or already left, i.e., gone out of the home back to the parents, or wherever, she is exhorted to "remain as she is" (in the separated state) or go back to her husband (not ex-husband). Divorce is *not* under consideration here. If a husband or wife actually ends the marriage by divorce this text no longer applies.

This links closely with Paul's similar comment in verses 27-28 that those who are divorced should not remarry because of "the present distress" (verse 26), but that if such persons do remarry, then they are to understand that they "have not sinned."

Conclusion:

Those who use 1 Corinthians 7:10-11 to teach that divorced persons have no right to marry are misinterpreting Paul's teachings. They do grave injustice to the crux of Paul's teaching, which is that we must allow marriage for people who need it so they can "avoid fornication" (1 Cor. 7:2).

The primary teaching of the apostle Paul is that those who are married should remain that way, and not only that but also they should be faithful (Col. 3:9; Eph. 5:22). If a couple has problems and they become separated, they should not make unwise and hasty decisions, especially during the time of distress, but be patient and endeavor to work things out.

Suggested Reading:
Open Bible Study: Who Has A Right to Marriage?
http://www.totalhealth.bz/Open-Bible-Study-Regarding-Who-Has-Right-To-Marriage.pdf

CHAPTER 17:

FORBIDDING TO MARRY THE DEVIL'S MOST SUCCESSFUL DOCTRINE (1 TIM. 4:1-3)

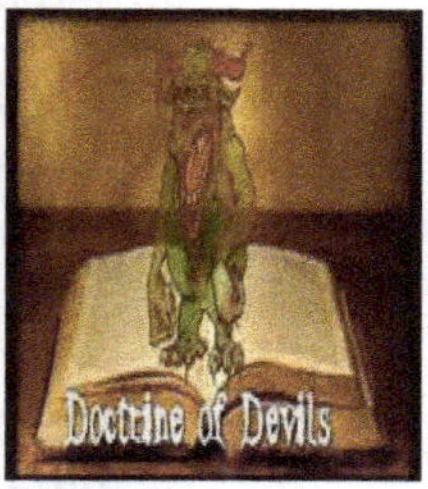

The doctrine that divorced people are ineligible for marriage, which is contrary to the teachings of the apostle Paul but nonetheless commonly believed, has numerous scriptural and hermeneutical problems and has unacceptable consequences. This doctrine has served and continues to serve the devil well.

The Devil's Doctrine:

1. Denies the right of some to marry. This makes them easy prey for various temptations.
2. Requires the biblically unprecedented breaking up of homes in cases involving a second marriage for at last one of the partners, which virtually always drives them from the church and Christ.
3. Denies Paul's teaching that those who are *loosed* from a spouse may marry.
4. Discourages evangelists (if they believe and practice the devil's doctrine) because a majority of prospects for conversion will be lost (after much effort and time is expended) when told they must break up their homes, live celibate, and forget sex for the rest of their lives.
5. Makes God and Christianity appear to be unjust by punishing even those innocent of marital sin and making it appear that it is God's doing.
6. Causes many who want to follow Jesus to reject him.
7. Causes many who have obeyed the gospel to turn away from Jesus.

8. Causes division in churches and discord among brethren.

9. Results in fornication when some "cannot contain" because marriage, God's means to help us "avoid fornication," is forbidden for certain ones deemed "not eligible" for marriage (1 Corinthians 7:2, 9).

10. Has been the cause for an enormous amount of time to be expended by Christians that could otherwise be used in spreading the gospel.

11. Promotes a meritorious works-based salvation, rather than a grace-based salvation (one must suffer and do penance to earn salvation).

12. Denies God's statement that it is not good for man to be alone.

13. Makes not only initiating divorce an unforgivable sin, unless it is initiated for fornication, but makes being divorced by another an unforgivable sin.

14. Encourages a race to the courthouse to be the one to "put away" the other first so as to "have a right to remarry"—thus, actually promoting and encouraging divorce.

15. Tends to cause (among those who set out to defend the devil's doctrine) a deterioration of certain important intellectual faculties because biblical hermeneutics have to be ignored or rejected.

16. Makes God's Word appear to have a loophole whereby the cunning and powerful may avoid celibacy yet remain in fellowship with the "church," after murdering their spouse, which is a forgivable sin.

17. Makes the Bible appear to be contradictory as it requires the assumption that Moses taught what God did not want, then Jesus contradicted Moses, then the apostle Paul contradicted Jesus when he said to let the *unmarried* marry (1 Corinthians 7:8, 9), and then Paul contradicted himself.

18. Requires the belief that Jesus transgressed the Law by changing it from "The divorced may marry" to "The divorced may not marry," from which it must then be concluded that the New Testament is not inspired and that Jesus was not the Son of God.

19. Denies the words of both Jesus and Paul, who said some cannot remain celibate. The fact that Jesus mentioned eunuchs indicates that some can and some cannot remain celibate.

20. Elevates the Law of Moses over the gospel of Christ in that Moses freed the woman to marry again while Christ leaves her like an animal chained and deserted with no one to meet her needs and with no hope of finding anyone.

Many other biblical principles could be added to this list to illustrate the conundrums inherent in the traditional view on "divorce and remarriage." The idea that the divorced may not marry is derived from a misunderstanding of one verse. That verse is used as a foundation for a dangerous and harmful doctrine, and other scriptures that show that Jesus's teaching was misinterpreted have to be viewed through the lens of traditional MDR teaching. Some need to reevaluate their understanding of the various passages related to the subject of divorce and marriage. We must determine to take all the Bible says on the subject and seek a conclusion that will allow harmony of the scriptures. Otherwise, we are like those who say we are saved by "faith only" while ignoring other teachings and commands in the Bible that teach all that is involved in salvation, such as grace and the blood of Christ etc.

"Now the Spirit speaketh expressly, that in the latter times some shall depart from the faith, giving heed to seducing spirits, and doctrines of devils; [2] Speaking lies in hypocrisy; having their conscience seared with a hot iron; [3] ***Forbidding to marry***, *and commanding* to abstain from meats..."

1 Timothy 4:1-3

CHAPTER 18:

THE "EXCEPTION CLAUSE" (MATTHEW 5:32 AND 19:9)

Aside from the subject of salvation, what Jesus meant when he said, "except it be for fornication" is of utmost importance. This is because of the divergent views, some of which have resulted in many Christians, or prospective Christians, turning away from Christ, churches splitting, preachers being maligned and marked as heretics, and countless hours spent in study and debate that could have been spent in more profitable ways. If indeed a divorced person is "living in adultery" if he/she marries another, then it is right to be dogmatic in one's teaching and practice regarding the issue. But think of the harm that has been done by forbidding marriage for those who need it. Many "faithful" have been deprived of the pleasure of sex and joy and security of a family, which can result in serious emotional issues. Considering the fact that the apostle Paul classified "forbidding to marry" as "doctrines of devils" (1 Timothy 4:1–3) it is obvious that God was actually warning against taking a certain position—the one that requires those divorced to remain celibate.

> ***"...Whoever marries a woman who is separated but not divorced, commits adultery"*** **(Matt. 5:31-32)**
> **George Lamsa Translation**

Previously, we discussed Jesus's condemnation of the Jewish men's practice of sending away their wives but not divorcing them according to the Law (by giving them a certificate of divorce) so they could "go be another man's wife" (Deuteronomy 24:1, 2). The meaning of "except it be for fornication" makes sense only if one understands the error Jesus was addressing. One view has Jesus correcting a unique problem but the other has Him contradicting Moses' teaching, which was God's Law that was not yet abrogated.

The so-called MDR texts are: Matthew 5:32, 19:9; Mark 10:11; and Luke 16:18. Many miss some very important information contained in these texts.

Three Important Things to Note:

First, only the women would commit adultery by marrying another. The text does not say a man who is guilty of "sending away" a wife is guilty of adultery if he marries another. Since under the Law the men were allowed more than one wife, it is apparent that the sin was in the men's dealings with the wife whom they "put away" rather than a sexual sin in a new marriage. That is made very clear by Jesus in Mark's account as discussed below.

Second, Jesus said the action the men took in sending away a wife and marrying another is "adultery against her" (Mark 10:11). Jesus's statement conflicts with the idea that the man who sends away a wife without the cause of unfaithfulness commits adultery with the woman he marries. This text indicates Jesus's concern was with the woman being "put away." In what situation does a man commit *adultery* against his wife? Remember, tradition says *adultery* is a sexual sin—the sex act with one that is the spouse of another or sex with one who is not your own spouse; therefore, since this important point (the woman having adultery committed against her) is often missed, is it not possible that the exception clause has been misunderstood and misapplied? And what a tragedy if it has been because this is a key text!

Third, the "exception clause" is found only in Matthew's account. If the exception clause is significant and important as many have assumed and taught, why is it not taught in all the Gospels? And why is it left out of the New Testament epistles? Surely, if Jesus intended for the world to understand that all divorced persons must remain celibate unless they actually initiated the divorce because of adultery, He would have declared it in no uncertain terms. But instead of making the foregoing clear, He tells the world, through an inspired apostle's teachings, to allow the "unmarried" (which includes those divorced) to marry so they can "avoid fornication" (1 Corinthians 7:1, 2, 7-8; 27-29) and states that they do not sin if they marry. Paul answered questions that were asked by Christians relating to who may marry, yet in all his writing, we do not find even a hint that the *reason* for a divorce has anything to do with whether the divorced may marry another.

Matthew 5:32

> "Here the exception clause may refer to a situation in which those married are already closer related and whose marriage, according to Jewish law, would technically be sexual immorality (Cf. Lev. 18:6-18; Acts 15:20; 1 Cor. 5:1)"
>
> The Believer's Study Bible, NKJV, (c) 1991, Nelson / Editor: W. A. Criswell, PhD.

The "exception clause" means exactly what it says just as the rest of the text regarding *put away* and committing adultery means exactly what it says, when properly translated. Perhaps it is best explained by a paraphrase:

> Whosoever shall put away (send out of the house) his wife, except in the case of fornication (*an illicit or unlawful marriage*) and marrieth another causeth her to commit adultery: and whosoever shall marry her that is put away committeth adultery.
>
> Matthew 5:32

If a marriage was not legal/scriptural, then no certificate was needed. If the man sent away his wife, or woman, after learning that fornication is being committed because it is an unlawful relationship, his actions would not constitute adultery "against her."

John told Herod, regarding his brother's wife whom he had married, "It is not lawful for thee to have her" (Matthew 14:3; Leviticus 20:21; Deuteronomy 25:7). (The Law did not allow a man to marry his brother's wife, even if legally divorced, yet it required it if the brother died childless.) This is a case when sending away (no divorce) was proper and right. This is the exception of which Jesus spoke. Herod would not commit adultery against his illicit wife by sending her away.

In 1 Corinthians 5, we read about a young man who "had his father's wife." Most likely, he married his stepmother after his father died. This was an unlawful relationship, one that even the Gentiles did not practice. The relationship needed to end. Obviously, the "exception clause" would apply.

The following versions lend support to the accuracy of the paraphrase above, but unfortunately, they render *apoluo* as divorce:

The New Jerusalem Bible:

> But I say this to you, everyone who divorces his wife, except for the case of an illicit marriage, makes her an adulteress; and anyone who marries a divorced woman commits adultery.
>
> Matthew 5:32

New American with Apocrypha:

> But I say to you, whoever divorces his wife (unless the marriage is unlawful) causes her to commit adultery, and whoever marries a divorced woman commits adultery.
>
> Matthew 5:32

Holman Christian Standard:

> It was also said, Whoever divorces his wife must give her a written notice of divorce. But I tell you, everyone who divorces his wife, except in a case of sexual immorality, fornication, or possibly a violation of Jewish marriage laws causes her to commit adultery. And whoever marries a divorced woman commits adultery.
>
> Matthew 5:32

Also, George Lamsa was on the right track but failed to accurately translate *apoluo*:

George Lamsa's Translation of the New Testament:

> It has been said that whoever divorces his wife, must give her the divorce papers. But I say to you, that whoever divorces his wife, except for fornication, causes her to commit adultery; and whoever marries a woman who is separated but not divorced, commits adultery.
>
> Matthew 5:31–32

Lamsa makes it quite clear that the meaning, according to the context, is that marrying a woman that has been separated from her husband but has not received the "bill of divorcement" results in adultery.

Wuest Word Studies and the *Wuest* translation give support to the idea that the "put away" are not legally divorced:

Wuest Word Studies:

> "The words 'to put away' are apoluo, literally, 'to release.' When used in connection with divorce, it means, 'to repudiate.'
>
> Mark 10:11

Wuest Translation:

> "And having come to Him, Pharisees kept on asking Him whether it is lawful for a man to repudiate a wife, putting Him to the test."
>
> Matt. 5:32

> Whoever marries her who has been dismissed commits adultery.
>
> Wuest

The common thinking is that the woman *put away* is actually *divorced*, and because she did not do the divorcing because of the husband's fornication, the man who marries her also commits adultery. The fact that this position has problems is seldom denied. The explanation is simple. The woman who is *put away* commits adultery in marrying another because she is not legally/scripturally released from her husband. The man who marries this woman commits adultery because he marries the wife of another man.

In Jesus's exception clause, He did not mean that the spouse committed fornication, which either broke the marriage bond or allowed the "innocent" one to so do through divorce proceedings. His words simply had reference to the *relationship*—it was not a legal or scriptural marriage. If a man found that he had married someone who was already married, who was close kin (incest), or otherwise contrary to the Law, he would not need to do anything but "put away," which amounted to separation—not divorce. This situation was the scenario about which the exception clause applied.

CHAPTER 19:

UNDERSTANDING THE "EXCEPTION CLAUSE" TEN RULES TO OBSERVE

Is the Bible unintelligible when it comes to the subject of divorce and marriage? Did God intend for people to have difficulty with this subject, or is it only difficult because of the error that has been taught and because of the influence of those who teach it? Another possible reason that people miss the true teaching of the Bible is because of their failure to use good hermeneutics. Surely there is a simple explanation for Matthew 19:9 that contains the phrase "except it be for fornication" that is free of unacceptable consequences and that does not require one to ignore hermeneutical difficulties. There undoubtedly is one such explanation; otherwise, the Bible is unintelligible and not inspired by God. To find what our loving and merciful God wants us to know, we cannot overemphasize the importance of a proper study of the context of key passages. Matthew 19:3–13 is one such passage.

One must follow some simple rules when studying any Bible subject. Those who refuse to acknowledge these rules while continuing to teach and practice questionable and potentially harmful doctrines are simply being foolish, thoughtless, and imprudent, if not outright rebellious. The words of the apostle James should incite godly fear in all who would endeavor to teach God's word:

> Not many [of you] should become teachers (self-constituted censors and reprovers of others), my brethren, for you know that we [teachers] will be judged by a higher standard *and* with greater severity [than other people; thus we assume the greater accountability and the more condemnation].
>
> James 3:1 *AMPC*

Below are some rules that are applicable to the divorce and remarriage issue or study:

1. **Consider who is being addressed and all surrounding circumstances such as the intentions of the querist and the dispensation or law in effect at the time.**

The Pharisees were attempting to entrap Jesus by tempting him to take sides and to contradict Moses's Law regarding divorce (Deuteronomy. 24:1–4). They knew that Jesus, who lived under the Law of Moses, was obligated to respect and follow that law. Without a doubt, the Jews would have charged Jesus with sin had He contradicted Moses's teachings. It is interesting to note that the enemies of Jesus did not make such a charge, but that so-called "friends" are now saying he did contradict Moses.

2. **Use common sense in studying the Bible just as you would in studying any book.**

Are teachers really using good common sense when they assert that one who has no marriage, having been legally divorced by his/her spouse, is still "bound" or still "married" to the spouse who divorced him/her?

Does it make sense to argue that a divorce frees one person in the party but not the other? Where is the sense in teaching that one is "bound" to a previous spouse but not still married to him?

Does it make sense to insist that a faithful woman, legally divorced by her husband according to God's law that "she may go and become another man's wife" (Deut. 24:1, 2) must remain celibate? She may even be the "innocent party" and actually have had opportunity to divorce him first—and therefore, assure her "right" to marry according to tradition.

Do defenders of the traditional doctrine make sense when they, seeking to avoid the force of an argument, assert that their doctrine does not have Jesus contradicting Moses because Jesus's teachings were not applicable until after the cross? Indeed, because Jesus clearly addressed the Jews, they knew his words applied to them; and if Jesus did not mean what he said to be applicable at the time he said it, then he lied—making people feel guilty when they had not yet broken an effective law.

3. **Do not interpret one statement in a manner that contradicts other clear statements or principles in the Bible.**

Jesus's statement recorded in Matthew 19:9 is interpreted to mean that a divorced person cannot marry another. This idea contradicts the Old Testament teaching that "it is not good that man should be alone" (Genesis 2:18) and New Testament teachings that a spouse is needed to avoid fornication: "Nevertheless, to avoid fornication, let every man have his own wife, and let every woman have her own husband" (1 Corinthians 7:2).

4. **Study the context of a statement and all of the related material in the rest of the Bible.**

A statement taken out of context is a pretext. If one's theory is based upon a passage taken out of context and is not in complete harmony with other scriptures on the matter, it must be rejected.

5. **Obscure (difficult) passages may be understood in light of other passages on the same subject that are clear in their meaning.**

One must not draw a conclusion based solely on an obscure passage and then twist all the other passages on the same subject to harmonize with the preconceived conclusion.

6. **A correct understanding is what it says, not what someone else says it says.**

Dictionaries, lexicons, and commentaries were written by men who were known to have been influenced by tradition. Such helps may be beneficial as we study but the Bible itself is the best commentary.

7. **On important issues God will provide sufficient evidence for an honest person to have a confident and clear understanding.**

Jesus said, "Ye shall know the truth and the truth shall make you free" (Mark 7:7). There is nothing like having the truth and being free from the traditions and doctrines of men that Jesus says causes religion to be vain (Matthew 15:9).

8. **Do not seek to derive something from a passage that is not there, or is more than what the author intended.**

This rule is always important but is particularly important when studying divorce and marriage. The three main passages that are used to support the position that denies people who have no marriage the right to marry are Matthew 19:9, 1 Corinthians 7:11, and Romans 7:1–3. None of these passages says what many, seeking to defend the traditional teaching, assert that they say. When other rules are applied, it becomes apparent that celibacy for the divorced is not being taught.

9. A correct understanding of the passage will violate no logical hermeneutical rules and will be in harmony with all truth.

The correct understanding of a passage may contradict tradition, but it should not be our intention to harmonize a passage with the teachings of men. Rather, we must seek to learn what the inspired writer intended. One can be confident he is correct if his position is based upon diligent and honest study using good hermeneutics.

10. Have a love for truth and a determination to find it regardless of what the earthly consequences might be.

The life of a preacher can be difficult when he bucks tradition. But only the truth can make you free. God speaks to you through the Bible. Listen to Him and trust Him for the outcome. "If God be for us, who can be against us?" (Romans 8:31b)

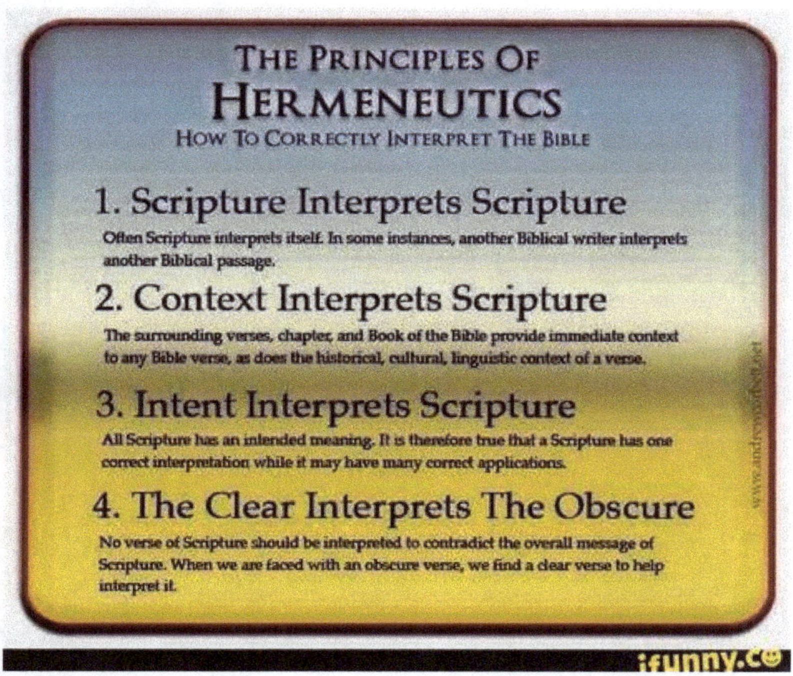

THE PRINCIPLES OF
HERMENEUTICS
HOW TO CORRECTLY INTERPRET THE BIBLE
1. Scripture Interprets Scripture
Often Scripture interprets itself. In some instances, another Biblical writer interprets another Biblical passage.
2. Context Interprets Scripture
The surrounding verses, chapter, and Book of the Bible provide immediate context to any Bible verse, as does the historical, cultural, linguistic context of a verse.
3. Intent Interprets Scripture
All Scripture has an intended meaning. It is therefore true that a Scripture has one correct interpretation while it may have many correct applications.
4. The Clear Interprets The Obscure
No verse of Scripture should be interpreted to contradict the overall message of Scripture. When we are faced with an obscure verse, we find a clear verse to help interpret it.
ifunny.co

CHAPTER 20:

UNDERSTANDING THE "EXCEPTION CLAUSE": A CLOSE LOOK AT THE CONTEXT (MATTHEW 19:3–12)

This part of the study is an exegesis of the entire text of Matthew 19:3–12.

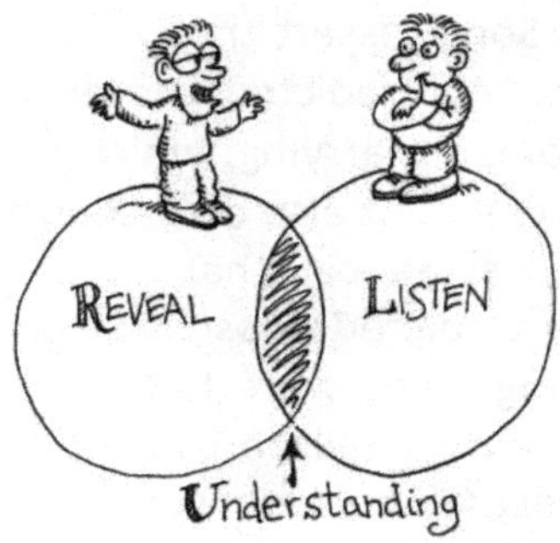

> The Pharisees also came unto him, tempting him, and saying unto him, Is it lawful for a man to put away his wife for every cause?
>
> Matthew 19:3

At the time when Jesus lived on the earth, a dispute had been raging for about a century between the schools of Shammai and Hillel over the proper interpretation of "something indecent" (Deuteronomy 24:1). This was but one of numerous attempts by the Pharisees to entrap Jesus. They evidently had two motives: to pit Jesus against Moses and thus charge him with teaching contrary to the Law; or to get Jesus to take sides on the controversial divorce issue that would cause Him problems.

Context
Context
Context

What was the answer the Pharisees were seeking in response to their question? Would they not have been satisfied if Jesus had answered "yes" or "no"? Indeed, they would have, but Jesus perceived their intentions and did not respond as they had hoped. Thus, they failed in their effort to cause Jesus to take sides on the issue that so divided the Jews. And so this would explain why at

Jesus's trial no charge was made that He had taught contrary to Moses regarding the marriage law.

How did Jesus respond? The conclusion of some today is that Jesus took sides with the Shammai school, which would mean He fell for the Pharisees' trap. Since nothing in this passage or scripture (or elsewhere in the Bible) gives any credence to the idea that the Pharisees or the Hillel school understood Jesus to have taken sides with the Shammai school, then it would seem imprudent to conclude and teach that Jesus sided with Shammai.

Some assert that Jesus not only took the Shammai position but also contradicted Moses in teaching *new* law regarding divorced woman marrying, which is intended to mean that not just divorced *women* but also divorced *men* could no longer marry. Again, we find no evidence that the Pharisees understood Jesus to have contradicted Moses. Since that was apparently one of the main things they were hoping Jesus would do, it is prudent to conclude that their failure to note (even at His trial) that Jesus contradicted Moses means they did not understand Jesus to have done so by teaching a new and different law.

Jesus Said He Was Not Making New Law

> Let there be no thought that I have come to put an end to the law or the prophets. I have not come for destruction, but to make complete. Truly I say to you, Till heaven and earth come to an end, not the smallest letter or part of a letter will in any way be taken from the law, till all things are done. Whoever then goes against the smallest of these laws, teaching men to do the same, will be named least in the kingdom of heaven; but he who keeps the laws, teaching others to keep them, will be named great in the kingdom of heaven.
>
> Matthew 5:17–19 (BBE)

A Feeble Quibble

Some preachers are now saying Jesus's words were not applicable to the Jews but were just teachings that would go into effect when his law went into effect after his death. In other words, a command was given to the hearers (Jewish men) but they were not really expected to do anything. How does that theory harmonize with the following passage?

> What thing soever I command you, that shall ye observe to do: thou shalt not add thereto, nor diminish from it.
>
> Deuteronomy 12:32

Asserting that what Jesus said to sinners under the Law was not applicable to them, that it did not apply to them, and that they could practice what He condemned is not only a dodge or quibble, but it also implies that Jesus spoke without authority and did not tell the truth.

On the other hand, if Jesus did change the Law, many of the Jewish men would have had to violate the Law by immediately ceasing to be faithful to their wives. Let me repeat that: they would have had to violate the Law in order to obey Jesus. Who can believe it? In addition, even if we were to accept that Jesus's words did not apply before the cross, no New Testament scripture teaches by command, example, or necessary inference that the people taught on the day of Pentecost, or thereafter, were told their legal marriages were *adulterous*. The only examples we have are marriages that were not legal (Mark 6:18, Leviticus 20:21, 1 Corinthians 5:1), and that is in perfect harmony with what Jesus actually taught and which, hopefully, you will clearly see before you complete this reading.

Which school was correct, Hillel or Shammai?

> When a man taketh a wife, and marrieth her, then it shall be, if she find no favor in his eyes, because he hath found some unseemly thing in her, that he shall write her a bill of divorcement, and give it in her

> hand, and send her out of his house. And when she is departed out of his house, she may go and be another man's wife. And if the latter husband hate her, and write her a bill of divorcement, and give it in her hand, and send her out of his house; or if the latter husband die, who took her to be his wife; her former husband, who sent her away, may not take her again to be his wife, after that she is defiled; for that is abomination before Jehovah: and thou shalt not cause the land to sin, which Jehovah thy God giveth thee for an inheritance.
>
> Deuteronomy 24:1–4 (ASV)

The text does not really give a specific reason at all for the divorce, and I draw this conclusion because of verse three, which says, "And if the latter husband hate her…" Thus, it seems reasonable that the same criteria (he just did not love her) would have been applicable to the first husband who was commanded to write the "bill of divorce" (Mark 10:3) if he was intent on ending the marriage. It is also true that the men's decision was not questioned. Thus, the certificate did what it was intended to do regardless of whether the husband's "reason" was a good one or not.

Neither the Hillel nor Shammai School of Thought Was Correct

The Shammai school held that "something indecent" meant "marital unfaithfulness," which some today insist is the same thing as "except for adultery"; however, the Law required the death penalty for this offense, which means a divorce would not be needed. Thus, adultery was never a reason for divorce under the Old Testament.

The Hillel school held that the reason for divorce included anything that becomes displeasing to the man. This was certainly not what Moses intended to be understood as the reason for his command. Those of the Hillel school were looking at Moses's command as being something that was for *their* benefit, but this was not the case at all. They concluded that, being men, they had God's approval to discard or "put away" a wife with no more reason than they might have to discard a garment. Such was not the will of God as is evident from the following passage:

> For the Lord, the God of Israel, saith that he hateth putting away: for one covereth violence with his garment, saith the Lord of hosts: therefore take heed to your spirit, that ye deal not treacherously.
>
> Malachi 2:16

> Moses's aim was "to regulate and thus to mitigate an evil which he could not extirpate." The evident purpose was, as far as possible, to favor the wife, and to protect her against an unceremonious expulsion from her home and children.
>
> *International Standard Encyclopedia*

Those who were not hardened in heart would be obedient to the command of God and "deal not treacherously" with his wife, which forbade putting them out of the house. The question of whether adultery was the reason for the command to give the "bill of divorce" is easily settled by noting the following:

> And the man that committeth adultery with another man's wife, even he that committeth adultery with his neighbor's wife, the adulterer and the adulteress shall surely be put to death.
>
> Leviticus 20:10

> If a man be found lying with a woman married to a husband, then they shall both of them die, the man that lay with the woman, and the woman: so shalt thou put away the evil from Israel.
>
> Deuteronomy 22:22

Again, since physical sexual adultery was punishable by death, we must rule out the possibility that "adultery" was given as a reason for one to divorce.

The true meaning of Deuteronomy 24:1–4 is ably explained by Mike Willis, a conservative preacher and long-time editor of *Truth Magazine:*

> A reading of this passage demonstrates that Moses was trying to legislate in such a way as to aid the woman because of the manner in which man was abusing her. According to what I can understand was happening in the days of Moses, a man would put away his wife without any concern for her future. She would not be free to go out and marry another man and yet she could not live with her husband. This left her in destitute circumstances quite frequently. Hence, what Moses was trying to legislate was something that would aid women who had been put away by their husbands.
>
> The Mosaical legislation said that if a man was going to put away his wife, he had to give her a bill of divorcement that showed that she was free from him and had the opportunity to remarry. Hence, it was designed to protect the women from the harsh treatment husbands were giving to them.

That the Jews were doing as Mike Willis suggests is evident from the fact the Jews are still practicing the same treachery against their wives. Considering that the Mosaic text (Deuteronomy 24:1–4) was actually a command that gave specific instructions as to how to divorce (when one was determined to do it), rather than a *privilege* for the men (as is evident from the words of Jesus, Mark 10:3), and that the command to provide the "bill of divorcement" was not applicable in the case of marital unfaithfulness, *both* the school of Hillel and the school of Shammai were wrong. Thus, Jesus did not take sides with either of them.

We have already discussed the idea that Jesus did not contradict Moses. As we begin to understand the text from Matthew, we will begin to see (if we have not seen already) that indeed Jesus did not contradict Moses, which explains why the Pharisees did not make a charge against Him on that matter.

> And he answered and said unto them, Have ye not read, that he which made them at the beginning made them male and female, And said, For this cause shall a man leave father and mother, and shall cleave to his wife: and they twain shall be one flesh? Wherefore they are no more twain, but one flesh.

> What therefore God hath joined together, let not man put asunder.
>
> Matthew 19:4–5

What the Law of Moses said was in contrast with what was from the beginning, because God gave no provision for divorce in the beginning. What Jesus said was in contrast with what was from the beginning because it agreed with the Law of Moses. Yet, in rebuking those who took their marriage vows lightly, Jesus did point out God's ideal and that was that marriage is intended for life.

> They say unto him, Why did Moses then command to give a writing of divorcement, and to put her away?
>
> Matthew 19:7

First, we see that the "writ of divorce" was a command. Jesus's reply (Mark 10:3), "What did Moses command you?" is proof.

Second, the reason for the command was that men were dealing *treacherously* with their wives. This was evidently God's way to give relief to the wives. If they could be legally free, they could marry another. A man who deliberately refused to set his wife free, simply casting her out without a divorce decree, was dealing treacherously with her, or committing adultery "against her," as Jesus put it (Mark 10:11).

> He saith unto them, Moses because of the hardness of your hearts suffered you to put away your wives: but from the beginning it was not so.
>
> Matthew 19:8

Moses "suffered," that is, he exacted no penalty for what they were doing—it was just allowed to continue. God gave the command to give the "bill of divorcement," but men continued to disobey. One of the reasons men would "put away" and not give the "bill of divorcement" was the fact that they would have had to return the dowry they received from the woman's father. And so we see they had a motive—a thing often necessary to prove someone guilty of a crime. Of course, we know that men were allowed more than one wife under the Law. (There was no condemnation for polygamy among the Jews for about another 1000 years.) Thus, it was nothing for a man, if he should get tired of a woman, to simply put her away or "send out of the house", which is similar to *abandonment*. Nevertheless, when it was done, the man and woman were still married. This put the woman, who was not allowed to have multiple husbands, in a position of having no man to care for her and no legal or scriptural right to marry. She needed to be released according to the command of Moses (Deuteronomy 24:1–4). This act of "putting away" was a *treacherous* deed by the husband, but the Law contained no provision to punish the men if they did not comply. Jesus did refer to such an act as committing adultery "against her" (Mark 10:11) but He said it was "suffered." Even to this day, it is suffered among the Jews. Women in the United States are not affected because they are allowed to divorce their husbands.

> And I say unto you, Whosoever shall put away his wife, except it be for fornication, and shall marry another, committeth adultery: and whoso marrieth her which is put away doth commit adultery.
>
> Matthew 19:9

First, what Jesus said was not in contrast with the Law of Moses because it was identical to the Law of Moses. Certainly, Jesus was not saying, "Moses said this, but I'm changing it to this…" That would have resulted in an immediate uproar and stoning. Yet it was not even brought up at his trial.

Paraphrase of verse nine:

> *Whoever shall send his wife out of the house and marry another, commits adultery against her, unless he sent her away because of fornication, which is being committed because of the unlawful relationship.*

Holman Christian Standard:

> Except in a case of sexual immorality, fornication, or

> possibly a violation of Jewish marriage laws causes her to commit adultery.
>
> Matthew 5:32

The above must be the meaning because the Mosaic text (which was the basis for the discussion) was needed (and therefore written) because of the treacherous practice of Jewish men who were sending their wives away without completely freeing them from the marriage, which would enable them to marry another.

The Pharisees' first question was about "putting away". We cannot go back and read their mind regarding whether they had legal divorce in mind or merely *putting away*. We do know that Jesus responded to what they *said*. But when Moses was mentioned, they answered with both "put away" and "bill of divorcement." It seems plausible that Jesus went back to their original question about "putting away" without the "bill of divorcement" and that He made His succeeding comments with such in mind.

The Exception Clause

The exception clause, found in verse nine of Matthew 19 and verse thirty-two of Matthew chapter 5, has been the root of more controversy than perhaps any other biblical text. I shall briefly try to explain how it relates to what we have already learned. Note the following passage:

> Now therefore make confession unto the Lord God of your fathers, and do his pleasure: and separate yourselves from the people of the land, and from the strange wives.
>
> Ezra 10:11

God gave no command to *divorce* those "strange wives." Why? They were not legal marriages. The relationships were not pleasing to God and simply needed to end. The translators of the *New Jerusalem Bible* were on the right track (except in rendering *apoluo* as divorce). They translated the passage as follows:

> But I say this to you, everyone who divorces his wife, except for the case of an illicit marriage, makes her an adulteress; and anyone who marries a divorced woman commits adultery.
>
> Matthew 5:32

> His disciples say unto him, If the case of the man be so with his wife, it is not good to marry.
>
> Matthew 19:10

First, it was not the Pharisees but the disciples who commented on Jesus's teachings. Certainly, they were not intending to place doubt upon the wisdom of God in instituting marriage. They understood Jesus to be saying that if the marriage is not going to be legitimate, such as the case when the woman is a forbidden foreign wife, brother's ex-wife, or other forbidden relatives, it is best not to marry that particular woman (Genesis 24:37; Matthew 14:4; Leviticus 20:17; 20:21).

> But he said unto them, Not all men can receive this saying, but they to whom it is given.
>
> Matthew 19:11

Those who could receive the saying would simply be the ones to whom it applied—those whose marriages were illegal/unscriptural and resulted in fornication. No one would "receive it" if the situation was not applicable to them.

> For there are eunuchs, that were so born from their mother's womb: and there are eunuchs, that were made eunuchs by men: and there are eunuchs, that made themselves eunuchs for the kingdom of heaven's sake. He that is able to receive it, let him receive it.
>
> Matthew 19:12

To understand the above passage, we must go back to verse ten. The disciples stated that it was not good to marry if the "case of the man be so with his wife." What case? He was talking about an illegal or unscriptural marriage. In the above passage, Jesus states that men who cannot find a woman, except one that is not lawful to marry, had best remain celibate. Those who are eunuchs, having not the capability to have sex, certainly would have no problem with not marrying. They would have no problem accepting the saying.

This exegesis is logical, scriptural, and hermeneutically sound and allows for God, Jesus, His apostles, and His disciples to be seen as fair and just. All should be able to accept the teaching in this thesis because the original teaching of God on marriage is respected—no families need to bust up (if their marriage is legal) and legally divorced persons, innocent of sin or not, need not remain celibate. The practice of requiring celibacy is something that is contrary to the very reason given for marriage (1 Corinthians 7:2).

Marriage is dissolvable (contrary to Catholic decree) if done legally, and those who have been through an unfortunate divorce are NOT still *bound*. This is evidently true because of the clear teaching of Paul and the lack of biblical or historical evidence to support the practice of breaking up legal marriages and imposing celibacy.

When a divorce takes place, one or both parties may have been guilty of sin, but the sin(s) is forgivable. The last thing that should happen to one disheartened because of a divorce is that he/she be required to maintain a permanent position that makes the endeavor to live the Christian life even more difficult.

CHAPTER 21:

MEANING OF THE "EXCEPTION CLAUSE" ILLUSTRATED

The exception clause of Matthew 19:9 has often been used to support breaking up marriages (homes) and imposing celibacy when a divorce has taken place and the divorce was not *for fornication*. The word for *fornication* comes from *porneia*, which involves incest. It is important to note that Jesus could not have meant *adultery* in speaking to the Jews at the time because *adultery* was never a reason for divorce— "uncleanness," or "some unseemly thing" (ASV), was something different (Deuteronomy 24:1–2) and likely was not even intended to be taken as a justifiable "reason" for divorce. Certainly the men were not questioned regarding it and the woman's divorce papers were accepted without having to look into the man's "reason".

Recently, Yahoo news reported a case that illustrates what Jesus was really teaching regarding the exception clause:

> Twins who were separated at birth and adopted by different sets of parents later married each other without realizing they were brother and sister, a peer has told the House of Lords.
>
> Friday, January 11, 12:15 p.m., ET London (AFP)

David Alton, an independent, pro-life member of the Lords, said the brother and sister were granted an annulment after a high court judge ruled that the marriage had never validly existed.

In view of the factual case documented above, let us take another look at the context of an often misused MDR text:

> And I say unto you, Whosoever shall put away his wife, except it be for fornication, and shall marry another, committeth adultery: and whoso marrieth her which is put away doth commit adultery. His disciples say unto him, If the case of the man be so with his wife, it is not good to marry.
>
> Matthew 19:9

Many use verse ten to support the idea that those who marry after a divorce commit adultery and that the people who marry them also commit adultery; however, for Jesus's disciples to have thought that to be true, they would have had to understand him to be teaching contrary to the Law. If that were the case, the response would have been: "But Lord, the Law has always allowed the woman who was given a bill of divorcement to go be another man's wife." And, of course, the Pharisees would have used such a comment to destroy our Lord. The disciples' statement was actually in perfect agreement with what is being taught in this chapter. "If the case of the man be so with his wife (or woman), it is not good to marry." Surely the disciples understood Jesus to be talking about a case like, or similar, to the one noted in the article above.

The couple (twins) in the recent news did not need a legal divorce because they were not legally married—the relationship was *incestuous*. They needed to do what Jesus taught; being married to each other, they were committing fornication—the same fornication to which Jesus was referring; therefore, they needed to separate. They did not need a *divorce* because their marriage was invalid, being incestuous.

Such illicit marriages were common in Old Testament days. In Ezra 10:2–11, we have an example of confession of sin with regard to the taking of foreign wives, and a covenant was made with God to "put away" the strange forbidden wives. It is interesting that God said to "separate" yourselves from them, to include the children (verse three), and that divorce proceedings were not mentioned.

Also, after the Babylonian captivity records were nonexistent; therefore, it was often impossible to know for sure if a marriage was legal/scriptural. At any rate, fornication, due to an illicit marriage, was all Jesus was talking about when He mentioned the exception to a man's putting away a woman and marrying another being an adulterous act. The versions noted below support the point just made:

New Jerusalem:

> But I say this to you, everyone who divorces his wife, except for the case of an illicit marriage, makes her an adulteress; and anyone who marries a divorced woman commits adultery.
>
> Matthew 5:32

New American with Apocrypha:

> I say to you, whoever divorces his wife (unless the marriage is unlawful) and marries another commits adultery.
>
> Matthew 19:9

Holman Christian Standard:

> But I tell you, everyone who divorces his wife, except in a case of sexual immorality, fornication, or possibly a violation of Jewish marriage laws causes her to commit adultery. And whoever marries a divorced woman commits adultery.
>
> Matthew 5:32

In Mark's account, Jesus makes it clear that the sin in question is *against* the wife that is *put away*, unless this sending away is justified because of an *illicit marriage*. He tells us the "adultery" is "against her" rather than *with* the woman the man marries (Mark 10:11). This being true, according to the Law, if there is, in fact, a divorce, the sin of adultery is not committed. Thus, the English phrase "put away," translated from the Greek word *apoluo*, must mean only what lexicographers give as its primary meaning, rather than the meaning that has been generally assumed due to misunderstanding of Jesus's teachings.

To further illustrate the true teaching regarding the "exception clause" that has so often been used to unjustly and unscripturally (1 Corinthians 7:8, 9) impose celibacy on the "unmarried" (including those who are divorced), I present the following scenario:

Bill marries Sue (who has never been married). Bill finds out that Sue is actually his blood sister; therefore, the marriage is not legal. Since there is no legal marriage, there is no need for a divorce.

Bill "puts away" Sue by saying, "We must end this relationship, which is sinful (fornication)," and they divide the goods and separate.

CHAPTER 22:

A SOUND AND POWERFUL ARGUMENT AGAINST MDR TRADITION FROM GALATIANS 5:11

A rhetorical question is....

- **When a question is asked to make a point, not because you want an answer?**
- **The answer is obvious and does not need to be stated.**
- **Or, it is to create a stronger effect than stating what you mean directly.**

Although the Pharisees sought diligently to entrap Jesus in his words in order to find him guilty of something for which they could kill him, they did not charge Him with contradicting Moses on MDR. Thus, we can confidently conclude that they did not understand Jesus to have taught contrary to Moses. Unlike some people today, these men of Jesus's day, who understood His words far better than we can, did not hear Him say that a divorce is no longer a divorce unless it was done because of adultery. Nor did they hear Him say that all divorcees who are remarried are living in adultery.

Unfortunately, this argument is often completely ignored. But some have argued, "A question does not prove anything." Well, let us look at some teaching from Paul to see whether or not a question can prove something. From the scripture below, it is clear that a question, like the one noted above, can indeed be a valid and powerful argument.

In writing to the church at Galatia, the apostle Paul made an argument that follows the same line of logic as the one I have noted that is often ignored. He said (Galatians 5:11):

> Brothers and sisters, if I am still preaching that circumcision is necessary, why am I still being persecuted? In that case the cross wouldn't be offensive anymore.
>
> (*GW*)

Some in the church at Galatia were teaching justification by the Law of Moses and that circumcision was essential. The above passage, which is basically a question, was an argument—a valid and powerful argument. Paul argues that he is not still teaching circumcision (as was the case before his conversion) because if he were, the Jews would not be persecuting him. Thus, instead of stating outright that he is not contending for circumcision, as some may have charged, he presents an argument in the form of a question. Now, if Paul can use this kind of argumentation, and we can see the power of it, why can we not use the same type of argumentation and see the power of it when it comes to the MDR issue? If Jesus had indeed taught contrary to the law on MDR, why would the Pharisees not use His words against him? Why did they not say at Jesus's trial, "This man has taught contrary to Moses by saying all who have divorced (unless for adultery), or been divorced are now living in adultery"? Only one answer makes sense: Jesus did not say what many have attributed to Him. If he had done so, He would have contradicted Moses and been viewed as a transgressor of God's Law.

Rather than assume that Jesus taught something that has consequences we cannot accept, we must believe what Jesus actually said. Some try to prove from the context that Jesus had divorce, as we understand it, in mind, but the context does not bear this out. If the context indicates that Jesus had divorce in mind (when using the word *apoluo*) in the discussion recorded in Matthew 19, why do we have no indication that the Pharisees used Jesus's teaching against him?

CHAPTER 23:

DIVORCED ("UNMARRIED") BUT STILL BOUND?

The earliest published material that I have been able to find that teaches that a divorced ("unmarried") person is still *bound* "in the eyes of God," while admitting that the marriage is dissolved by the legal divorce, as described in Deuteronomy 24:1, 2, is in *Searching the Scriptures* (STS). The articles were written by J. T. Smith in 1984. In the same journal, back in 1977, he made a statement that should not have gone unchallenged. He said, "We are also informed that the Lord binds us together, and that what God has bound together that no man can put asunder." The text simply does not say, "No man can put asunder." Certainly, one can follow God's instructions and "put asunder" (Deuteronomy 24:1, 2), and adultery is not "the only reason" because for that sin, the Law required the death penalty. Since the statement apparently went unchallenged, J. T. evidently felt confident that he could later be successful in teaching his theory about divorced persons still being bound.

How can one person in a marriage be loosed by divorce but not the other?

Let us look at some reasons to question the above noted theory:

1. God gave a procedure for dissolving a marriage so the woman could "go be another man's wife," yet this strange doctrine is saying that a divorce really does not do what it was designed to do. When a couple is divorced, how can one remain *bound* while the other is *loosed*? Marriage is the *only* thing that the Scriptures teach binds a couple together. Take away the marriage, and the bond no longer exists. This is true except in the minds of those who have accepted the theory espoused by Smith in 1984 and echoed by hundreds

since. If the bond still exists after divorce, then the "bill of divorcement" that God commanded be given to the wife means nothing (Deuteronomy 24:2; Mark 10:3–5). Smith actually published an article by Jesse Jenkins that set forth this very supposition. Here is what he said:

> In Deuteronomy 24:1, 2, the writing of divorcement was not an integral part of a divorce. It was a statement that he had divorced her and the provision by which the divorced woman could marry another. If a man sent his wife out of the house, but refused to give her the writing of divorcement, she would nevertheless be a put away (divorced) woman.

To Smith's credit, I was allowed to write a rebuttal in *Gospel Truths.*

2. The theory is based upon the assumption that Jesus stated to the Jews that "divorcing" and marrying another was tantamount to committing adultery. But Jesus could not have meant *divorce* because that would have been contrary to Moses's teachings. To get around this argument, an illogical argument has been made. Some are arguing that the teaching of Jesus (Matthew 19:9) was not contrary to the Law because it applied only when the new covenant would go into effect. This is obviously false because Jesus was speaking to the people who addressed Him, and He told them that such a practice would result in adultery. If a man did what Jesus spoke against, was he guilty or not? If the man was not guilty, then did Jesus lie to these people? Isn't it really obvious Jesus was not talking about the future?

3. The theory assumes that when Jesus and others used the word *apoluo*, a complete and legal divorce was under consideration, even though many of the best translations never translate *apoluo* as *divorce*.

4. The theory forbids those who are "unmarried" but still "bound" to have a marriage. This seems to be doing what Paul condemned in 1 Timothy 4:1–3.

5. The theory allows one who has been divorced to marry again, but he must marry only the one who divorced him—the one to whom he is still "bound." It matters not that his previous spouse has married another and had children. The only hope of a "scriptural marriage" (they say) is to break up this marriage and remarry the original spouse. But God, in no uncertain terms, condemned this practice that many in the church today are encouraging. He said it is "abomination before the Lord: and thou shalt not cause the land to sin" (Deuteronomy 24:4). Also, according to the theory, the person that did the divorcing is free to marry. Therefore, the one divorced would have to break up a marriage that is admittedly legal before he/she could marry again.

The theory that one can be divorced but still bound is obviously laden with problems and is supported only by assumptions and circular reasoning. It evidently was dreamed up as a way of explaining Paul's teaching in 1 Corinthians 7 to harmonize with the idea that Jesus taught that the *divorced* commit adultery when they marry.

CHAPTER 24:

THE THEME OF 1 CORINTHIANS 7

"Now concerning the things you wrote unto me…"

Verse 1

The seventh chapter of 1 Corinthians may be one of the most controversial chapters in the epistles, but it is certainly one of the most informative. The chapter deals primarily with questions that Christians asked the apostle Paul regarding marriage. This is evident from the first verse of the chapter: "Now concerning the things whereof ye wrote unto me: It is good for a man not to touch a woman" (1 Corinthians 7:1). We do not have a copy of the letter, but from the answers, we could construct a list of questions that would likely resemble the ones that were sent to Paul.

When intelligent, truth-seeking Christians fail to come to a confident understanding of the truth revealed in chapter 7, it is likely because of at least one of the following reasons:

1. Many, from the outset, have in their mind that Jesus taught that divorced people must remain celibate; thus, they feel that whatever Paul meant must harmonize with what they think Jesus taught. Therefore, any exegesis or explanation of Paul's teachings that does not harmonize with their previously conceived notion is rejected.

2. Some fail to acknowledge that the questions were asked in view of the "present distress" (verse twenty-six), i.e., persecution, and that all the advice isn't necessarily applicable to all under all circumstances. For example, some argue that Paul argued for *celibacy*, but it is imprudent to contend that Paul took issue with God who said, "It is not good that man should be alone." When talking to those who were *separated*, he said that they should "remain unmarried" or "as they are." This should be interpreted in light of the "present distress."

   If Paul had been teaching the doctrine that is attributed to Jesus (*celibacy* for one involved in divorce unless he initiates the divorce for fornication), he surely would not have failed to mention the "exception clause." Therefore, Paul must have intended his advice only for those Christians who get separated to remain as they are while trying to work things out during the "present distress." The passage, therefore, was not about legal divorce but was applicable to a couple who had separated—a common occurrence to this day.

3. Some are not willing to apply good hermeneutics, or even to be consistent in the rules they do apply. For example, some argue that the "unmarried" in verse eight and nine does not include the divorced. Yet, in verse eleven, where Paul speaks to those who have "left" or "departed" and are therefore *separated*, they contend that the phrase "let them remain unmarried" refers to the divorced.

4. Finally, passages in the chapter are interpreted in a way that is not consistent with the apparent theme of the chapter, which we shall now address.

In several passages in the chapter under study, Paul emphasizes the need for marriage and sexual release, so that a man or woman might avoid sexual immorality. He begins by saying: "Nevertheless, to avoid fornication, let every man have his own wife, and let every woman have her own husband" (verse two). Then, he said:

> Let the husband render unto the wife due benevolence: and likewise also the wife unto the husband. The wife hath not power of her own body, but the husband: and likewise also the husband hath not power of his own body, but the wife. Defraud ye not one the other, except it be with consent for a time, that ye may give yourselves to fasting and prayer; and come together again, that Satan tempt you not for your incontinency.
>
> 1 Corinthians 7:3–5

In verse seven, Paul speaks of his gift (celibacy) but recognizes that not all possess such a gift. Therefore, he advises:

> However, if they cannot control themselves, they should get married, for it is better to marry than to burn with passion. (*ISV*)

In several different places in chapter seven, the reader is urged, even commanded, to allow marriage. These passages include verses one and two, eight and nine, twenty-seven and twenty-eight, and thirty-six. To avoid misunderstandings, the apostle gave the reason marriage should be allowed ("to avoid fornication") and he noted who was *eligible* for marriage—the "unmarried."

Verse fifteen is a controversial passage. It says:

> But if the unbelieving depart, let him depart. A brother or a sister is not under bondage in such cases: but God hath called us to peace.

In this verse, the inspired apostle tells us that sometimes, maybe even when we have been a good and faithful spouse, our spouse may leave. When that happens, we are "not under bondage." Some say this does not give us a right to marry again, but not having that right would be bondage. (This passage is dealt with exclusively in another chapter.)

Let us now observe some things taught in verses twenty-seven and twenty-eight:

> Art thou bound unto a wife? seek not to be loosed. Art thou loosed from a wife? seek not a wife. But and if thou marry, thou hast not sinned; and if a virgin marry, she hath not sinned.

Some insist that Paul is only speaking of virgins, since they are included at the end, and therefore argue that when Paul said, "But and if thou marry, thou hast not sinned" it only applies to virgins. Let's back up to the beginning of the context.

> "Now concerning virgins I have no commandment of the Lord: yet I give my judgment, as one that hath obtained mercy of the Lord to be faithful."
>
> Verse 25

The first thing we need to observe is that he says he has no commandment, evidently regarding virgins marrying in the distressful situations that were apparent due to persecutions (Verse 26). Second, we should observe, as pointed out by Pulpit Commentary, that when speaking of virgins he is speaking of both men and woman. “Rather, for a person—whether man or woman” (*Pulpit Commentary*). But beginning in verse 27 it becomes clear that Paul switches and begins answering questions that pertain to whether a man should stay with his wife and whether if divorced he may marry another. The fact that he is no longer speaking of virgins is evident because of the following facts: 1) they do not have a wife; 2) they are not *bound;* and 3) they are not *loosed*. But each of these things is applicable to divorced men.

After taking about the virgins exclusively, Paul contrast those “bound” (married) with those “loosed” (divorced) and then says, “But and if thou marry, thou hast not sinned.” Who is given permission to marry? The answer is very clear; those who have been “loosed” from a wife. The fact that virgins are included in the statement that they do not sin, in no way takes from the teaching regarding those “loosed”, which is from a Greek word, used in the form of a verb, that refers to divorce (*luo*). If any single word in the New Testament refers to the entire process of divorce, this has to be it as it is used in this context. There are at least 8 English versions that translate *luo* as divorce in 1 Cor. 7:27. Virtually all versions make it clear that *divorce* is implied.

The word *apoluo*, as we have shown, does not refer to legal divorce, but we must conclude that “loosed” (*luo*) does. One can “put away” (*apoluo*) yet not give the bill of divorcement (*apostasion*). But if a woman is *loosed* from a spouse, she has divorce papers to prove it. The Bible gives absolutely no indication that one is *loosed* (divorced) except by a “bill of divorcement” (Deuteronomy 24:1, 2). Yet some contend that the word *loosed* here does not refer to divorce. They contend that one can be *divorced* but not *loosed*, which is a concept that does not harmonize with what we know the Bible to teach, nor does it make any sense.

Thayer evidently understood the word *luo* to refer to a divorced man, rather than only virgins. He stated:

> To loose any person (or thing) tied or fastened; 1a) bandages of the feet, the shoes; 1b) of a husband and wife joined together by the bond of matrimony; 1c) of a single man, whether he has already had a wife or has not yet married.

Why would one who contends that *apoluo* means divorce argue that *luo* does not mean *divorce* in the context of 1 Corinthians 7:27? The former is an assumption based on usage by unbelievers that has serious hermeneutical problems, whereas the latter is abundantly clear from the context. The answer is they are seeking to make it harmonize with their preconceived idea as to what Jesus taught.

One who is *loosed* (divorced) is advised by Paul not to seek a wife, apparently because of the "present distress," but is told that if he does marry, he does not sin. Nothing in Paul's teaching leads us to believe that a divorce does not end a marriage and free the parties to marry another. Some have argued that verse eleven does, but that argument poses serious problems. Even if this text did refer to *divorced* Christians, rather than those merely *separated* (as is supported by the context, reliable respected versions, and other Bible scholars), it would apply only to Christians. Yet many refuse to so limit the text, but insist it is in harmony with their view of Jesus's teaching that one commits adultery unless he initiates the divorce because his spouse has committed adultery. (This text is dealt with exclusively in a separate chapter.)

CHAPTER 25:

"NOT UNDER BONDAGE": "THE PAULINE PRIVILEGE" OR "DOCTRINE OF ABANDONMENT" (1 CORINTHIANS 7:15)

> But if the unbelieving depart, let him depart. A brother or a sister is not under bondage in such *cases:* but God hath called us to peace. *KJV*

This text has been a challenge to many who seek to learn and teach the truth regarding the question "Who may marry?" There is much variance in the explanations given for this text, even though what is said appears to be clearly set forth. Perhaps one reason for lack of agreement is that some seem to be compelled to explain the text to harmonize with what they think Jesus taught, or maybe something they think Paul taught; so if they have misunderstood these texts, they are sure to be wrong in their exegesis of the text under study. Yet several great commentators, who might have been tempted to "explain away" this key text, have nonetheless dealt with it forthrightly. It is important that we understand that any view one might have on this passage cannot be true if it does not allow for harmony of the Scriptures. Thus, it is imperative that the reader endeavor to set aside preconceived ideas and simply seek to know and accept what the text actually says, which may help in fully understanding what Jesus and Paul taught regarding marriage.

> ***The most painful goodbyes are the ones that are never said, never explained and never made legal.***

We shall first look at how *chorizo* (*depart, separate*) is defined—to include comments from some respected commentators. Second, we will look at how various versions render the text. Third, comments from several scholars are presented. Fourth, the author's exegesis of the texts followed by the application we might make to those whose spouses have done what Paul addresses in the scenario. Finally, there will be a brief explanation of some things that both Jesus and Paul taught that should be helpful to those looking for harmony of the Scriptures.

The meaning of the Greek word "chorizo" (*depart, separate*):

Below is a quote from Albert Barnes who explains the situation Paul addresses in 1 Cor. 7:10, 11 regarding the situation where a woman simply leaves her husband. In Barnes' final statement he indicates that divorce is a different situation.

Albert Barnes New Testament Commentary:

> But and if she depart: if she have withdrawn by a rash and foolish act; if she has attempted to dissolve the marriage vow, she is to remain unmarried, or be reconciled. She is not at liberty to marry another. This may refer, I suppose, to instances where wives, ignorant of the rule of Christ, and supposing that they had a right to separate themselves from their husbands, had rashly left them, and had supposed that the marriage contract was dissolved. Paul tells them that this was impossible; and that if they had so separated from their husbands, the pure laws of Christianity, did not recognize this right, and they must either be reconciled to their husbands, or remain alone. The marriage tie was so sacred that it could not be dissolved by the will of either party.

> *Let her remain unmarried*: that is, let her not marry another. Or be reconciled to her husband: let this be done, if possible. If it cannot be, let her remain unmarried. It was a duty to be reconciled if it was possible. If not, she should not violate her vows to her husband so far as to marry another. It is evident that this rule is still binding, and that no one who has separated from her husband, whatever be the cause, unless there be a regular divorce, according to the law of Christ (Matthew 5:32), can be at liberty to marry again.

Jamieson, Fausset and Brown Commentary:

> But and if she depart: or "be separated." If the sin of separation has been committed, that of a new marriage is not to be added (Matthew 5:32).

Strong (quoted from SwordSearcher):

> [Grk. 5563] *chorizo* (*kho-rid'-zo*) from 5561; to place room between, i.e. part; reflexively, to go away:—depart, put asunder, separate.

Another highly respected scholar (below) notes that *chorizo* has reference to *separation* rather than *divorce*.

Bloomfield [The Greek New Testament]

> From the use of καταλλ [reconcile] and the air of the context it is plain that the apostle is not speaking of formal divorces, affected by law, but separations, whether agreed on or not, arising from misunderstandings or otherwise.

Versions:

(*ASV*) Yet if the unbelieving departeth, let him depart: the brother or the sister is not under bondage in such *cases*: but God hath called us in peace.

(*BBE*) But if the one who is not a Christian has a desire to go away, let it be so: the brother or the sister in such a position is not forced to do one thing or the other: but it is God's pleasure that we may be at peace with one another.

(*CEV*) If your husband or wife isn't a follower of the Lord and decides to divorce you, then you should agree to it. You are no longer bound to that person. After all, God chose you and wants you to live at peace.

(*ESV*) But if the unbelieving partner separates, let it be so. In such cases the brother or sister is not enslaved. God has called you to peace.

(*GNB*) However, if the one who is not a believer wishes to leave the Christian partner, let it be so. In such cases the Christian partner, whether husband or wife, is free to act. God has called you to live in peace.

(*GW*) But if the unbelieving partners leave, let them go. Under these circumstances a Christian man or Christian woman is not bound by a marriage vow. God has called you to live in peace.

(*ISV*) But if the unbelieving partner leaves, let him go. In such cases the brother or sister is not bound; God has called you to live in peace.

(*LITV*) But if the unbelieving one separates, let *them* be separated; the brother or the sister is not in bondage in such matters; but God has called us in peace.

(*MKJV*) But if the unbelieving one separates, let *him* be separated. A brother or a sister is not in bondage in such *cases*, but God has called us in peace.

Commentators:

Some scholars say the word "depart" (*chorizo*) does not mean divorce, while others insist that it does. Some declare that "bondage" does not refer to marriage, yet others contend otherwise. Regarding the phrase "not under bondage," some have said it means that the believer, being abandoned, cannot prevent the unbeliever from leaving and simply is not under responsibility to continue support, etc., but is NOT free to marry. Others say the believer and unbeliever were "never under bondage" because God does not recognize mixed marriages. The more likely meaning is that the believer (under the circumstances noted) is not *bound* (married), and is *free* to marry. This view was held by **Clark** and **Gil**, two commentators that are generally held in very high esteem for their scholarship and general sound teaching. **Foy Wallace Jr.** also held this position. To harmonize the text with his idea of what Jesus taught, Wallace maintained that the abandonment "presupposes a state of adultery."

Many other scholars have expressed the same sentiment regarding the abandoned one's freedom and right to marry. Below are quotations from those mentioned, above, that commented on the phrase "not under bondage," followed by the comments of several other scholars:

John Gil

> "being in such circumstances, that either Christ must be forsaken, or the unbeliever will depart, are they obliged to yield to such an one, but rather suffer a departure; nor are they bound to remain unmarried, but are free to marry another person, after all proper methods have been tried for a reconciliation, and that appears to be impracticable; desertion in such a

case, and attended with such circumstances, is a breach of the marriage contract, and a dissolution of the bond, and the deserted person may lawfully marry again; otherwise a brother, or a sister in such a case, would be in subjection and bondage to such a person:

Adam Clark

But if the unbelieving, depart --- Whether husband or wife: if such obstinately depart and utterly refuse all cohabitation, a brother or a sister --- a Christian man or woman, is not under bondage to any particular laws, so as to be prevented from remarrying. Such, probably, the law stood then; but it is not so now; for the marriage can only be dissolved by death, or by the ecclesiastical court.

Foy Wallace Jr.:

Verses 15-16, in the case of the abandonment of the believer by the unbeliever, whereby the believer is "not under bondage" and is therefore set free. If the bondage here does not refer to the marriage bond, then the believer would still be in the bondage of it. To advocate, as some do, that the passage means the believer is not bound to live or remain with the departing unbeliever would be a truism, for it is set forth as a case of abandonment and the abandoned one obviously could not abide with the one who had departed. It appears evident that when the unbeliever so departs it presupposes a state of adultery which exists in the principle previously discussed, and here the apostle's inspired teaching is again projected beyond the Lord's own strictures and declares the abandoned believer "not under bondage." If that does not mean that the believer in these circumstances is free to marry, then it cannot mean anything, for if the one involved is not altogether free the bondage would still exist." (*The*

Sermon on the Mount and the Civil State; p. 45)

"The word adultery in New Testament usage does not necessarily refer to the sinful physical [sexual] act, it is not restricted to the one way of violating the bond. In the four passages in Matthew, Mark and Luke the term adultery is given the sense of ignoring the bond, of which a man is guilty who formally puts away his wife unjustifiably and regards himself unhitched. The passages n Matthew 19: Mark 10 and Luke 16 discuss hypothetically the man who manifests this view by marrying again. His sin of adultery consisted in treating the original contract as null and void when it was not. The phrase "put away" in the verses means to formally divorce, not merely to "send away," or separate, and he thereby assumed the bond to be wholly dissolved." (*The Sermon on the Mount and the Civil State;* p. 42)

"With no course of action legislated, revealed or prescribed, we cannot make one without human legislation. The course of some preachers in demanding separations and the breaking up of family relations, and the refusal to even baptize certain ones whose marriage status does not measure up to his standard of approval, is a presumptuous procedure. It reveals the tendency to displace God as the Judge of us all, and a preacher ascends to the bench. More than teaching the moral principles involved, the preacher has no course of action revealed, and to establish one would result in human legislation, more far reaching in evil consequences than the moral effects of divorcement limited to the persons involved. There are some things that are not subject to the law of restitution, things done in certain circumstances which cannot in later circumstances be undone, which remain as matters between God and the individual, and therefore reserved for the judgment. It is certain, however, that if the Lord Jesus Christ had intended a course of action in these cases, he would not have left it for preachers to prescribe, but would have himself legislated it." (*The Sermon on the Mount and the Civil State*; p. 41)

Thomas Coke Commentary on the Holy Bible

1 Corinthians 7:15. *Is not under bondage,* &c.— That is, says *Hilary,* "The Christian in this case is free to marry to another Christian." "He is free," says *Photius,* "to depart, because the other has dissolved the marriage." "If he depart," say Chrysostom, OEcumenius, and Theophylact, "because thou wilt not communicate with him in his infidelity, be thou divorced, or quit the yoke, &c." But it must be remembered, that the present subject refers only to marriages between Christians and those who were professedly heathens. A brother or sister, in the case above mentioned, after all due means of peace and reconciliation have been in vain attempted, (for *God hath called us to peace,*) is not enslaved.

Greek Testament Critical ExegeticalCommentary

The meaning is, 'let the unbeliever depart, rather than by attempting to retain the union, endanger that peace of household and peace of spirit, which is part of the calling of a Christian.'

Observe, (1) that there is no contradiction, in this licence of breaking off such a marriage, to the command of our Lord in Matthew 5:32,—because the Apostle expressly asserts, 1 Corinthians 7:12, that *our Lord's words do not apply* to such marriages as are here contemplated. They were spoken to those *within the covenant*, and as such apply immediately to the wedlock of *Christians* (1 Corinthians 7:10), but *not to mixed marriages*.

1 Corinthians 7:15. Paul had before enjoined that the *Christian* partner should not make a separation if the non-Christian consents to remain. But what if the *non-Christian* partner seeks separation? In that case they were to let such a one go without detention (χωριζέσθω, permissive, see Winer, p. 291 [E. T. Since *desertion* (χωρίζεται) appears here as an admissible ground for divorce, this has been thought to conflict with Matthew 5:32; Matthew 19:9, and various explanations have been attempted (see Wolf *in lo*[(1134)]). But the seeming contradiction vanishes, if we consider 1 Corinthians 7:12, according to which Jesus had given no judgment upon *mixed* marriages; Matthew 5:32, therefore, can only bind the believing consort, in so far that he may not be *the one who leaves*. If, however, he is left by the non-believing partner, then, as this case does not fall under the utterance of Christ, the marriage may be looked upon as practically dissolved, and the believing partner is not bound.

Matthew Poole's English Annotations on the Holy Bible

If the unbelieving husband or the unbelieving wife will leave his or her correlate, that is, so leave them as to return no more to live as a husband or as a wife with her or him that is Christian, **let him depart.** Such a person hath broken the bond of marriage, and in such cases Christians are **not under bondage,** they are not tied by law to fetch them again, nor by the laws of God to keep themselves unmarried for their perverseness. But it may be objected, that nothing but adultery, by the Divine law, breaketh that bond.

Answer. That is denied. Nothing but adultery is a justifiable cause of divorce: no man may put away his wife, nor any wife put away her husband, but for adultery. But the husband's voluntary leaving his wife, or the wife's voluntary leaving her husband, with a resolution to return no more to them, breaks also the bond of marriage, frustrating it as to the ends for which God hath appointed it; and, after all due means used to bring again the party departing to their duty, doth certainly free the correlate. So that although nothing can justify repudiation, or putting away a wife or a husband, and marrying another, but the adultery of the person so divorced and repudiated; yet the departure either of husband or wife without the other's consent for a long time, and refusal to return after all due means used, especially if the party so going away doth it out of a hatred and abomination of the other's religion, will justify the persons so deserted, after due waiting and use of means to reduce him or her to their duty, wholly to cast off the person deserting; for no Christian in such a case, by God's law, is under bondage.

The Bible Study New Testament

However. This is the "Pauline privilege." Note that it only covers the specific condition of an *unbeliever* deserting the Christian partner. There was and is much controversy about Christianity (compare Matthew 10:34-36), and sometimes the unbelieving partner is so fanatically opposed to Christianity that he or she refuses to continue the marriage. Is free to act. The Christian partner ABANDONED by the unbeliever is free from the former relationship. The marriage has terminated.

Marriage Matters (1 Corinthians 7:6-24) (Copied from Bible.org)

But although the believer should not initiate the divorce, if the unbeliever should do so, the believer is no longer bound to the marriage (7:15). Paul granted permission for divorce in the case of a believer being deserted by an unbeliever.[28]

This is stated in 7:15, where Paul writes that the believer is "not bound in regard to marriage" (i.e., free to remain single or to remarry).[29] In 7:39-40, there is a conceptual parallel where a wife is said to be "bound" (a different word in Greek, but the same concept) as long as her husband lives. But if the husband dies, she is "free" to marry as she wishes, only in the Lord. If the parallel holds, then not bound in 7:15 also means "free to marry another."[30]

The greater part of the commentaries understand "not under bondage," to deny the necessity of remaining unmarried, and infer from it the lawfulness of taking another spouse under the conditions specified by the apostle Paul.

Lenski (1 Cor. P. 294 and 295) and Fisher (p. 219) support the idea that "not under bondage" is that the marriage bond has been severed and that the believer is no longer enslaved to it.

The Text

After dealing with various questions regarding marriage, that addressed various groups, Paul then addresses the *rest*. Included in this group would be those disciples whose spouses were not Christians and did not want to continue the marriage. The text speaks of the non-Christian spouse as *departing*, *leaving* or *separating*. Based on the meaning of the word used here, the fact that one can *depart* (desertion) and not *divorce* and the fact that a divorce certificate (a requirement for divorce according to Deut. 24:1, 2 and Jer. 3:8) is not mentioned, it would seem to be presumptuous to conclude that legal divorce is what is meant by *depart* in the particular scenario addressed. In view of what the text says, our concern now is to determine whether the abandoned spouse is free to marry, needs to divorce, or may not marry even with a legal divorce.

The text addresses the situation in which a child of God is married to an unbeliever. It may be possible that neither spouse was a Christian at the time they married but that one obeyed the gospel. In either case Paul, through inspiration from God, addresses a problem for which the solution, it would seem, is one that would benefit Christians rather than the devil who opposes all that is good.

Under most circumstances the Law did not allow God's people to intermarry with unbelievers. Such marriages were "unlawful" and considered to be "fornication." The New Testament contains examples of illegal marriages: 1 Cor. 5:1 and Matt. 14:4. Clark contends that the former case was one of incest—a man's marrying his father's divorced wife, but who may have only been his step-mother. The latter verse refers to Herod, who married his brother's divorced wife, which was contrary to the Law as long as the brother was living (Lev. 20:21) In his second letter to the Corinthians, Paul writes about being *unequally yoked* with unbelievers. While marriage may not be under consideration, the reader has to be impressed with God's thinking regarding ties with the heathen.

> Be ye not unequally yoked together with unbelievers: for what fellowship hath righteousness with unrighteousness? and what communion hath light with darkness? 15 And what concord hath Christ with Belial? or what part hath he that believeth with an infidel? 16 And what agreement hath the temple of God with idols? for ye are the temple of the living God; as God hath said, I will dwell in them, and walk in them; and I will be their God, and they shall be my people. 17 Wherefore come out from among them, and be ye separate, saith the Lord, and touch not the unclean thing; and I will receive you, 18 And will be a Father unto you, and ye shall be my sons and daughters, saith the Lord Almighty.
>
> 2 Cor. 6:14

While we might conclude from the above passage that it is sinful for a Christian to marry an unbeliever, we cannot conclude that such a marriage necessarily should be terminated. Paul makes it clear in his remarks preceding the statement that while "a brother or sister is not under bondage in such cases" the marriage is nevertheless genuine, and the Christian should remain in hopes of converting his/her mate. But considering what Paul said, above, and that it has never been God's will for His people to marry unbelievers, it is not unreasonable to conclude that a divorce would not be needed if an unbeliever abandoned a believer. (This would certainly be applicable in a case in which there was no divorce law or it might be impossible to get a divorce, such as a Jewish man who *sends away* his wife [*apoluo*] but refuses to give the "git" or divorce paper so he does not have to pay back the dowry she brought to the marriage.) This reasoning is also supported by the example of the Jewish priests who acknowledged their sin of taking foreign wives. Ezra told the priests to *separate*.

> And Ezra the priest stood up, and said unto them, Ye have transgressed, and have taken strange wives, to increase the trespass of Israel. Now therefore make confession unto the LORD God of your fathers, and do his pleasure: and separate yourselves from the people of the land, and from the strange wives.
>
> Ezra 10:10–11

It seems apparent, from this reading and the preceding verses, that the priests understood that they were not legally/scripturally bound to those women and that it was their duty to *separate* from them. We recognize today that where no legal marriage exists there is no need for divorce proceedings. For example, at one point in our history marriage between two men was not legal. It was an "illegal marriage" (fornication). But after a state made it legal several homosexuals married. Later there was a national ruling that such unions were "not lawful." The couples did not need to divorce because there was never a legal marriage. A more applicable situation would be a case wherein a brother and sister learn they had married each other. They would need only to separate. While this is not entirely applicable to the situation in which a Christian has been abandoned by the unbelieving spouse, it makes it understandable that when the unbeliever abandons the believer (leaves, departs, separates with the intention of ending the marriage) then the bond is broken and a legal divorce proceeding, at least in the situation Paul addresses there at Corinth, was not needed.

Those who seek to defend the traditional position on MDR insist that *chorizo* means divorce in 1 Cor. 7:10, 11 and verse 15. But if this is true, that *chorizo* means divorce, then it logically follows that "not under bondage" should be interpreted to mean freedom from the marriage bond and freedom to marry.

Unlike the case in verses 10-11, where the *Christian* married couple *separate* and are exhorted to remain "unmarried" (or in the state they are in), verse 15 deals with the situation in which an *unbeliever* separates. Paul says the believer is not bound to the marriage. Marriage is what Paul had in mind, not some imaginary bond that releases the brother only from his obligation to keep house for the ungodly unbeliever. There is no indication in the text that Paul intended to put a limit on the believer's freedom from the unbeliever. Paul said the believer is "not under bondage." To put limits on the believer's freedom, or the freedom of anyone that is legally divorced, is to make laws where God did not legislate and is presumptuous action.

Understanding the Teaching of Jesus

As we noted in the beginning, some are not able to accept the teaching of 1 Corinthians 7:15, because this would be "another cause for divorce" and thus contrary to what Jesus taught. But did Jesus really teach that a divorce is not a divorce unless it is for adultery? After many years of careful and diligent study I came to the conclusion that Jesus' concern was with the Jewish men who had not only perverted God's ideal (marriage for life) but had disregarded Moses' command to give a divorce certificate in cases wherein the man intended no longer to love and support the wife. This is based on the true meaning of the word *apoluo,* which is translated "put away" in most of the older, trusted versions. Of course, "put away" (send away) does not mean *divorce*, as defined by Moses and confirmed by God Himself, using a personal example (Deut. 24:1, 2; Jer. 3:8). *Putting away* is only one of the parts noted and LACKS the "bill of divorcement" that makes it legal and final.

The words "put away" are used 52 times in the KJV. In most instances they refer to getting rid of false gods. Only in a few instances is the phrase even assumed to mean divorce. Translating *apoluo* as *divorce* has Jesus contradicting the Law that allowed the woman to "go and become another man's wife" (Deut. 24:1, 2). This is something Jesus, before He taught on this issue, promised not to do (Matt. 5:17-19) so that there would be no misunderstandings. The Jews, who sought reason to kill Jesus, evidently did not misunderstand His teaching because they did not charge Him with contradicting Moses on this issue.

The Exception Clause

Below is the quotation from the KJV, followed by my paraphrase of this passage:

> And I say unto you, Whosoever shall put away his wife, except it be for fornication, and shall marry another, committeth adultery: and whoso marrieth her which is put away doth commit adultery.

> *And I say unto you, whoever shall put away his wife without a certificate of divorcement, except for the cases of an illicit or illegal marriage, and shall marry another, committeth adultery: and whoso marrieth her that is put away without a certificate of divorcement doth commit adultery.*

Two versions lend support to the accuracy of the above paraphrase: *The New Jerusalem Bible* and *the New American with Apocrypha.*

Many believe Jesus taught that the only time God recognizes a divorce is when fornication has been committed, which they insist has to be the *cause* of the divorce and that it frees only the *initiator* of the divorce to marry. This is based on their idea of what Jesus was teaching in Matthew 19:9. This idea has many hermeneutical problems, the first being that *apoluo* has to be FORCED to mean divorce. The logical meaning is that the man whom Jesus said "committeth adultery against her" (Mk 10:11) would not be guilty of so doing if the "putting away" (*apoluo*-ing) is a situation in which the marriage is not legal, resulting in fornication. (Two New Testament examples were previously noted.) Thus, Jesus never taught only one reason for divorce (that being fornication) and that if a divorce is not for said reason it is not a divorce at all. The New Testament does not actually give a reason for divorce. Rather, Jesus pointed Jewish men, who were abusers of wives and violators of the Law, to God's ideal from the beginning. In addition, Paul taught men to "love your wives" and women to "honor your husbands." Nevertheless, God designed divorce for a reason and it still does what it was designed to do, when His definition is followed. The believer who has been abandoned, in cases wherein divorce is not possible, seems to be an exception—a case in which divorce is not needed. The text says the believer whose spouse has abandoned him/her is not under bondage in such cases. While many scholars have sought to explain or define bondage (*douloo*) to harmonize with their ideas of what Jesus taught, the *International Standard Bible Encyclopedia* stayed true to scholarship and conscience when they wrote, "(*c*) Marriage is once referred to as a bondage (1Co 7:15) (verb δουλόω, *doulóō*)."

CHAPTER 26:

EZRA VERSUS MALACHI

Ezra was a prophet of God. He and the people confessed their sin of taking strange wives that God had forbidden. They promised to *put away* their wives. We can learn a lesson here that will help us in our study of MDR.

> Now when Ezra had prayed, and when he had confessed, weeping and casting himself down before the house of God, there assembled unto him out of Israel a very great congregation of men and women and children: for the people wept very sore. And Shechaniah the son of Jehiel, one of the sons of Elam, answered and said unto Ezra, We have trespassed against our God, and have taken strange wives of the people of the land: yet now there is hope in Israel concerning this thing. Now therefore let us make a covenant with our God to put away all the wives, and such as are born of them, according to the counsel of my Lord, and of those that tremble at the commandment of our God; and let it be done according to the law. Arise; for this matter belongeth unto thee: we also will be with thee: be of good courage, and do it. Then arose Ezra, and made the chief priests, the Levites, and all Israel, to swear that they should do according to this word. And they swore. And Ezra the priest stood up, and said unto them, Ye have transgressed, and have taken strange wives, to increase the trespass of Israel. Now therefore make confession unto the Lord God of your fathers, and do his pleasure: and *separate yourselves from the people of the land, and from the strange wives* [emphasis added]. And they gave their hands that they would put away their wives; and being guilty, they offered a ram of the flock for their trespass. All these had taken strange wives: and some of them had wives by whom they had children.
>
> Ezra 10:1

The commonly accepted position on MDR is that Jesus taught that divorced persons commit adultery when they marry another. But is that what the Bible actually teaches? Do we have reason to conclude that Jesus contradicted the Law with his teaching? Did he indeed teach contrary to the Law or did he instead teach contrary to the Jewish notions and customs of the day, which were contrary to Moses's teaching?

Those who argue as noted above insist that Malachi 2:16 teaches that God *hates divorce*. Divorce is bad as hearts are often broken and physical, mental, and spiritual health is harmed. But was God talking about divorce, or was he talking about something much worse? The text says he *hateth putting away*. By studying the text in Malachi and Ezra, we can get a good picture of what is involved in the "putting away" that God hates, and the putting away that God requires when a marriage is not legal/scriptural, and thus have a better understanding of *divorce*, which sometimes is necessary and right (Jeremiah 3:8).

If the "putting away" in the Book of Malachi is *divorce*, and that is what God hates, then how do we explain the "putting away" in Ezra? How do we harmonize the idea that Malachi 2:16 says, "God hates divorce" with the teaching in Ezra that indicates that the same "putting away" is not divorce, as defined by Moses (Deuteronomy 24), but is in fact something that is required by God whether the man wanted to continue the relationship or not? How could God be pleased with his children's "divorcing" their wives in one text while requiring it in another? Many insist that every time the Bible speaks of a wife's being *put away, divorce* is the meaning; but if such is the case, how do we explain how God was pleased with these men who followed Ezra's teaching to "put away" their wives?

Evidently, the people were committing fornication by having wives to which they were not scripturally married—wives they were not supposed to have. They were to "separate" from them. Thus, it becomes apparent that divorce, as defined by Moses, was not in the picture in this case. And so, evidently, one can "put away" yet not divorce, and it can be evil or it can be the right thing to do. This text also helps us to understand the meaning of the exception clause in Matthew 19:9. Jesus taught that to "put away" a wife and marry another would be to commit adultery and the woman "put away" would commit adultery if she married (Mark 10:11). Obviously, in contrast to the case of Ezra, the application of Jesus's words was to *illegal* marriages. The only way Jesus's statement could harmonize with Moses's teaching, which allowed the divorced woman to marry another, is that he was speaking of merely "putting away" rather than first giving the "bill of divorcement" and then sending her "out of the house." The "exception" is really very simple and is not a 42nd cousin to what is commonly taught and practiced. Adultery does not take place when a man "puts away" his wife for fornication, or because the marriage was not legitimate, as was the case with the men of Israel discussed in the Book of Ezra. The putting away that God *hates* is not referring to situations where the marriage is illegal or unscriptural, nor is it referring to divorce in cases of unfaithfulness, but its application is to men who were sending away wives and refusing to give them the "bill of divorcement" so that they could marry another. This is an evil that continues to be practiced by Jewish men to this day.

CHAPTER 27:

WILL FRIENDS OF JESUS ACCOMPLISH WHAT THE JEWS COULD NOT?

FACTS AND OBSERVATIONS

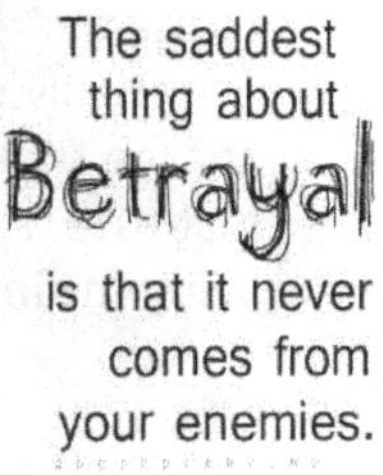

The saddest thing about
Betrayal
is that it never comes from your enemies.

1. A law was in effect while Jesus lived. It was known as the Law of Moses (Job 8:31).
2. It was possible to do things "contrary to the law" (Acts 18:13; 23:3).
3. Penalties existed as punishment for those who contradicted or taught contrary to Moses's law (Deuteronomy 17:8–13; Leviticus 26:14–24).
4. Those who were in a position to punish lawbreakers viewed Jesus as just another man—subject to the Law of Moses, as were others.
5. The Jews were looking for anything with which to charge Jesus. Entrapment was their motive when they questioned Jesus on the matter of "putting away."
6. After Jesus answered, the Jews did not charge Him with teaching contrary to the Law, but were silent on that matter.
7. Certain teachers, who claim to be *friends* of Jesus, are now charging Jesus with teaching contrary to the Law.
8. Jesus had the authority to change the Law, and He did, but He did not do it while He lived (Hebrews 7:12; 9:17).
9. Had Jesus taught that a person who had been divorced could not marry then He would have clearly contradicted Moses (Deuteronomy 24:2).
10. Anyone, including Jesus, contradicting Moses could, quite rightly, be accused of sin.
11. Jesus is the Son of God, and according to the Scriptures, He committed no sin (2 Corinthians 5:21; 1 Peter 2:22).
12. Therefore, those who teach that Jesus contradicted and changed the Law of Moses, while He lived, are teaching error.

13. If Jesus contradicted the Law of Moses, then His accusers would have succeeded in both discrediting and exposing Him as a pretender.

14. Those who continue to teach that certain legal marriages must be broken up and that certain people who have no marriage must remain celibate, charging that Jesus taught such, are not friends of Jesus at all. No friend of Jesus would claim He taught a doctrine that God put into the category of "doctrine of devils" ("forbidding to marry," 1 Timothy 4:1–3). Why, even his enemies who eventually crucified him on trumped-up charges did not make the charge that Jesus contradicted Moses, or that He sought to institute a new law whereby the divorced who marry again are living in sin (adultery).

CHAPTER 28:

THE POLYGAMY FACTOR

Living in twenty-first-century America, most proclaim that polygamy is wrong and incontrovertible. The only reason polygamy might be an important issue to someone is if he happens to live in a country where polygamy is legal and he has more than one wife or he is a Bible teacher and has to deal with converts who have more than one wife. I know a man who spent some time evangelizing in South Africa. He converted a man that had five wives. The African convert was informed that he would have to get rid of all of them but one. He asked, "Which ones do I send away?" He was told, "Send them all away except your first wife." He replied, "I married my first two wives at the same time."

Situations like the above should cause us to be interested and open to a study of polygamy. Are we doing right when we break up marriages by teaching men to "put away" a legal wife?

Polygamy is a very important, and usually overlooked, factor in our study of divorce and marriage (MDR). First, the idea that polygamy was practiced by faithful men of God is not even questioned by serious students of the Bible. Also, Jesus said not one word about polygamy. Now, let us get to the point. The traditional MDR doctrine says that if a man legally divorces his wife (unless she committed adultery), Jesus teaches that both he and she must remain celibate and that if either marries another, he or she commits adultery.

But when we apply the polygamy factor, we see a very big problem for the theory noted above. At the time of Jesus's teachings, a man could have more than one wife, so whether *he* was "still bound" to a particular wife after he divorced was irrelevant, as far as whether he could marry another. Yet it is claimed that the man who "divorced" her commits adultery with the woman he marries. How can that be? It makes no sense, especially when we look at Mark 10:11 and see that Jesus explains that the *man* commits adultery "against her," or the wife he "put away," rather than, as commonly asserted, *with* the person in the second marriage.

Think about it. Why would God give a divorce law for the *women* (because of evil men with hardened hearts) so the *men* could marry another, but then come back later and say to the women (through Jesus), "Oh, but you are *still married* or *still bound* unless your husband committed adultery"? All the while, the *man* continues to have as many wives as he likes or can afford.

The Bible teaches that a marriage is *ended* by divorce, but some insist that the guilty one is still *bound* to the other unless he initiated the divorce for fornication. If Jesus had actually taught this then He would have been in a real predicament when He taught it to the Jews. They would have understood Him to say, "From henceforth, you don't have a right to marry another unless you divorced your wife for adultery. Moses was wrong. I'm teaching what God intended from the beginning. I'm changing this now because Moses was not speaking for God. God just allowed him to write the law because of your "hardness of heart."

And we are left to wonder why God went all those years without explaining to the Jews that divorce did not free the woman or man to marry another unless the divorce writ stated that it was for *adultery*. He just let them commit adultery for hundreds of years; then Jesus came along, right before the end of the dispensation and Law of Moses, and *finally* told them it was *adultery*—but still said not one word about *polygamy*. And even though the Jews sought to entrap Jesus by enticing Him to say something contrary to Moses, these so-called "friends" of Jesus are saying Jesus did indeed contradict Moses. They say this even though the Jews accepted Jesus's saying regarding "putting away" and did not even charge Him with teaching contrary to Moses on the issue. Who can believe it?

CHAPTER 29:

"BUT I SAY UNTO YOU"

> ***Did Jesus take issue with Moses (who taught God's will) or with the false notions of the Jewish teachers?***

Let us carefully study Jesus's statement, from which some have concluded that He changed the Law from the idea that a woman who has been divorced *may* marry another, to the idea that anyone who has been divorced *may not* marry another. The issue involves the question, "Did Jesus contradict Moses?" Most will agree that Jesus did not speak contrary to Moses, who taught what was inspired of God. Yet many are confused about what Jesus meant when he said, "But I say unto you." To understand Him one must carefully examine the text, commonly known as *The Sermon on the Mount.*

Matthew 5:20 is a key passage that helps us understand what Jesus was meaning when he said, "But I say unto you."

> For I say to you, that unless your righteousness surpasses that of the scribes and Pharisees, you shall not enter the kingdom of heaven.

Jesus stressed that righteousness is necessary to be part of the kingdom. He made it clear that this righteousness must be greater than that of the scribes and Pharisees. In the previous two verses, Jesus declared that He was not going to change the Law; and now, He finishes setting the stage, seeking to alleviate the possibility of present and future misunderstandings of what He is about to say. Nevertheless, Jesus addressed a number of issues in His Sermon on the Mount that have been misunderstood and misapplied by careless Bible students.

When Jesus said, "But I say unto you," what did he mean? There are two possibilities: 1) He took issue with Moses's teachings (which were God's teachings), asserting that Moses's Law no longer applied because He was changing it (as he spoke); or 2) He took issue with the unrighteous scribes and Pharisees, who held false notions about Moses's teachings. That Jesus was taking issue with the false notions (interpretations) of the Jews, rather than Moses's or God's teachings, is fundamental and generally accepted by scholars and teachers in the church.

Now back to Matthew 5:17–18:

> Think not that I am come to destroy the law, or the prophets: I am not come to destroy, but to fulfil. For verily I say unto you, Till heaven and earth pass, one jot or one tittle shall in no wise pass from the law, till all be fulfilled.

Before Jesus says *anything* about the men's mistreatment of wives (putting away in verses thirty-one and thirty-two), or what has been interpreted to be "divorce and remarriage," He makes it clear that He is not going to say anything that should be interpreted to mean that He is changing what the Law of Moses taught.

Again Jesus said:

> For I say unto you, that except your righteousness shall exceed the righteousness of the scribes and Pharisees, ye shall in no case enter into the kingdom of heaven.
>
> Matthew 5:20

The above passage is important to our understanding the teachings of Jesus in the Sermon on the Mount because it was the scribes and Pharisees, interpreters of the Law, with whom he was about to take issue.

> Ye have heard that it was said by them of old time, thou shalt not kill; and whosoever shall kill shall be in danger of the judgment: But I say unto you, That whosoever is angry with his brother without a cause shall be in danger of the judgment: and whosoever shall say to his brother, Raca, shall be in danger of the council: but whosoever shall say, Thou fool, shall be in danger of hell fire.
>
> Matthew 5:21–22

Albert Barnes New Testament Commentary:

> **Ye have heard.** Or, this is the common interpretation among the Jews. Jesus proceeds here to comment on

> some prevailing opinions among the Jews; to show that the righteousness of the scribes and Pharisees was defective; and that men needed a better righteousness, or they could not be saved. He shows what he meant by that better righteousness, by showing that the common opinions of the scribes were erroneous.

> Jesus did not set himself against the Law of Moses, but against the false and pernicious interpretation of the law prevalent in his time.

The phrase "Ye have heard" has been erroneously interpreted. From whom had they heard? It sounds like Jesus is taking issue with someone who had been saying something that was inaccurate. Moses's writings were inspired of God and therefore not something contrary to God's will. Thus, it is certain that Jesus was referring to the interpreters of the Law.

Next, Jesus said, "Thou shalt not commit adultery." It is probable that the Pharisees had misinterpreted this teaching to extend only to the external physical act; and that they regarded evil thoughts of affairs with another and treacherous actions against their spouse of no consequence, or as not forbidden by Moses.

Albert Barnes notes:

> Our Saviour assures them that the commandment did not regard the external act merely, but the secrets of the heart, and the movements of the eye. That they who indulged a wanton desire; that they who looked on a woman to increase their lust, have already, in the sight of God, violated the commandment, and committed adultery in the heart.

With this explanation in mind, it is reasonable to conclude that Jesus was expounding on the Law, rather than making *new* law. Thus, Jesus was not saying, "Moses said *this*, but I am changing it to *this*." He was saying, "*Men* have been saying this but here is what is intended to be understood." And He made it clear how men (the unrighteous "scribes and Pharisees") were out of harmony with truth.

In this setting, and with a number of issues to address, Jesus, for the first time recorded, addresses another misunderstood teaching of Moses:

> It was said also, whosoever shall put away his wife, let him give her a writing of divorcement.
>
> Matthew 5:31, ASV

Who was going about saying, "Whosoever shall put away his wife, let him give her a writing of divorcement"? Moses? No. Moses's teachings were *written*; therefore, it must have been the scribes and Pharisees. This means Jesus was not teaching new law, which explains why there was no great negative response from the Jews who sought to kill him.

At the time of Jesus's great discourse on the Mount, the Jews were following their own traditions, known as *Talmud*. The Talmud resembled God's Law, but it was different—it was *new law*. Jesus endeavored to bring his people back to a proper understanding of Moses's teachings, which would involve a change in their practices.

A number of the Jews evidently had in mind that Moses's Law gave men permission to divorce a wife at will. So long as the divorce certificate was given, she could be cast out like a sack of potatoes that had gone bad. But some believed the divorce had to be for a certain reason. Many in our day assume that Jesus was taking sides (exactly what the Pharisees wanted him to do) and was presenting the only *reason* or *situation* where a divorce actually ended the marriage and freed the parties to marry. But Moses's divorce text was designed to protect and free the woman regardless of any reason the hardhearted men might presume justified their actions. A man determined whether to divorce or not, and whatever his actions, it was not questioned by a higher authority, except God in cases where it was unjust.

In many cases, a man wanted rid of a woman but chose not to actually give the woman a divorce. He would just send her out of the house." This would avoid the financial loss of having to pay back the dowry the woman's father gave him when they married, and it was a treacherous and adulterous act "against her."

With the above in mind, let us now consider the following:

> But I say unto you, that every one that putteth away his wife, saving for the cause of fornication, maketh her an adulteress: and whosoever shall marry her when she is put away committeth adultery.
>
> Matthew 5:32

(The next chapter deals with the latter part of the above text.) In the above passage, Jesus deals with one of the options that a man might select for discarding a wife. He dealt with the "legal divorce" option (verse thirty-one) and then proceeded to deal with the "put away" option. This *option* was contrary to the command of Moses to give her a bill of divorcement "so she may go be another man's wife" (Deuteronomy 24:1–2; Mark 10:3). Because of the men's unfaithfulness to their wives in putting them out the house, marrying another, and acting as if the previous marriage was nonexistent, Jesus says they were committing adultery "against her" (Mark 10:11). While it may well have been sinful to divorce her legally, if she was a faithful wife, a man would commit a *greater sin* in merely putting her away. In doing so, he rejected the command of Moses and sinned against the woman as well.

By now, it should be apparent to the reader that Jesus did not take sides with one of the Jewish schools of thought regarding divorce, but merely explained Moses's teaching (Deuteronomy 24:1–4) in light of what it was intended to accomplish.

CHAPTER 30:

"MAKETH HER AN ADULTERESS"

> But I say unto you, that every one that putteth away his wife, saving for the cause of fornication, maketh her an adulteress: and whosoever shall marry her when she is put away committeth adultery.
>
> Matthew 5:32

In this chapter, we are concerned mainly with the last part of the text above. First, if Jesus is saying everyone that *divorces* his wife makes her an adulteress, He is definitely contradicting Moses. This is something most Bible students understand is not an acceptable conclusion. We must try to understand this passage in a way that harmonizes with the idea that Moses allowed divorced persons to marry. This concept is in harmony with proper hermeneutics.

It is my understanding that "putteth away" describes part of the divorce process but does not imply the word *divorce* where the whole legal process is understood. The "putting away," without giving the "bill of divorce," is what Jesus had in mind here. He said that every man that does it, saving for the cause of fornication, makes his wife an adulteress. If a woman is *put away* occurs because of fornication (not unfaithfulness, not adultery specifically, as often affirmed, but because fornication is being committed in the relationship due to its not being legal/scriptural) then there is an exception—the one *put away* is not caused to commit adultery. Examples would include:

1. a man marrying his brother's wife while his brother lives—Herod (Matt. 14:3, 4; Lev. 20:21);
2. a man marrying his father's wife (1 Cor. 5:1); and
3. men marrying forbidden foreign woman (Gen. 28:6).

The "exception clause" explains that if a man "puts away" his wife when the marriage is not legal/scriptural, which is to end the relationship by permanent separation, it *does not* cause the woman to be an adulteress. Naturally, she could marry, and the one she married would not be guilty of adultery, as would be the case if a legal wife were merely "put away" and not given the "bill of divorcement."

What Is Meant by "Maketh Her an Adulteress"? (Matthew 5:32b)

Below are four possible explanations as to how the woman Jesus speaks of is made an adulteress just by being put away:

1. She is, in fact, an adulteress because Jesus said it. She does not have to do anything—she will be caused to be an adulteress if she is divorced.
2. She is viewed as an adulteress but is not, in fact, an adulteress.
3. She will likely go and be with another man and, in fact, be an adulteress.
4. If a man merely puts his wife out of the house, he makes it impossible for her to carry out her duties as a wife. She commits adultery—adultery meaning "failing to live up to the covenant" or "breaking covenant."

In view of what we have already learned, the latter is clearly the most logical explanation. The man commits adultery against the woman (Mark 10:11) by his putting her away but not fully releasing her "so she may go and be another man's wife" (Deuteronomy 24:1–2), and she commits adultery because her ability to carry out her responsibilities is taken away.

Obviously, if the woman who is "put away" marries another man, she commits adultery because she is *still married* to the man who sent her away. This explains why the man who marries her also commits adultery—he would be marrying a woman that legally belonged to another man.

CHAPTER 31:

EXAMINING SOME IMPORTANT TEXTS

The Bible, having been inspired of God, exhibits amazing accuracy and harmony. Government regulations and other documents that are wholly the product of men, often contain contradictions. This makes it very frustrating for employees to administer programs. But it is comforting and reassuring to know that God's Word contains no such contradictions; therefore, we find various passages throughout the Bible upon which to build faith. Below are a number of passages that relate to our study:

ISAIAH 50:1

> Thus saith the Lord, Where is the bill of your mother's divorcement, whom I have put away? or which of my creditors is it to whom I have sold you? Behold, for your iniquities have ye sold yourselves, and for your transgressions is your mother put away.

This passage emphasizes the importance of the "bill of divorcement" and teaches us that until there is an actual legal divorce (which requires a written document) hope remains for a reconciliation. It also clearly illustrates that "put away" does not mean "divorce." Evidently, God did not deal treacherously with Israel by simply putting her away and leaving it at that. He had effected a "separation" but no divorce at this point.

Jamison Fausset Brown gives an accurate explanation of the above text:

EZRA 10:19, NKJV

> And they gave their promise that they would put away (*yatsa'* H3318) their wives; and being guilty, they presented a ram of the flock as their trespass offering.

The *putting away* in this example was not due to "adultery" or "unfaithfulness" on the part of the wives, yet the husband's action received God's blessings. The reason God approved was because the "marriages" were not legal/scriptural.

It is worthy of note that the text offers no indication that the priests did anything other than "put away" or *separate* from their foreign wives according to the will of God. They did not need to actually divorce these women because the marriages were not legal—divorce is needed only to dissolve a legal marriage. Not long ago, one of the states made a law that persons of the same sex could marry. But it was quickly overturned by a higher court. Those of the same sex who got married didn't need to get a divorce as no current law backed up their claim to marriage.

The priests God condemned in the Book of Ezra were committing sin by living with the women they had wrongfully married. It is the same type of thing as "fornication" (*porneia*), which includes "incest," according to Strong. The fact that these men did not formally divorce their wives is in perfect harmony with Jesus's "exception"— "except for fornication."

MALACHI 2:16
"God Hates Divorce"

The above passage is dealt with in chapter 26.

EZRA 10:1–44
"Ezra Versus Malachi"

The above passage is dealt with in chapter 26.

DEUTERONOMY 24:1–4

What is significant about Deuteronomy 24:1–4? When I began to seriously study and debate (with numerous individuals) the MDR issue, this text was scarcely being considered at all, which is unbelievable considering that it is the hub of the issue. Moses commanded: write a bill of divorce, put it into her hand, and "send her away" (*shalach*). That there are three separate commands involved in a divorce is evident. The Hebrew word *shalach* is translated "send her away" and is equivalent to the Greek word *apoluo*, which means the same thing but is often translated "put away." It is important to note that Strong, Vine, Thayer, Gloss and others nowhere mentions divorce in their definition of *shalach*. If the "sending away" in Deuteronomy 24:1–4 does not mean divorce, on what basis can we conclude that the Greek equivalent does?

JEREMIAH 3:1

> They say, 'If a man put away (*shalach* H7971) his wife, and she go from him, and become another man's, shall he return unto her again? shall not that land be greatly polluted? but thou hast played the harlot with many lovers; yet return again to me,' saith the Lord.

In the above passage, the word *they* was doubtless a reference to the Jews who had come to misunderstand and misuse Deuteronomy 24:1–4. The text forbids the husband to take back a wife to whom He had actually given a "bill of divorce" if she had married another. He was not forbidden to take back a woman He had "put away" or merely sent out of the house, as we have seen from Isaiah 50:1, though it seems apparent from this text (Jeremiah 3:1) that such had become the thinking of the people. God said, "Regardless of this erroneous thinking I will take you back." He was saying, "We have been *separated* and you have played the harlot; nevertheless, I will take you back." Was God asserting that he would do something that was against the Law, and therefore, would mess up the paradigm He had given? No, God would take her back through the marriage of another person—Jesus Christ. See Romans 7:1, 4.

JEREMIAH 3:8

> And I saw, when for all the causes whereby backsliding Israel committed adultery I had put her away (*shalach* H7971), and given her a bill of divorce (*keriythuwth* H3748); yet her treacherous sister Judah feared not, but went and played the harlot also.

After alluding to the fact that he had been previously dispatched to plead for Israel's return during the separation, Jeremiah stated that God had "given her [Israel] a bill of divorce," thus, dissolving the marriage and relieving God of any responsibility to Israel as his "chosen" or as his "wife" whom he had married (Jeremiah 3:14). In verse fourteen, we see that the Lord had instructed Jeremiah to plead with his "backsliding wife" to return and He would take her back. Considering verse twelve, it is indisputable that Jeremiah was talking about what he had been told to say *before* the divorce had actually been given.

Note in the text that God gave her a certificate of divorce and sent her away—separate and distinct actions. The sending away was part of the divorce but not *the* divorce.

EZEKIEL 44:22

> Neither shall they take for their wives a widow, nor her that is put away (*garash* H1644): but they shall take maidens of the seed of the house of Israel, or a widow that had a priest before.

The *New King James Version* says, "driven out" instead of "put away."

The command to the priests restricted them to marrying a *virgin* or a *widow* of another priest. By obeying this command, it would prevent the possibility of marrying a woman who might still be married to another. The above passage may be an indication that misunderstandings were prevalent among the Jews regarding what was an acceptable divorce. Marrying a *virgin* or the *widow* of another priest that knew the Law assured that the woman the priest had married had no legal ties to another. When you consider their responsibilities, it is understandable that God would require such of these men.

MALACHI 2:14–16

> Yet ye say, Wherefore? Because the Lord hath been witness between thee and the wife of thy youth, against whom *thou hast dealt treacherously* [emphasis added]: yet is she thy companion, and the wife of thy covenant. And did not he make one? Yet had he the residue of the spirit. And wherefore one? That he might seek a godly seed. Therefore take heed to your spirit, and let none deal treacherously against the wife of his youth. For the Lord, the God of Israel, saith that he hateth putting away: for one covereth violence with his garment, saith the Lord of hosts: therefore take heed to your spirit, that ye deal not treacherously.

The Septuagint and Arabic versions say, "whom thou hast left," whereas the KJV says, "against whom thou hast dealt treacherously."

Some have used this text to try to uphold the idea that "put away" is legal divorce but gave up on that notion when it became apparent that their efforts hurt their own position. The text indicates that the woman who was *put away* was yet the "wife of thy youth." But how can that be if a divorce does what God intended it to do and which he says it does: "She may go and be another man's wife"? Well, evidently the treacherous dealing, of which God speaks, and of which men were guilty, was not legal divorce. The reason it could be said that she was still the "wife of thy youth" was because the woman was not divorced. The woman "whom thou hast left," or the woman who had been treated "treacherously," received much harsher treatment than if she had been legally divorced, as divorce would have allowed her to marry again. What a terrible thing for a man to do to a woman! In most countries today, this cannot happen because women can get a divorce. But what are well-meaning religious leaders doing when they tell the divorced they may not marry? Isn't it pretty much the same thing? Someone might insist: "That is what Jesus said." Is it really, or is this the voice of tradition? Paul said it is "forbidding to marry" and put it into the category of "doctrines of devils." Malachi speaks of the action as being a treacherous act.

HOSEA 2:7

> And she shall follow after her lovers, but she shall not overtake them; and she shall seek them but shall not find them: then she shall say, I will go and return to my first husband, for then it was better for me than now.

Those who contend that a marriage cannot be dissolved might try to use this text to support their position. While the *New International Version* indicates that "husband" is in the present tense, virtually all other versions say "first husband." But even if we were to acknowledge that the original text does not say "first husband," verse two makes it abundantly clear that the marriage was dissolved. It says, "Plead with your mother, plead: for she is not my wife, neither am I her husband."

One might contend that God took her back or at least made the offer to so do. But nothing in the text indicates that Israel married another. She would "follow after lovers, but she shall not overtake them"; however, the text (as well as Jeremiah 3:1) does speak of her as having "lovers." But because she had not married another, God could take her back without violating Deuteronomy 24:4, which forbids the former husband from taking back a wife that had actually married another man.

According to Jeremiah 3:8, both Israel and Judah played the harlot (committing adultery) and were divorced, i.e. given a bill of divorcement and put away. God was no longer bound or obligated to Israel in any way, and she was free to marry Christ (See chapter 14). Thus, the idea that one can be "divorced but still bound" is certainly not supported by any text noted above.

MARK 10:11

A number of New Testament texts shed light on the subject under study, and most have been dealt with throughout this book. But considering the importance of this text and the fact that it, like Deuteronomy 24:1–4, was hardly considered until a few years ago, we shall make some comments here.

> And he saith unto them, Whosoever shall put away his wife, and marry another, committeth adultery against her.

This text indicates that *adultery* was what the Jewish men were doing to their *previous* wife—not *with* one in another marriage. That the men could have more than one wife under the Law is indisputable. (See chapter 27: “The Polygamy Factor.”) Therefore, to insist that Jesus was teaching that one who *divorces* his wife and marries commits adultery when he has sex with the new wife is unfounded and erroneous.

Why do Discussions on Divorce and Marriage often go Nowhere?

Could it be because people do not look to the same standard or same authority?

One loves, supports and defends ONE or the OTHER.

Human Tradition

When speaking of the “*loosed*” the Bible says “**if thou marry, thou hast not sinned** ,” but *human tradition* says the divorced will sin if they marry. Therefore, those who love tradition argue to support that which means the most to them. www.TotalHealth.bz

1 CORINTHIANS 7:11

See chapter 16: "The Unmarried (Agamos): Who Are They?"

John 4:17-18
"The Woman at the Well"

> He said to her, "Go, call your husband and come here." The woman answered and said, "I have no husband." Jesus said to her, "You have correctly said, 'I have no husband'; for you have had five husbands, and the one whom you now have is not your husband; this you have said truly."
>
> John 4:18

The above scripture has often been used to try to prove that people who have been divorced are living in adultery when they marry again because they are still married to a previous spouse, even though divorced. The basic argument is that divorce does not end marriage, and that one divorced and married to another is not really married "in God's eyes."

Not only does the above passage not support this assertion but it actually defeats it. Jesus stated that the woman had previously had five husbands but the man she was now with was not her husband. Thus, He recognized the previous husbands.

It might be argued that the word translated "husband" can mean "man" and therefore Jesus did not necessarily say the woman had actually been married to EACH of the five men. But the translation is evidently correct because Jesus noted that the man she was now with was not one that she had married. He was NOT a "husband," although he was obviously a "man."

A woman's being divorced and married to another was common in Jesus' day, and one divorced was neither shunned nor considered a second---class citizen. Yet, for this teaching of Jesus to be true, the traditional MDR theory would require that all the five husbands actually died. The probability of that having been the case is unlikely. Certainly the more probable explanation is that at least some of those five husbands had divorced this woman. Yet, we are supposed to accept that even though Jesus said this woman had had five legitimate husbands, the one she was with at that time was not her husband only because God did not recognize a second marriage, and that Jesus was telling the woman she was living in adultery.

1 Corinthians 7:39

The context of this passage indicates that the woman had indeed been married five times but, after divorce, was living with another man who was not her husband because she had not married him. In view of this, can we in good conscience believe that Jesus came preaching a new doctrine, different from the Law of Moses, that suggested that this Samaritan woman had married the man she was living with but was not married “in God’s eyes” and thus was committing adultery? What is more problematic is that such thinking suggests that she was not sinning, having been divorced and married again, until Jesus changed the Law—thus, suddenly changing her status from being legally and scripturally married to being an adulterous. Yesterday she was legally married; but today, because the law was changed, she was thrust into adultery. That is what the traditional MDR doctrine requires. Who can believe it?

"A wife is bound for as long a time as her husband lives. But if the husband dies, she is free to marry whom she wishes, only in the Lord."

The above is one of a few passages that is often misused to teach that divorce does not end a marriage. Of course, the idea that a marriage cannot be ended contradicts God's definition of divorce (given as law) and makes a mockery of God's having divorced Israel, which teaches us by example (Deut. 24:1,2; Mark 10:3; Jer. 3:8). This being true, what did Paul mean when he said, "A wife is bound for as long a time as her husband lives"?

The question of whether divorced persons (both men and women) could marry had been previously answered by the apostle (verses 1-2; 8-9; 27-28). He now addresses other questions likely similar to the following: "If a woman’s husband dies is she still bound to him and if not may she marry who she wishes?" The answer given is that she is only bound as long as he lives and that if he dies she must marry "only in the Lord."

The above text only addresses questions that pertain to women, therefore is cannot be used to teach that only death ends a marriage. Death ends a marriage, but the word ONLY is neither explicit nor implied.

CHAPTER 32:

A DOCTRINE BASED UPON ASSUMPTIONS

Many Christians teach that one who is divorced may not marry, and if he does, he is sinning and cannot go to heaven. Their position is based upon what they think Jesus taught. But these notions are mere assumptions, as they are not based upon fact nor soundly and unequivocally grounded in scripture.

These teachers make the following mistakes: They assume that what Jesus supposedly taught *overrides* what Paul taught and that Paul's teachings are to be explained in a way that harmonizes with Jesus's teaching. Jesus dealt with a rather unique problem among the Jews while Paul answered questions asked by Christians, which he he straightforwardly answers.

> ***We make all sorts of assumptions because we do not have the skills, courage, or will to investigate.***
>
> Robert Waters

1. They assume that Jesus was talking about *divorce* when He said, "Whosoever shall put away his wife, except it be for fornication, and shall marry another, committeth adultery." But "put away" does not mean *divorce* in English; therefore, well-qualified and trusted translators were accurate when they did not translate *apoluo* as *divorce*.
2. They assume that one can be divorced yet still be "bound" even if the other spouse is free to marry and does marry another.
3. They assume that since the scripture says, "Let not man put asunder," man *cannot* end a marriage unless God gives his approval. First, that is obviously wrong as death definitely ends a marriage and people are known to murder their spouses. God certainly would not approve of this way of ending a marriage, but the marriage ends nonetheless. Second, while it is true that man may not end a marriage the way Jewish men were attempting to do (merely sending away), one can/ may end a marriage the way God prescribed (Deuteronomy 24:1–2). Whether the action is just

and proper has no bearing on whether the divorce does what God intended it to do.

4. They assume that since God binds a couple, only God can unbind. But marriage is a *covenant* or *contract* between a man and a woman. Thus, either party can terminate the relationship by following God's instructions.

5. Those who say the divorce must be for *fornication* before either party is free to marry assume that we can ascertain the facts, even though there are often numerous vague circumstances. And we do not have the equipment to judge hearts; however, we can be certain when a marriage ends (freeing the parties) by assuring that the simple procedure that God gave us, and practiced Himself, was followed.

6. They assume that "forbidding to marry" (1 Timothy 4:1–3) does not mean it is wrong to tell people they may have no marriage if they are divorced and that the text noted above applies only to practices within Catholicism. Nevertheless, if *anyone* asserts that a person who has no marriage may not marry without sin, then that person is doing what Paul condemns.

7. They assume "unmarried" does not mean not married, or without a marriage, and that Paul's words apply only to those that are "eligible" for marriage.

> I say therefore to the unmarried and widows, It is good for them if they abide even as I. But if they cannot contain, let them marry: for it is better to marry than to burn.
>
> 1 Corinthians 7:8–9

8. They assume that some people are not eligible for marriage based entirely upon what they have *assumed* Jesus taught. But Jesus was clearly teaching and explaining the Law of Moses, and if He taught contrary to that Law, which allowed the divorced to marry, He contradicted Moses. Virtually, all serious Bible students affirm that Jesus did not contradict Moses.

9. Some assume that Jesus's teaching was not applicable at the time Jesus spoke but was to be applicable when the New Covenant went into effect. This is an assumption deemed necessary to get around the above conundrum, but basic hermeneutics must be disregarded to accept the theory.

10. They assume that the phrase "let them marry" does not mean, "let them marry," except in the circumstances that fit or support their preconceived ideas.

11. They assume "loosed" means in the "eyes of God," or "a case where God approves of the divorce because it is due to unfaithfulness" rather than a legal/scriptural divorce.

> Art thou bound unto a wife? seek not to be loosed. Art thou loosed from a wife? seek not a wife. But and if thou marry, thou hast not sinned;
>
> 1 Corinthians 7:27–28

12. They assume that "not good for a man to be alone" does not apply to certain people who are on the wrong end of a divorce and that these people should be punished.

13. They assume that "every man" of 1 Corinthians 7:2 does not apply to those who are divorced.

> Nevertheless, to avoid fornication, let every man have his own wife, and let every woman have her own husband.
>
> 1 Corinthians 7:2

14. They assume that Paul's statement, "If they cannot contain let them marry," means, "If they will not contain do not let them marry." They believe all people have the power to contain if they wish to be faithful to God.

> But if they cannot contain, let them marry: for it is better to marry than to burn.
>
> 1 Corinthians 7:9

15. They assume that some marriages between a man and a woman that are legal, and recognized by the people as legal, are not marriages "in God's sight."

16. Many assume that "fornication" breaks the marriage bond "in God's eyes," but they assume that this fornication is adultery, which no text specifies. Actually, the act of adultery does not end a marriage in God's sight, for if it did the offended spouse could not forgive, which is contrary to Christianity, and would have to divorce the unfaithful spouse.

17. They assume that *adultery* is only a sex act committed by one married person with someone to whom he is not married. But Israel committed adultery with "stones and stocks" (Jeremiah 3:9), which obviously was not sexual. Also, Jesus said the man who *puts away* his wife and marries commits adultery against her, i.e., the wife he *put away.*

CHAPTER 33:

GROUNDS FOR DIVORCE

This chapter has little to do with the doctrinal issues pertaining to the "exception clause," about which much has been said in this book. We intend to present some practical thoughts pertaining to divorce. The quotation below is copied (by permission) from *Marriage for Moderns* by Henry Bowman was published in 1954 but is still true and relevant.

> Grounds for divorce may be considered from two related points of view. They are the reasons alleged by a person seeking divorce on the basis of which he asserts that he has been injured and claims that a divorce should be granted. Grounds are also the categories of reasons for which the law permits divorce and the courts grant it. Grounds and causes are not necessarily the same, either for divorce in general or for divorce of a specific couple. Usually what happens is something like this. A couple are incompatible. This leads one or both of them to commit some act—such as desertion, nonsupport, adultery—which is a symptom of maladjustment but does fall within the categories of the law. On this basis, one seeks divorce; or, being incompatible, they may agree that both want a divorce. They then fit their situation into the most convenient legal categories so that the plea of one conforms to legal requirements and a divorce may be decreed. In many cases, this amounts to a deliberate "trumping up" of grounds to satisfy the court. In New York, for example, where the only ground acceptable is adultery, a couple may agree to get a divorce. Then the husband hires an accomplice and witnesses to assist him in "proving" his "adultery," and a divorce is granted on this ground. For reasons such as these, statistics of divorce grounds do not give an accurate picture of conditions.

> This disparity between true causes and grounds alleged is both made clear and dramatized by what ordinarily happens in court when divorces are granted. In a typical court… no case is contested. The judge seldom challenges anything a plaintiff says. He seems to depend upon the attorneys to get the facts, although few of these facts are brought out in court. He has no way of getting at the facts himself. The court provides no agency for counseling or for attempting to reconcile the couples. The judge later admits that in his opinion at least half the plaintiffs did not deserve decrees on the basis of the evidence submitted; but he also feels that he was helpless to do anything about it and that refusing them divorces would only make them perjure themselves further and would not affect marital readjustment. He is earnest, honest and sincere, but has no background in psychology or sociology.

First, Mr. Bowman makes the valid point that couples seek divorce because they are incompatible and that "grounds" are often *forced*, or conjured up, so that the divorce might be granted. Second, in view of the difficulties that professional judges have determining the facts in marital affairs, on what basis can we be reasonably certain we have the facts necessary to make judgments as to who is "innocent," and therefore, allowed to marry, and who is "guilty," and therefore, doomed to a lonely life of celibacy? One particular comment by Foy Wallace Jr. is worth repeating here:

> With no course of action legislated, revealed or prescribed, we cannot make one without human legislation. The course of some preachers in demanding separations and the breaking up of family relations, and the refusal to even baptize certain ones whose marriage status does not measure up to their standard of approval, is a presumptuous procedure. It reveals the tendency to displace God as the Judge of us all, and a preacher ascends to the bench. More than teaching the moral principles involved, the preacher has no course of action revealed, and to establish one would result in human

legislation, more far reaching in evil consequences than the moral effects of divorcement limited to the persons involved. *The Sermon on the Mount and the Civil State*, p. 41.

It is neither the preacher's nor the elder's job to "ascend to the bench" in an attempt to determine (by human judgment) who is innocent and who is guilty and pronounce the judgment: "You are living in adultery" or "You will be committing adultery if you marry and must live the rest of your life celibate."

Next, comes the efforts to enforce the decree, which almost always result in the "recalcitrant" brother's rejection of the church and the Lord. What a distressing job preachers and elders often assign to themselves! Why not just obey the command of Paul who said, "Let them marry" (1 Corinthians 7:2, 8, 9, 27, 28)?

CHAPTER 34:

THE PROCESS OF DIVORCE IN THE OLD TESTAMENT

BY SAMUELE BACCHIOCCHI, PHD, ANDREWS UNIVERSITY
(Deceased)

The procedure required of a man intending to divorce his wife was for him to write out a bill of divorce and give it to her: "He writes her a bill of divorce and puts it in her hand and sends her out of his house... " (Deuteronomy 24:16). The wording of the bill of divorce was probably similar to the one generally used by the Jews of the Diaspora, which reads:

> On the _______, in the year__________from the creation of the world, in the city of___________, I,_____ ______________, the son of_________________, do willingly consent, being under no restraint, to release, to set free, and to put aside thee, my wife,___________ _______, daughter of_, who has been my wife from before. Thus I do set free, release thee, and put thee aside, in order that thou may have permission and the authority over thyself and to go and marry any man that thou may desire. No person may hinder thee from this day onward, and thou art permitted to every man. This shall be for thee from me a bill of dismissal, a letter of release, and a document of freedom, in accordance with the laws of Moses and Israel.____________the son of____________, witness._____the son of _________, witness.

The bill of divorce served several purposes. It deterred a hasty action on the part of the husband by restraining frivolous and rash dismissal. It testified to the woman's freedom from marital obligations from the husband who sent her away. It protected the woman's reputation, particularly if she married another man.

The process of divorce that Moses required was not a license to repudiate the wife at will, but rather “a stringent requisition that whoever did so should secure his wife from injury by certifying that she was not chargeable with unchaste conduct, but divorced upon some minor pretext.”

CHAPTER 35:

DEALING WITH SOME COMMON OBJECTIONS

Whenever something is presented to a person that is new and contrary to what they have been taught, it is natural that they will have objections and these must be met. Also, false accusations must be answered; therefore, I have endeavored to forthrightly deal with every objection I have heard to the position I hold on marriage and divorce. Below are some that might not have been dealt with previously.

"From the Beginning It Was Not So" Matthew 19:8

> "He saith unto them, Moses because of the hardness of your hearts suffered you to put away your wives: but from the beginning it was not so."

The above is often set forth as an argument that Jesus changed Moses' Law to how it was in the beginning when there was no divorce. While it certainly is true that Jesus was not happy with the Jewish men's idea that God was okay with the way they treated their wives, indication that He changed the Law at that moment not only lacks evidence to support such a claim but is met with insurmountable problems.

Back in verse three we see that the Jews asked about putting away for "every cause." Jesus responded that marriage unites two as "one flesh" (joined by God) and then noted that man should not seek to end the marital relationship due to trivial matters. The Jews replied, "Why did Moses then command to give a writing of divorcement, and to put her away?" In Mark's account of His response we see that Jesus strongly rebuked the evil practice of "putting away" (*APOLUO*ing) but not divorcing when He asked, "What did Moses command you?" (Mark 10:3). But defenders of tradition generally ignore Jesus' answer recorded in Mark's account, then proceed to twist what He said in Matthew's account to conform to the idea that Jesus was condemning the divorced to a life of celibacy.

Our text gives the reason Moses did nothing about the evil practice of putting away. Jesus said it was because of the "hardness of your hearts." This is often errantly interpreted to mean that Jesus was saying, "Moses allowed 'divorce' because of your bad hearts, but I'm taking it away—I'm changing it to how it was in the beginning." But think about it: Would the Jews not have immediately taken up stones to kill Jesus if He had actually asserted that He was making such a major change in the Law of Moses? Certainly they would have at least brought it up at His trial. Since they did not we must conclude that Jesus made no such declaration.

There is absolutely nothing in the statement "from the beginning it was not so" from which we can conclude that Jesus was doing anything more than condemning the Jews for their actions in thinking it was okay for them not to honor their commitment in marriage. The only reason anyone would want to change the meaning of *apoluo* to mean divorce or say Jesus changed the Law of Moses is to justify the traditional false teaching regarding divorce and subsequent marriage.

"We Have to Accept What Jesus Said"

It goes without saying that we must accept the words of Jesus, at least when His teaching is applicable to us. But we must be sure we are right regarding whether His words are applicable and also regarding what He actually said. We cannot accept a conclusion that makes our religion vain. If Jesus said what is attributed to Him by traditional MDR teachers, then he contradicted the Law of Moses. This means He sinned, and therefore, is not the Savior. If we really want to accept what Jesus said, we must be willing to give up tradition that, when put to the test, does not measure up. We must apply good hermeneutics in our study before we can be sure we believe and practice what Jesus actually said.

"So, One Can Divorce and Remarry as Many Times as He Wants?"

I have often heard the above objection to the teachings set forth in this book. The statement is somewhat inflammatory and seems to be designed more for building prejudice than as an argument. At any rate, one man argued that if Jesus was dealing only with *putting away*, then we don't have any scripture to teach against *divorce*, but that is not true.

First, the Jewish men under the Law of Moses, to whom Jesus's teaching was directed, were allowed to have more than one wife. And it seems to be evident that it was commonly thought by Jewish men that they could divorce and marry as often as they wanted to; but their actions received no justification from Jesus who explained Old Testament law. Let us now look at some Old Testament passages that refute the idea that one may divorce and remarry as often as he likes:

> Let thy fountain be blessed: and rejoice with the wife of thy youth. Let her be as the loving hind and pleasant roe; let her breasts satisfy thee at all times; and be thou ravished always with her love. And why wilt thou, my son, be ravished with a strange woman, and embrace the bosom of a stranger? For the ways of man are before the eyes of the Lord, and he pondereth all his goings. His own iniquities shall take the wicked himself, and he shall be holden with the cords of his sins.
>
> Proverbs 5:18–22

> Live joyfully with the wife whom thou lovest all the days of the life of thy vanity, which he hath given thee under the sun, all the days of thy vanity: for that is thy portion in this life, and in thy labour which thou takest under the sun.
>
> Ecclesiastes 9:9

Here are some New Testament passages that forbid Christians from divorcing:

> And unto the married I command, yet not I, but the Lord, Let not the wife depart from her husband: But and if she depart, let her remain unmarried, or be reconciled to her husband: and let not the husband put away his wife.
>
> 1 Corinthians 7:10–11

Since one cannot legally divorce without *departing*, *leaving*, or *putting away*, the above text teaches against doing so; however, it does not require a life of celibacy, as some insist.

In addition to the above, we have clear teaching that wives must "submit yourselves unto your own husbands" (Ephesians 5:22; Colossians 3:18; 1 Peter 3:1) and be "obedient to their own husbands" (Titus 2:5). Husbands are commanded to "love their wives" (Ephesians 5:25; Colossians 3:19). And, of course, the Bible teaches against lying, the need to keep one's promise, and the need to comply with the terms of a covenant (marriage).

In view of the passages noted above, it is clear that the objection discussed in this part is invalid; therefore, it is not necessary to twist Jesus's teachings in order to have a passage that teaches husbands and wives of their responsibility to be faithful to each other.

Let's now back up to what I said in the beginning: "One man argued that if Jesus was dealing only with *putting away*, then we don't have any scripture to teach against *divorce*, but that is not true." Let's turn the argument around. If Jesus was not dealing with the sin of putting away but not divorcing according to the Law, then we have Him ignoring the sin and no other teaching condemning the practice. Of course, He did condemn it clearly when He said the man "committeth adultery against her" (Mark 10:11).

"Legal Divorce Is What Moses 'Suffered,' which means the Context of Jesus's Teaching Was about Legal Divorce"

Mark's account of the gospel answers the above objection:

> And the Pharisees came to him, and asked him, Is it lawful for a man to put away his wife? tempting him. And he answered and said unto them, What did Moses command you? And they said, Moses suffered to write a bill of divorcement, and to put her away. And Jesus answered and said unto them, For the hardness of your heart he wrote you this precept.
>
> Mark 10:2–5

After Jesus answered the Pharisees' question with a question (verse three), they then made the statement: "Moses suffered to write a bill of divorcement, and to put her away." Notice that Jesus did not ask what "Moses" suffered—he asked, "What did Moses command you?" Then "they" (the Pharisees) replied to Jesus's question, but not exactly as it was asked. They added the word *suffered*, which means: "liberty, license, allow." We might be able to understand how they thought Deuteronomy 24:1–4 was something that was suffered. But Jesus replied, "For the hardness of your heart he wrote you this precept." The Pharisees changed the wording from "precept" to "suffer," but Jesus did not let them get away with it. He set them straight. This helps confirm the fact that Jews were failing to obey the precept or command to give the wife the "bill of divorcement" if the marriage was ended and that this non-legal putting away is what Jesus said is "adultery against her."

"Since the Time of John, New Testament Law Has Been Preached"

> For all the prophets and the law prophesied until John.
>
> Matthew 11:13

> The law and the prophets were until John: since that time the kingdom of God is preached, and every man presseth into it.
>
> Luke 16:16

The above passages are sometimes used in an effort to get around the fact that traditional teaching has Jesus contradicting Moses. Having read numerous commentators, I have yet to read one that even hints at the idea that the above passages support the idea that Jesus could teach contrary to the Law in effect while he lived.

These texts indicate that at the time the kingdom began to be preached, all the Jews had, as far as written record, were "the law and the prophets." From the time of John, as well as Jesus, those writings took a backseat to more *pressing* matters—the kingdom of God. When John, an Old Testament prophet, began his ministry, the Law was clearly in force, and it remained in force until the death of Christ (Hebrews 9:16–17).

"Divorce for Any Cause Encourages Divorce"

First, it is unfair and inaccurate to charge that teaching that a divorce ends a marriage and frees the parties to marry makes one guilty of encouraging divorce. It is also unfair and inaccurate to suggest that I believe that one may divorce for any reason. While the Bible teaches that a divorced woman may "go and be another man's wife" and that we are to let the "unmarried" marry, it also teaches the need for faithfulness. A true Christian will make every effort to obey Paul who tells husbands to "love your wives and be not bitter against them" (Colossians 3:19), and tells wives to "submit yourselves unto your own husbands, as unto the Lord" (Ephesians

5:22). People in the world are going to continue to divorce and be divorced regardless of what Christians teach. Christians will not think of divorcing their faithful spouse, and thereby breaking the covenant they happily made but instead will work diligently to make the marriage the best it can be.

Actually, it is the traditional position on MDR that encourages divorce. One preacher who I debated admitted that his teaching encourages "a race to the courthouse." He believes that only the one who initiates the divorce for fornication is free to marry, as he is the one that did the putting away "for fornication"; therefore, having been persuaded by such teachings, to assure that he is not the one divorced and required to remain celibate, he would immediately file for divorce if he learned his spouse has been unfaithful.

"You Are Promoting Adultery"

I have had the above statement directed at me a few times. It is obviously inflammatory and may have been designed to build prejudice. But since it is an objection the author has heard to his teaching it should be addressed.

It is easy to hurl out accusations—anyone can do it. But the question is, can it be proven? If Jesus really did teach that the divorced who marry are living in adultery, then the objection would be valid. But in view of the problems associated with that doctrine (which we have discussed at length), it must be rejected. Whether the objection is to be confirmed or deemed invalid must be based upon what the Scriptures actually teach. If *apoluo* (in Jesus's teachings) means *put away*, rather than *divorce*, and it does, one is not promoting adultery by allowing marriage after a legal divorce. This teaching, according to Paul, actually helps the divorced to "avoid fornication" (1 Corinthians 7:1, 2; 8, 9; 27, 28). In the case of the divorced, those who are most vulnerable to sexual sins, the traditional position on MDR takes away God's means of avoiding fornication, some of which could be adultery, and the charge therefore backfires.

"The Way of the Transgressor is Hard"

When it is pointed out that the traditional MDR position forbids marriage for those who need it, and it is therefore unjust punishment, often the reply is: "The way of the transgressor is hard." The first part of the text says, "Good understanding giveth favour" (Proverbs 13:15). Two verses previous the wise man said, "Whoso despiseth the word shall be destroyed: but he that feareth the commandment shall be rewarded" (Proverbs 13:13). Therefore, the emphasis is to have a good understanding of the will of God. Actually, when a man rejects what God's Word says because it differs with his tradition, he despises the Word. When one follows human tradition instead of God, he is a transgressor, and the way is "hard." The "way" for preachers who hold the traditional position on MDR is not easy. They diligently seek to teach souls the gospel but often see their efforts become fruitless because of their doctrine—the hard "way" they have chosen.

It is not easy for teachers of traditional MDR doctrine to tell a husband and wife, who they have taught and who are ready to obey the gospel that they must break up their marriage and family and live celibate if they want to be saved.

It is not easy for traditional MDR church leaders to tell new members who have moved into the neighborhood (after investigating or getting a confession) that they will not be accepted into fellowship because their marriage is "unscriptural."

It is not easy for a preacher of the traditional MDR position to stand before the assembly and preach that one who is divorced (to include those innocent of marital sin) is not eligible for marriage unless he/she marries the one who divorced him/her, which is often impossible and/or unscriptural (Deuteronomy 24:4). And it is not easy for these teachers to teach their doctrine in a forum where informed brethren are allowed to point out inconsistencies and various hermeneutical problems and present what the Bible actually says. Below is a scenario that sets forth the ultimate nightmare for the traditional MDR preacher. Put yourself in his shoes:

After you have taught the gospel to a young couple (with children), both of whom show all the signs of repentance and of being happy to have learned the truth, they are ready to obey the gospel and begin the Christian life. But you must do your duty and ask about previous marriages. The woman replies, "I was married once, but he divorced me so he could marry a woman he met at work." You are now deeply disturbed because of what you must now try to teach this couple. If they hear you and do as you suggest, you are devastated; but if they reject your teaching and reject the gospel, you are even more distraught. You tell the young woman that Jesus said a divorced person may not marry, that her present marriage is adulterous, and that before she and her husband may be baptized, they must agree to break up the marriage. You have to tell the woman she cannot ever marry again because she was divorced.

She replies, "You showed me where Jesus said 'My yoke is easy and my burden is light,' yet you say he demands that I remain celibate the rest of my life? How can this be? I want and need my husband, and my children need us to be a family. What have I done to deserve this? Your doctrine is not in harmony with the nature of God."

All you can think of is the usual response: "The way of the transgressor is hard." But she quickly responds, "What sin have I committed?"

Indeed, the way of the transgressor is hard, but who is the real transgressor in this scenario? In view of the apostle Paul's clear teaching regarding whether the "unmarried" are to be allowed to marry (1 Corinthians 7:8, 9, 27, 28), the answer is obvious.

Yes, the way of the transgressor is hard. But the teacher can be the transgressor if he teaches error. If the error he teaches causes a "little one" who believes on Christ to stumble, woe to him.

> And whosoever shall offend one of these little ones that believe in me, it is better for him that a millstone were hanged about his neck, and he were cast into the sea.
>
> Mark 9:42

"Your Idea That 'Put Away' Does Not Mean Divorce Is Contrary to Scholarship"

It is unfortunate that many have turned a deaf ear to the reasonable position set forth in this book for no other reason than that it differs with the teachings of many scholars. We must take the inspired advice of Paul who said "...not to think of men above that which is written, that no one of you be puffed up for one against another" (1 Corinthians 4:6). Scholars who define words are mere men. They are not inspired, and therefore, are subject to error. Divorce and marriage is a subject that has been tainted by Catholicism, which (generally) does not allow divorce no matter what the cause. Most of the great scholars of the past were either Catholic or were highly influenced by Catholic tradition.

We have noted a number of scholars that have supported the teaching set forth in this book by translations of the biblical language and their comments. Many of them are highly respected. Whether one is a scholar or just an ordinary Bible student, sometimes the only way he can determine the meaning of a word is by its usage in the context. When this is necessary, having a doctor's degree in the language does not give one a great advantage.

The text that is perhaps most often applied in defense of the idea that *apoluo* was "used of divorce" is the case of Joseph who was of a mind to "put away" Mary (Matthew 1:19). The text says, "Then Joseph her husband, being a just man, and not willing to make her a public example, was minded to put her away privily." Because it is assumed that Joseph and Mary were married at that time, the conclusion is commonly derived that the phrase "put her away" had reference to legal divorce. But the word for "husband" is the same word that is translated "man," and therefore, does not mean Mary and Joseph were married. It is clear that they were only *betrothed* or *engaged*, which is not *marriage*. They were, in fact, married later, which is further proof they were not married at the time Joseph considered putting Mary away (repudiating) for what he thought was an evil act on her part.

Actually, the context lends more support for the author's position than for the traditional position. Joseph, being a just man, intended to end the relationship because of her mysterious pregnancy. It was specified that this would be done privately. A legal divorce is not private. It requires a public document, and public declaration is made. Often divorces are published in local newspapers.

We find no biblical evidence that Joseph intended to divorce Mary. The scriptures do not speak of a need for divorce when no marriage exists. Some assert that it was a custom to actually go through some legal process to end an engagement. Nevertheless, God, not the people, gave the Law. Marriage is a marriage, engagement is engagement, and the terms are different. The thinking and custom of people do not change this fact, nor do they change God's Word.

Note the following from a highly-respected scholarly source:

> The fact that Joseph had in mind the putting away of his espoused wife, Mary, without the formality of a bill or at least of a public procedure proves that a decree was not regarded as absolutely necessary.
>
> (Matthew 1:19) *International Standard Encyclopedia*

The author quoted above made the point that Joseph did not have a mind to formally divorce. Thus, he evidently understood that what Joseph had a mind to do ("put away") was not equal to the formal procedure of providing the "bill of divorce."

The case of Joseph and Mary actually supports the position that "put away" is something that is done *without* papers and is not divorce. Jesus's teaching in Matthew 19:9, particularly the "exception clause," takes on a whole new meaning once we understand and accept what he actually said. We then see that Jesus did not contradict the Law and that he was not teaching that divorced persons commit adultery if they marry. This means that we do not have to practice "doctrines of devils" in "forbidding to marry" (1 Timothy 4:1–3), and we may (as commanded) allow marriage for those who are "unmarried" and have no marriage (1 Corinthians 7:2; 8, 9; 27, 28).

"That's Old Testament—We Can't Use It"

A common argument against using Deuteronomy 24:1-2 and Jeremiah 3:8 to teach that divorce ends a marriage is that these passages are found in the Old Testament; and, since the Law was abolished at Christ's death, we cannot turn to the Old Testament to establish doctrine (Jeremiah 31:29-31; Hebrews 8:6-9). On the surface, considering that that the church receives its authority from the New Testament, we might view the above contention as worthy of consideration. However, we must not overlook some important matters.

One, the Old Testament is God's word. It is "profitable for doctrine, for reproof, for correction, for instruction in righteousness" (2 Tim. 3:16). We cannot simply dismiss its principles without a just reason, particularly in matters pertaining to the institution of marriage, which existed prior to the church.

Two, the Old Testament, not the New, contains God's teaching on this subject, including the definition of marriage and divorce. These instructions were not included in the New Testament because, contrary to Catholic tradition, the church does not have authority in this area.

Three, we violate no church ordinance by following God's definition of marriage and divorce as contained in the Old Testament. No New Testament passage requires us to change the meaning of the terms "marriage" and "divorce."

Four, the focal point of the discussion Jesus had with Pharisees about divorce and marriage was the Old Testament. The whole basis of His argument is the information contained in Deuteronomy and Jeremiah.

Let's summarize what we have considered here: 1) The Old Testament is God's word; 2) the definition of divorce is found only in the Old Testament; 3) we violate no church regulation by accepting Old Testament authority on the subject of divorce and subsequent marriage; and, 4) Jesus confirmed the definition of divorce contained in the Old Testament. Based on these facts, it follows that rejecting God's proclamations in Deuteronomy 24:1-2 and Jeremiah 3:8 is simply to reject God's will regarding divorce.

"Moses' Law (Deut. 24:1-2) Did Not Release the Woman to Marry"

Those who teach the above reject what the KJV clearly says, but virtually ALL versions imply that a divorce obtained according to this law indeed freed the wife to marry. Verse FOUR gives an even stronger implication. It says the woman was defiled in regard to the FIRST husband after he divorced her, and he could not take her back. (To do so would amount to wife swapping.) There is no mention that another man could not marry the woman without committing adultery, or that she was "defiled" and could not marry another man. The very fact that she was given the divorce certificate indicates that it was designed to free her to marry another. Additional evidence that this was the case is that when God divorced Israel He made the point that He did not merely "put away" (repudiate, send away) but also followed the Law in giving the certificate. Why was this important? It was to end the marriage and free the wife. This wife of God is the same wife Paul referred to when he addressed "them that know the Law"—Israel. Israel (the church) is now married to Christ—she is His bride (Rom. 7:1, 4). Say what you want about verses 2 and 3. It will not change the fact stated in verse 4. It will still remain true that Israel ("them that know the Law") "should be married to another, even to him who is raised from the dead, that we should bring forth fruit unto God."

Those who hold the doctrine noted in the heading would have people believe that divorce as practiced under the Law did NOTHING. They evidently do not see a problem with God's allowing His people to believe their women were free to marry for thousands of years and then, right before the end of the dispensation, God sent Jesus to correct the Jews on their many errors but, on this law, He corrected Moses. This teaching is TWISTED, and those who teach it are WARPED. It is error gone to seed! It proves there are no limits to what people will say and do to defend their tradition.

"There Is Nothing in the New Testament That Addresses Giving a Bill of Divorcement to Your Covenant Spouse"

First, marriage predates even the Old Testament and is an institution that is applicable to all people of all times. The divorce law (Deut. 24:1, 2) was given to God's people and remains applicable to God's people. The New Testament provides no definition of divorce, but Christians who understand what "loosed" means respect God's law and when someone becomes "unmarried" (by divorce) we obey the command to "let the marry" (1 Cor. 7:7, 8). We believe and accept that they do not sin if they marry (1 Cor. 7:28).

Second, while it is true that we have no examples or teaching in the New Testament about giving a bill of divorcement to end a marriage, this does not mean that divorce is not found in this document or that God ceased to recognize divorce. The discussions

Jesus had with the Pharisees indicate the importance of the "bill of divorcement." Those who reject divorce as accomplishing what God intended it to do are happy to ignore Jesus' question found in Mark 10:3— "What did Moses command you?" And, of course, we know that God, in exemplifying His own divorce, emphasized the importance of providing the bill of divorcement as opposed to merely sending away, which would be contrary to the Law.

Third, the New Testament church has no authority over marriage and divorce. This might explain why we have no examples of actual divorce or examples of church leaders asking questions about marriages, investigating, making judgments, and issuing punishments in the form of breaking up marriages and imposing celibacy.

Some insist that Jesus did away with divorce, but there are serious problems with that idea, which we have discussed previously. He dealt with the sin of putting away but not divorcing according to the Law. He called such action adultery against the woman (Mk 10:11).

The WHOLE WORLD, including virtually all professed Christians (except for Catholics), has for thousands of years recognized divorce as making one *unmarried* and *loosed*, and it still does, and it is based on the teaching of the Bible.

"Moses Taught That the Divorced Woman Is *Defiled*"

Most commentaries follow and support the ancient position of the Catholics regarding Jesus' teaching on the "MDR" issue; therefore, they seek to interpret Deuteronomy 24:4 (as well as the first three verses) to make sense of what they think Jesus said. But a noted commentator, John Gil (Exposition of the Entire Bible), is an exception. Regarding the woman's being *defiled*, he writes:

"...with respect to her first husband, being by her divorce from him, and by her marriage to another, entirely alienated and separated from him, and so prohibited to him..."

Verse four states that the man who divorced this woman may not take her back—she is *defiled* as far as he is concerned. But, there is no reason to conclude that the woman even committed a sin based entirely on the fact that her husband divorced her. Nor is there reason to conclude that, after being divorced and married to another, the woman as well as the man she married would commit adultery or "live in sin." Many contend that this is what Jesus said, but would it not be strange for God to wait until the very end of the Mosaic dispensation to inform His people regarding this very important matter? Furthermore, is it not strange that the Jews did not understand Jesus to have taught such a doctrine contrary to Law?

Now, it makes sense that if a woman was merely *put away* (with no certificate) she would commit adultery if she married, as would the man she married (Matt. 5:32). But if a man was tired of a woman and divorced her, why would God punish the woman by saying she had committed some great sin, i.e. that the word *defiled* had reference to making her *impure* or *polluted*, and that she was not free to marry? Indeed, why require a certificate in the first place if it did not entirely free the woman of bondage to her husband "so she may go be another man's wife" and actually have a life?

"Moses Suffered Divorce—Not Putting Away" Mark 10:2-5

And the Pharisees came to him, and asked him, Is it lawful for a man to put away his wife? tempting him. 3 And he answered and said unto them, What did Moses command you? 4 And they said, Moses suffered to write a bill of divorcement, and to put her away. 5And Jesus answered and said unto them, For the hardness of your heart he wrote you this precept.

Let's look at this text step by step.

1. Pharisees came asking Jesus, "Is it lawful for a man to put away his wife? tempting him."
2. Jesus answered with a question: "What did Moses command you?"
3. The Pharisees replied that Moses allowed them to write a bill of divorcement and THEN "put her away."

4. Jesus responded, "For the hardness of your heart he wrote you this precept."

The Pharisees tried to entrap Jesus but instead got themselves entangled. They asked if it was lawful for a man to "put away" his wife, which Jesus could not answer with "yes" or "no" because of the ambiguity (and misuse) of the word "apoluo." Were the Pharisees referring to a true divorce, according to the Law, or were they using the word for what it actually means—merely putting away? Jesus simply asked them what Moses commanded on the matter. Their reply was that Moses "allowed" them to WRITE a bill of divorcement and THEN "put her away."

In their answer they actually clarified the matter regarding a true divorce, as opposed to what Jesus had previously condemned (mere putting away) in His sermon on the mount (Matt. 5). But the Pharisees sought to justify their evil actions against their wives by asserting that Moses "allowed" them to do this divorce, which they had accurately defined. At that point Jesus told them that the command (about which they had just spoken) was given because of their evil hearts. Thus, the divorce law was not what was "suffered"—it was a command. What was "suffered" or allowed (which is to say nothing was done about it) was putting away but not divorcing. Even though such action was "adultery against her" (Mark 10:11) it was mere separation (a common occurrence to this day), and at any time the man could take the woman back. Since it was difficult to determine whether a separation was intended to be permanent, and because the husband was the judge in the matter, no law was set up to deal with him regarding this mistreatment of his wife.

A lie may take care of the present,

but it has no future.

Are You One Who Debates Divorce and Marriage?
If so, then you should know:

1) **The issue is not** a matter of whether it is wrong to divorce a faithful wife or husband—it obviously is.
2) **The issue is**, does divorce do what God intended it to do (Deut. 24:1,2; Jer. 3:8)?
   a) It is one thing to say one commits sin by divorcing a faithful spouse.
   b) It is another thing to say the spouse he/she divorced is not divorced and must remain celibate the rest of his/her life, which might even involve breaking up a happy marriage with children. (See 1 Tim. 4:1-3)

www.TotalHealth.bz/marriage-and-divorce.htm

The phrase "God hates divorce" has often been quoted as an argument that divorce is sinful. And, yes, divorce can be sinful. It is wrong to divorce a faithful legal spouse.

But the word in Malachi 2:16 that is translated as "divorce" (in some versions) is not divorce as God defines it in Deuteronomy 24:1-2 and Jeremiah 3:8. The word in Malachi is the same word that is found in the last part of Deuteronomy 24:2, which is the LAST part of the divorce process. The word means sending away or putting the woman out of the house. Since one can do this sending away, or putting out, without completing the divorce process, it stands to reason that this word does not refer to divorce.

The corresponding Greek word is *apoluo* - it has the exact same meaning. Have you ever wondered WHY scholars do not, way down in the definition, add that this Hebrew word means, or is used of, divorce while they do so when defining *apoluo*? The reason is that the word came to be "used of divorce" (Thayer) but only by people who either did not know the word of God (His command regarding divorce, Mark 10:3) or who had no respect for it. See Strongs below and then Vines:

>"H7971

חלשׁ

shâl̀,lach

shaw-lakh'

A primitive root; to send away, for, or out (in a great variety of applications): - X any wise, appoint, bring (on the way), cast (away, out), conduct, X earnestly, forsake, give (up), grow long, lay, leave, let depart (down, go, loose), push away, put (away, forth, in, out), reach forth, send (away, forth, out), set, shoot (forth, out), sow, spread, stretch forth (out)."

Vines says *shalach* means: "to send, stretch forth, get rid of."

It was, and is, putting away, that does not free the woman to marry, that God hates. Of course, breaking promises and covenants is something He hates. However, divorce is not only the Law He gave for the benefit of the woman, but He made it clear that divorce can benefit all when He revealed to us that He used it Himself. His divorce ended the marriage he had with Israel and freed Israel to marry another. That Jesus married Israel (Rom. 7:1, 4) speaks loudly that marrying a divorcee, even a woman who has been unfaithful to her husband, is not sinful.

CHAPTER 36:

WHAT MAKES THE MOST SENSE?

When searching diligently for the truth regarding any matter, how one proceeds will determine whether he succeeds or fails in his noble effort. Often, young people ask their parents about matters that concern them. At their young age, they feel that the answer given must be correct simply because of the source—their parents who they trust. Unfortunately, many never set out to determine truth regarding who has a right to a marriage; they simply have always accepted, without question, whatever their parents and/or church taught. They hear "sound" gospel preachers preach on the subject of marriage and divorce— asserting how simple it is, how we must believe and obey Jesus, and that "the way of the transgressor is hard." But to obtain the truth, one must look at the various theories and ask himself: "What makes the most sense?" Let us look at two theories:

Doctrine 1:

> It is commonly taught (the traditional view) that Jesus said one who is divorced commits adultery if he/she marries again, thus he/she must remain celibate or go back to his/her original spouse. Let's note some problems with this theory:

Jesus was a Jew and lived under the Law of Moses. He was viewed as a *man* and expected to follow the Law, not contradict it. It is significant that before Jesus began to teach what many think condemns the divorced to a life of celibacy, He first stated that he had no intentions of changing the Law (Matthew 5:17, 19). It is clear that the Law allowed divorced women to marry (Deuteronomy 24:1, 2). Thus, if Jesus said divorced people commit adultery when they marry, He did not keep His promise and He contradicted (transgressed) the Law. The basis for Jesus's being the sinless sacrifice for our sins is that He lived a sinless life. But if He contradicted the Law, our religion is vain.

So now ask yourself if doctrine one makes any sense. If one argument is not enough, think about the fact that God is a just God, that He requires us to be just, and He has never made a law that requires innocent persons to be punished.

Also, think about the fact that a divorced (*loosed*) person is "unmarried" and that Paul commands all to "let them marry" and explains, regarding the "loosed," "thou hast not sinned" (1 Corinthians 7:8, 9; 27, 28).

Here is another problem: Paul spoke of "forbidding to marry" as being "doctrines of devils." Can one tell another that he has no right to marriage and not be guilty of that which Paul condemns?

Here is yet another problem: divorce ends a marriage, and Paul said to let every man and every woman have a marriage (1 Corinthians 7:1, 2) so they can avoid fornication. Thus, if we deny the divorced a marriage, we put them in a vulnerable position to sin and may cause many to turn from Christ.

Finally, this doctrine has no biblical harmony. It has Moses teaching what God did not want: Jesus contradicting Moses, Paul contradicting Jesus, and Paul contradicting himself.

Doctrine 2:

> Jesus taught that persons who are *put away* or *sent out of the house* commit adultery if they marry.

Scholars generally do not support the above as it is worded—many insist that *legal divorce* is under consideration. Sadly, some use this observation as the reason for rejecting what the text actually says. But shouldn't we make our own determinations as to what is truth?

Shouldn't we, for ourselves, look at the words in the Bible and decide how they are used elsewhere and in the context of the passage we are studying? Doctrine two (which I hold) is also contrary to tradition. But what our church teaches, or what we have been taught, may be wrong.

It is argued that the Greek word *apoluo* also means *divorce*. That "put away" is a proper translation of *apoluo* is not argued, but many have allowed themselves, contrary to the evidence, to become convinced that "put away" means *divorce*. I will not argue that *apoluo* has never been used by some to mean divorce, as it evidently was used by the Romans and others, who did not believe nor respect God's definition of divorce, and it is obvious that "put away" is used to refer to divorce by a number of preachers today. Some use "put away" in their writings on MDR to the extent that they sound ridiculous. It would make more sense and would better communicate what is intended if they would just say *divorce*. When language is misused enough, it eventually takes on a new meaning.

Words sometimes only partially communicate and leave room for speculation, theory, and conjecture. Below is an example of what I mean:

I met an old friend a couple of years ago that I had not seen in more than twenty years. I knew she had married a doctor but did not know anything about him or the marriage. She said to me, "I had to get rid of him." Now, "get rid of" could be interpreted in various ways. She might have meant she divorced him. Maybe she meant she just told him "it is over—we are through" and moved out. Perhaps, she said nothing at all but simply left his house. If my friend had wanted to clearly communicate the idea that she had divorced her husband, she could certainly have used the word *divorced*, or even said, "I gave him his walking papers." But since she was not specific, I cannot be absolutely certain what she meant. There is a remote possibility that the man she married was already married when he married her or that he was a first cousin, both of which would have made the marriage illegal. Thus, in such case, she would not have needed to do anything more than "put him away," which would be an end to the relationship.

Apoluo is found sixty-two times in the New Testament, and several excellent versions never translate it as divorce. No lexicographer gives "divorce" as the first meaning of *apoluo*—it is usually near the end where you might see the words "used of divorce."

Some conservative members of the church, who insist that "put away" means divorce, are even arguing that a divorce takes place even without the "bill of divorcement" and that such was the case during the time of Moses. They argue that the "bill of divorcement" was "not an integral part of the divorce." So we see the importance of looking to the Bible for our answers. Indeed, God gave the definition, and it included a "bill of divorcement." In fact, it was a command (Mark 10:3–5). Without the bill of divorcement, there was/is no divorce, except possibly the case noted in 1 Corinthians 7:15 previously discussed. When a man tries to divorce his wife, by merely "putting away" instead of God's way (Deuteronomy 24:1–2; Jeramiah 3:8), he is doing contrary to the command: "Let not man put asunder."

Doctrine two is simple. It allows us to believe Jesus's words exactly as He said them. We can believe them without contradicting any rule of hermeneutics. Evangelists who know and practice this doctrine will be encouraged in their work, knowing that they will not drive away more than 50 percent of those whom they teach and who are ready to obey the gospel. They also will not have to present the news to anyone (as the traditional view requires in many cases) that to be a Christian the family must break up, even though the marriage is legal, and the parents live celibate the rest of their lives.

I have had to change my position on divorce and marriage. I first believed the traditional view, which I accepted because it was all that I had heard. Then Olan Hicks helped me to learn that I had been deceived. I finally accepted doctrine two because it has no hermeneutical problems—it makes sense.

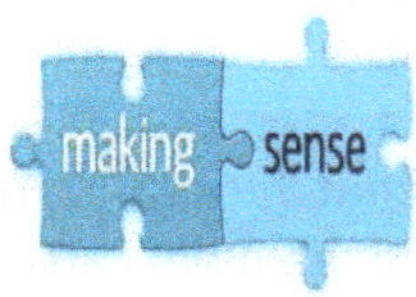

CHAPTER 37:

WHY ALL THE PASSION?

No subject has generated more passion among certain preacher circles in the last forty years than the popular MDR theory that attempts to determine "who may marry." This doctrine, which we shall refer to as the "traditional view," holds that the "divorced" must remain celibate. In recent decades, the concept has been vigorously promoted by Christian colleges and journals; however, I attended Florida College in the mid '70s, and I do not remember hearing it even mentioned. One has to wonder why many today are pushing their teaching with great fervor. Are they helping the Lord's cause or doing great harm? Are good hermeneutics being used when they study for their sermons, articles, books, tracts, and Facebook posts; or are brethren merely responding to the passion and jumping on the bandwagon? Evidently it is the latter, because the teachings of these men are unjust, morally wrong, and contrary to plain scripture.

All soldiers of Christ need passion for truth as well as love for the church and the lost. Love for truth will direct one to seek to understand Jesus and to hear Paul's teaching that demands that those who have no marriage be allowed to marry. People who love truth and seek the lost will think long and hard before attempting to twist Paul's teaching to harmonize with tradition that teaches the divorced must remain celibate.

Occasionally, someone accuses me of riding a hobby horse because of my passion and effort to reach others with what I believe to be the simple truth regarding marriage. Some have even accused me of not teaching on anything else. But a visit to my website www.TotalHealth.bz will reveal that my accusers are either uninformed or have deliberately made this false accusation. This illustrates that the problem is not just a matter of teaching. A number of preachers zealously seek to destroy the influence of those who disagree with their teaching and practice. Such criticism has little effect on me, and my detractors know it, but they also know that their attacks will be seen by others who will then be afraid to speak the truth. And their tactics are working. I know many preachers who have a correct understanding of marital issues but choose to keep a very low profile. They may teach individuals whom they view as honest and who love truth, in keeping with what Jesus said: "Give not that which is holy unto the dogs, neither cast ye your pearls before swine, lest they trample them under their feet, and turn again and rend you" (Matt. 7:6). This passage teaches that there are men who hate the truth that will seek to hurt us if we teach something they do not like.

Neither the apostles nor the pioneer preachers during the Restoration Movement taught that the divorced must be forbidden to marry. In the '60s several influential gospel preachers endeavored to divert the thinking, prevalent today, that churches must look into (investigate) and break up marriages that some question or deem to be unscriptural. And some clearly taught against the idea that the divorced may not marry. Below are some examples:

1) *Roy Lanier, Sr.*

> "Of course, my general advice to all is that they should obey the Lord's will, bring their lives into conformity with the demands of the Lord, but to determine whether a certain marriage is an adulterous relationship is not the preacher's responsibility, unless it is his own."
>
> 1 Corinthians 7:36, *Firm Foundation*, September 10, 1968, 588.
> Copied from *"The Truth About Divorce and Remarriage"* by Weldon Langfield.

2) *O.C. Lambert*

"There can be no doubt but that the church in the first century contained Christians who had been married more than once before conversion and were not required to separate."

Interview by James Woodroof (July 7, 1964) in Woodroof's *"Divorce and Remarriage."* Copied from *"The Truth About Divorce and Remarriage"* by Weldon Langfield.

3) *Foy Wallace Jr.*

"With no course of action legislated, revealed or prescribed, we cannot make one without human legislation. The course of some preachers in demanding separations and the breaking up of family relations, and the refusal to even baptize certain ones whose marriage status does not measure up to his standard of approval, is a presumptuous procedure. It reveals the tendency to displace God as the Judge of us all, and a preacher ascends to the bench. More than teaching the moral principles involved, the preacher has no course of action revealed, and to establish one would result in human legislation, more far reaching in evil consequences than the moral effects of divorcement limited to the persons involved. There are some things that are not subject to the law of restitution, things done in certain circumstances which cannot in later circumstances be undone, which remain as matters between God and the individual, and therefore reserved for the judgment. It is certain, however, that if the Lord Jesus Christ had intended a course of action in these cases, he would not have left it for preachers to prescribe, but would have himself legislated it."

The Sermon on the Mount and the Civil State, p. 41.

4) Dillard Thurman

> "When you try to teach a family about Jesus, do so without prying into their personal lives."
>
> *"Questions and Answers," Gospel Minutes,* August 1, 1980, 3.
> Copied from *"The Truth About Divorce and Remarriage"* by Weldon Langfield.

Had there been more, brave soldiers of Christ like these noted above, the tide might have been turned. Unfortunately, with few in number taking God's side the result was not unlike what happened when the ten spies contradicted Joshua and Caleb in their positive report to the people and their effort to embolden them to follow God's command to take the land. Those who lacked faith outnumbered the faithful spies and their great passion contributed to their disbelief, which influenced others; thus evil prevailed.

Friends, have you considered the implications of what many are teaching on MDR? First, their teaching actually has Jesus teaching the opposite of His actual intention, which was to put a stop to the evil practice of Jewish men's "putting away" but not divorcing, which He called "adultery against her" (Mark 10:11). The truth regarding the so-called "exception clause," the most perverted and misused phrase in all the Bible, can easily be seen once one understands that "put away," from the Greek word apoluo, is not divorce as defined by God (Deut. 24:1, 2; Jer. 3:8). It simply means that the man who sends away his wife, but does not follow Moses' teaching regarding divorce, does not "commit adultery against her" IF he is ending the "unlawful marriage" because of fornication. The context indicates that the type of fornication alluded to is a marriage that is not legal, and we have TWO examples of such illegal marriages in the New Testament (Matt. 14:4; 1 Cor. 5:1). Note the rendering of Matthew 5:31-32 by *Holman Christian Standard*:

> "It was also said, Whoever divorces his wife must give her a written notice of divorce. 32 But I tell you, everyone who divorces his wife, except in a case of sexual immorality, = fornication, or *possibly a violation of Jewish marriage laws* [emphasis added]

causes her to commit adultery. And whoever marries a divorced woman commits adultery."

While many think they are doing the will of God in "forbidding to marry" (which, by the way, Paul put into the category of "doctrines of devils") and are thereby helping God by preventing "adulterous marriages," their teaching actually benefits only the devil, and does so in many ways. Their teaching has: 1) Moses teaching what God did not like, even though he was inspired in his writings; 2) Jesus contradicting Moses who taught God's law; 3) Jesus breaking His promise not to change the Law before the cross; 4) Paul contradicting Jesus; 5) and Christians teaching that the divorced, even those innocent of sin in the matter, must remain celibate.

Requiring celibacy is contrary to the will of God that says "it is not good that man should be alone." Paul, who answered questions Christians asked regarding this important issue, said to let every man and every woman have a spouse; then he gave the reason: "to avoid fornication" (1 Cor. 7:1, 2). Thus, those who put tradition above Paul's teachings take away God's tool to help people avoid fornication. Paul went on to make it clear that the divorced are to be included among those whom religious leaders are commanded to allow to marry. Regarding the "unmarried" (divorced) he said, "let them marry" (1 Cor. 7:8, 9). Then he used different terminology to help assure it was understood that he was talking about the divorced. He contrasted the word bound (married) with the word loosed (divorced) and said in no uncertain terms that if a "loosed" man marries he does not sin (1 Cor. 7:27, 28). Unfortunately, some are teaching that one can be *bound* but not married and *loosed* but still *bound*. This theory arose due to desire to justify the traditional MDR teaching, but is nothing short of a denial of what Paul clearly taught.

At the beginning of this article I referred to the popular MDR teaching as a theory. It certainly is not factual because it is based on mere assumption regarding what Jesus meant, and the conclusion has many serious hermeneutical problems that make it unbelievable.

On the other hand, the truth is backed up by clear biblical teaching, such as presented above.

We SHOULD have passion for truth, as revealed in the Bible, and for the souls of those that are being lost because of the devil's most successful doctrine. He uses this "MDR" dogma to keep people out of the church, to cause people to leave the church, to divide churches, and to render ineffective sound preachers of truth. While unbridled passion, which Paul describes as "zeal without knowledge," can be a driving force for evil, passion for truth can be a driving force for good.

**Not everyone
or everything
deserves
your energy.**

CHAPTER 38:

LET NOT MAN PUT ASUNDER

> *Wherefore they are no more twain, but one flesh. What therefore God hath joined together, let not man put asunder* (Matthew 19:6).

In an effort to prove that there is no such thing as divorce, the above text has been interpreted by many to mean man CANNOT put asunder. But this is not what the verse says. It actually states that man SHOULD not do it; i.e., he should not attempt to do it HIS way. Rather, it should be done GOD's way if/when it is practiced. God explains how divorce is to be accomplished through Moses, and He even confirmed Moses' authority by revealing how He Himself procured a divorce from Israel (Deut. 24:1, 2; Jeramiah. 3:8).

> *Putting away* is merely PART of the divorce process, defined by God, and is therefore **not** THE process, or divorce itself.

Jesus addressed the problem of men's attempting to put asunder (divorce). He strongly rebuked an evil practice of the men of Israel when He said, "Whosoever shall put away his wife, and marry another, committeth adultery against her" (Mark 10:11). Most who attempt to teach on marriage and divorce get hung up at Matthew 19:9 and completely ignore Mark 10:11, which greatly helps us to understand what Jesus was teaching. Jesus said,

> "And I say unto you, whosoever shall put away his wife, except it be for fornication, and shall marry another, committeth adultery: and whoso marrieth her which is put away doth commit adultery."

In this text, Jesus was not attempting to change the Law of Moses that allowed the divorced woman to "go and be another man's wife." This law on divorce was to benefit women. Hence, to take away the law would be to undo a regulation that was designed for good rather than evil. Therefore, Jesus was attempting to correct the false Jewish notions regarding the Law, namely that they were wrong to break their vows in divorcing a faithful wife and wrong to "divorce" by merely sending away. God's law regarding divorce was just one of many laws the Jews had turned from, bringing on themselves condemnation (Matthew. 15:9; Colossians 2:22; 2 Pet. 3:16). Jesus addressed the concept of unbiblical divorce— "putting away" (man's putting asunder) but not giving the bill of divorcement; this action resulted in the woman's committing adultery if she took up with another man.

The Jewish men of Jesus' day had left the word of God and were practicing, to some extent, the type of "divorce" that was practiced by the world. John Trap said,

> "The Athenians and Romans had their divorces also. Their bill was only this, Res tuas tibi habeto, Take what is thine own, and be packing,"
>
> John Trap Commentary of the Old and New Testament, Mark 10:3.

In our day teachers of tradition who seek to justify their practice of breaking up marriages and imposing celibacy argue one of the follow: 1) Moses never taught that the divorced woman may marry; or it was taught, but God did not approve or recognize the marriage; or 2) Jesus changed the Law to how God intended it from the beginning—doing away with God's law on divorce. (Many argue that Jesus just changed the divorce law to add "fornication" as the only "reason" or "cause" whereby God would recognize the divorce.) The truth is, MAN is not to put asunder—it will not work because God will not recognize the divorce. Sending away, repudiation, putting out of the house, leaving or departing (resulting in separation) is not divorce as God defined it; and it will not dissolve a marriage.

CHAPTER 39:

TEN PIECES OF EVIDENCE THAT PROVE JESUS DID NOT SAY DIVORCED PEOPLE COMMIT ADULTERY IN A SECOND MARRIAGE

Let's begin this study by looking at the definition of two words that are very important to this topic: “evidence” and “prejudice.”

Evidence is:

> *"that which tends to prove or disprove something; ground for belief; proof"* (Dictionary.com);
>
> *"the available body of facts or information indicating whether a belief or proposition is true or valid"* (Web);
>
> *"A thing or things helpful in forming a conclusion or judgment"* (The Free Dictionary).

Evidence should be our sole criteria for making judgments pertaining to biblical issues. The word "prejudice" means to "pre-judge," and this is what we do if/when we make judgments or draw conclusions without first honestly evaluating evidence.

Prejudice is *"An opinion formed beforehand, esp an unfavorable one based on inadequate facts"* (World English Dictionary).

With the above defined words in mind let us now look closely at the following basic facts and comments so that we might draw a true and accurate conclusion pertaining to the question “Who may marry?”

1. Jesus said a woman that is "put away," which is only part of divorce process, commits adultery if she marries another. We must accept what Jesus said rather than what is assumed and asserted to be true by men who purport to be scholars (1 Cor. 4:6). Some scholars claim that *apoluo* is "used of divorce." The one text noted as evidence is Matthew 1:19 where the couple obviously were not yet married (Matt. 1:19); thus, it is apparent that using this as a reason to define *apoluo* as legal divorce is not warranted.

Divorce is defined in Deuteronomy 24:1-2, and Jeremiah 3:8-14 to include a certificate to be given to the woman so she may marry another. Good hermeneutics, when applied, will not allow for the idea that *apoluo* was used by Jesus to indicate any more than the common meaning of the word.

2. Jesus promised not to change the Law (any part of it) before "all is fulfilled" (Matt. 5:17-19). The Law (Deut. 24:1, 2) allowed the divorced woman to "go be another man's wife." Thus, Jesus could not have said a divorced person commits adultery if he/she marries because this would make Him a liar—a consequence that true friends of Jesus cannot accept. The Law allowed the woman to "go be another man's wife," and the man could have multiple wives.

3. If Jesus taught that a divorced person commits adultery in a subsequent marriage, he obviously meant during the time of the Mosaic dispensation since his comments were directed to the Jews while the Mosaic Law was in effect. Yet, Jesus' enemies, who sought to destroy him, did not charge him with teaching contrary to the Law regarding divorce. This must be given great consideration when seeking to determine what the Bible teaches regarding the question "Who may marry?" Some insist that this kind of argument proves nothing. Yet Paul used such logic to prove that he was not, as some charged, teaching the Law. He said, "And I, brethren, if I yet preach circumcision, why do I yet suffer persecution? then is the offence of the cross ceased" (Gal. 5:11).

4. If Jesus taught that a divorced person commits adultery in a subsequent marriage, then Moses taught what God did not want. It is argued that Jesus changed the Law of Moses because Moses merely allowed divorced women to marry because of the hardness of men's hearts. But is that really an argument that the divorce law was temporary? Have men changed?

5. If Jesus taught that a divorced person commits adultery in a subsequent marriage, then why do preachers today apply the

teaching to both women and men contrary to the context they use to support their teaching (Matt. 19:9)? This text simply does not say a man commits adultery if he marries another. Jesus explained that the man commits adultery "against her" (against the woman he sends away rather than with the woman in a new marriage, according to Mark 10:11). Since it is an indisputable fact that the man could have more than one wife, he was never forbidden to have a spouse or to take another—whether he divorced a current wife or just sent her away. The sin the man committed, explained in Mark's account, was not the sin of divorce (though that is not being justified by Jesus), but rather the sin of NOT following God's law for divorcing, which placed a hardship on the woman.

6. If Jesus taught that a divorced person commits adultery in a subsequent marriage, then God is not fair and just since such teaching would punish (with celibacy) innocent persons who are divorced against their will. Not only is God just, he teaches us to be just (Prov. 17:15, 26; Lev 19:26; Deut. 16:20).

7. If Jesus taught that a divorced person commits adultery in a subsequent marriage, we then are confronted with clear teaching of Paul that we must ignore, or accept the lame explanations of men that merely twist or pervert Paul's words (1 Tim. 4:1-3; 1 Cor. 7:1-2, 8-9, 27-28).

8. If Jesus taught that the divorced, who are then "unmarried" (see 1 Cor. 7:8, 9), may not marry, then why would Paul command Christians to "let them marry"? Could it be that the answer is given in 1 Corinthians 7:1-2—so that individuals (both men and women) might "avoid fornication"?

9. If Jesus taught that a divorced person commits adultery in a subsequent marriage, then why would Paul speak of the "loosed" (death and divorce are the only circumstances that loose one) as being able to marry without sin (1 Cor. 7:27-28)?

10. If Jesus taught that a divorced person commits adultery in a subsequent marriage, why did God make it very clear that his divorce of Israel, according to the Law (which teaches by example,

Deut. 24:1-2; Jer. 3:8, 14), freed Israel to marry another (Rom. 7:4)?

Conclusion

The gist of Paul's teaching in 1 Corinthians 7 is clear: marriage, when needed (because of sexual requirements), must not be forbidden. Yet, regardless of the biblical evidence against it, this is exactly what is being carried out in many churches (see 1 Tim. 4:1-3) by men who purport to be strongly against following the teaching of men but who agonizingly practice human tradition that destroys souls and churches, and discourages and stifles evangelistic efforts. Paul used such language as "if they cannot contain let them marry," and to the "loosed" (divorced or widowed) he said "if thou marry thou hast not sinned."

CHAPTER 40:

HOW IMPORTANT IS IT THAT WE BE RIGHT ON THE MARRIAGE AND DIVORCE ISSUE?

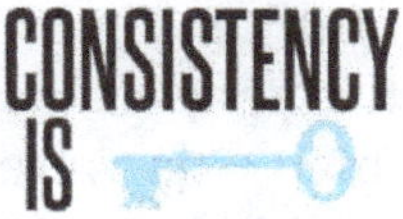

Since we will be judged by our individual actions it is prudent that we ask ourselves the above question, especially if we attempt to teach the word of God. Thus, if someone leads you to believe error on this important issue the consequences (and they are grave) will be suffered by more than the two of you. When you carefully and honestly consider the consequences you should appreciate the concern I have for being right on the matter of whether a divorced person should be allowed to marry.

> "What you need to learn, children, is the difference between right and wrong in every area of life. And once you learn the difference, you must always choose the right."
> D Jeanne DuPrau

First, what does it mean to be "right"? Well, it means we have the facts, the truth that the Bible teaches. Therefore, when we give advice as to what the Bible says to divorced people we will be giving advice that is what God wants them to hear. Their actions, based on that advice (should they listen), will then be for their benefit, rather than to their detriment.

Second, how can we know we are right? Because so many different opinions are out there some might conclude that we cannot really know. But if we use the applicable hermeneutical rules for studying this subject we can be certain, especially after our view has been tested by competent debaters, that we have the truth. Unfortunately, many preachers, who ordinarily use good hermeneutics, disregard this practice when studying about divorce and marriage. The standard, then, becomes something other than the word of God and the truth becomes a lie. (http://www.totalhealth.bz/marriage-divorce-remarriage-hermeneutics.htm)

When Christians, or potential Christians, are faced with the decision as to whether to remain as they are (1 Cor. 7:20, 24) or break up their home and live celibate, they want the truth. It is a serious matter, not only because vows have been made but because a new spouse's soul, as well as the children's, could be lost along with one's own if God's instructions are not followed. What are God's directives regarding those who have been divorced? The answer to this question is not as easy as it should be because of the various standards of authority to which people look. The following are the three main sources or standards of authority: 1) what Jesus said; and 2) what Paul said what tradition says. To learn the truth one must seek a position that allows the entire Bible to be in harmony. To do this, we need to know that Jesus addressed Jewish men who were *putting away* but not divorcing as the Law prescribed (Mark 10:3). Much evidence shows this to be true: 1) The word *apoluo* is found 111 times in the Greek New Testament. In several trusted English versions, like the ASV, it is not translated as divorce even one single time. 2) The men involved had a motive for putting away their spouses. You see, the old custom of men's giving a dowry to the bride's father had changed. The men were, at the time of Jesus, taking the dowry from the bride's father with the understanding that if they divorced their wives, they would give the dowry to the wives for their livelihood. 3) The declaration that a woman divorced according to Deuteronomy 24:1, 2 "may go and be another man's wife," must be in harmony with what Jesus taught, for He could not contradict what God had established. Thus, Jesus could not have been talking about divorce when He said a "put away" (GK *apoluo*) woman commits adultery if she marries another. 4) Some Jewish men are to this day failing to obey the command to give the divorce, or "get" as it is called. Thus, Jewish women are chained to men who neither love nor support them. Such actions by these Jewish men were, and are, no small matter. Jesus told the men of His day that they were committing adultery against their wives (Mark 10:11). But how could that be true if they actually gave their wives the divorce they wanted so they could marry another?

Does the Bible present TWO standards? No. God has only one divorce/marriage law, and it was given for all people for all time.

That law, of course, comes from the Bible. It just so happens that the first part of the Bible, the Old Testament, contains God's divorce law. It is found in Deuteronomy 24:1-4 and is confirmed by God Himself in Jeremiah 3:8. It is not problematic to appeal to these passages for guidance regarding divorce because the instruction is not found in the New Testament. Furthermore, since marriage is not regulated by the church, preachers cannot justly charge that those who appeal to these passages are seeking to be justified by the Law (Gal. 5:4).

We have seen that Jesus dealt with a unique Jewish problem. Through inspiration, the apostle Paul answered questions asked by Christians. In 1 Corinthians 7 Paul makes some very clear statements regarding whether or not a divorced person may marry. Unfortunately, many feel compelled to ignore or twist what he said because their standard is based on a misapplication of the problem Jesus dealt with among the Jews before the church was established.

Let us now note the clear teaching of Paul. In 1 Corinthians 7:1, 2, Paul says to let every man and woman marry and then gives the reason for the command— "to avoid fornication." In verses 8 and 9 he speaks of the "unmarried" (divorced people are definitely unmarried) and says "LET THEM MARRY." Then in verses 27 and 28 he contrasts those "bound" (married) with those "loosed" (divorced) and says they do not sin if they marry. Thus, the truth is to be found in this chapter written by Paul, to a society that certainly had problems with marriage and divorce. And, it is not out of harmony with what Moses taught nor with what Jesus taught.

When a Christian teaches error it might be due to ignorance and the consequences might not be great, depending on the specific issue. But if a preacher deliberately teaches what he knows is not true, or allows others to do the same without opposition, then the consequences for his own soul can be great. More importantly, he may lead others down the wrong path—the "path to destruction." Instructing a new convert, or potential new convert, that he/she must break up a marriage and live celibate is not action prescribed from God. The only New Testament examples we have of a marriage that is "unlawful" or "fornication" is that of Herod and Herodias and the man who "had his father's wife." Herod's marriage was illegal because he had married his brother's wife while the brother was still living, which was contrary to the law (Leviticus 18:16). The other example was a sinful situation that Paul said was not even practiced among the Gentiles (1 Corinthians 5:1). While many preachers of our day insist Jesus taught that a divorced person commits adultery by marrying, God made it clear that this doctrine did not come from Him, but, in fact, came from Satan (1 Timothy 4:1-3). To teach a doctrine that is of Satan and which benefits only him is to follow a path away from God, and it is not a narrow path. Jesus said many would follow it (Matthew 7:13).

Countless souls have been lost due to preachers giving an ultimatum to those whom they have diligently sought to save. Divorced people who have married again are told they must either live celibate, which often involves breaking up a happy and productive home, or they are refused baptism or fellowship with the church. Considering the fact that around one-half of the people an evangelist reaches with the gospel will be in what many consider to be an "unscriptural marriage," they will drive away about 95 percent when the ultimatum is presented. So the importance of being right becomes abundantly clear.

In the first century, the Lord's church grew very rapidly because of the "pyramid factor" ("each one teach one"). But the gospel would never have been preached to the world if the preachers had been persuaded of the need to investigate previous marriages that would have resulted in a very high number of potential converts being driven away.

Leaders of governments generally appreciate Christianity, when it is practiced according to the morals and principles of the Bible. But who cannot sympathize with leaders who would be unhappy having evangelists come to their country only to break up marriages and impose celibacy on many of their citizens?

CHAPTER 41:

SUMMARY

It seems to be taken for granted by many that when Jesus condemned the practice of "putting away" a wife, he was talking about divorce, as we understand it today. But if that was the case, why have translators not consistently used the word *divorce* instead of *put away* where *divorce* is supposedly (according to many) the meaning? It is argued that *put away* and *divorce* mean the same thing, but is this true? Is it possible that the Jews were practicing "putting away" their wives, and this practice was something different from a legal divorce and did not dissolve the marriage, regardless of the reason for the separation?

The Law under which Jesus lived (and was obligated to follow) made provisions for a marriage to be dissolved (Deuteronomy 24:1–2 and confirmed by God, Jeramiah 3:8).

> When a man taketh a wife, and marrieth her, then it shall be, if she find no favor in his eyes, because he hath found some unseemly thing in her, that he shall write her a bill of divorcement, and give it in her hand, and send her out of his house. And when she is departed out of his house, she may go and be another man's wife.

We see, then, that God laid down the procedure for a man to dissolve a marriage. This command was a procedure consisting of three separate actions (see below). Previous to this, men were simply *putting away* or *sending* their wives *out of the house* (women did not have the same rights). At that time, men were permitted to have more than one wife and received a dowry also, but if a man divorced his wife, then the dowry had to be returned. The dowry, however, did not have to be returned if there was no formal divorce. We can see, then, that simply sending his wife out of the house was a way for a man to avoid financial loss; however, the consequences were very serious for the wife: without a formal divorce, she was left without a home and a means of support; and, being still married, it was not lawful for her to marry. For a married woman to have sexual relations with another man was considered an act of adultery that was punishable by death (Leviticus 20:10). Husbands who dealt treacherously with their wives (by putting them away and marrying another, which was contrary to the teaching of Moses) were committing adultery against them—adultery meaning "covenant breaking" or "breaking wedlock." (See Mark 10:11 and Ezekiel 16:38, ASV, BBE, and CEV.)

In Luke's record of Jesus's teachings, we see that Jesus was talking to men who were lovers of money. He talked about the rich man and Lazarus and He brought in the issue of men's *putting away* their wives. He was showing that it was their greed that kept them from giving the decree so they wouldn't have to give back the dowry. Their actions were described as *adultery*. Mark's account observes that their actions were "adultery against her," i.e., the wife who was *put away* (Mark 10:11; Luke 16:14–20). The wife that was *put out* of the house may well have been innocent of any wrongdoing, yet she could not marry another without a certificate of divorcement that proved her marriage was legally dissolved. Thus, husbands who refused to give a bill of divorcement to women they had *put away* were disobeying God. It is interesting that the same evil practice among the Jews is still going on to this day. (See chapter 5: "Jewish Women in Chains.")

Nowadays, in most countries, wives, too, are permitted to divorce their husbands; consequently, women are not vulnerable to being left homeless and destitute the way Jewish wives often wee, and are to some extent, due to their husbands' refusal to present them with divorce papers. Nevertheless, the same sort of thing is experienced by both women and men today! People who have been divorced are being told by church leaders that, being divorced, they are ineligible for marriage and must remain unmarried or face the loss of fellowship in their church.

During the Mosaic age, a husband would often send (put) his wife away (Heb. *shalach*, Grk. *apoluo*) without a certificate of divorce. In God's sight, though, the husband committed adultery against her. Furthermore, his wife would find herself homeless and destitute and unable to marry; to do so would be to commit adultery, and any man who married her would commit adultery (see Mark 10:11; Matthew 5:31–32), a crime that was punishable by death (Leviticus 20:10).

However, God laid down a procedure to prevent such evils and protect wives from such treachery. This procedure consisted of three actions: writing her a bill of divorcement, placing it in her hand, and sending her away (Deuteronomy 24:1–2).

Interestingly, nothing in Jesus's teaching even suggests that the *man* who initiates "divorce" commits adultery (Matthew 5:31–32; Mark 10:11). Seeing this, some people, contending that the "put away person" has no right to marry, reason that a person needs only to ensure that he is the one filing for divorce. (This suggestion is imprudent as it tends to encourage divorce because people feel compelled to divorce when they have the "grounds" and before the other spouse divorces them, making them a "put away person" and "ineligible for marriage.") But the real significance to this observation is that the men would not commit adultery in the marriage with another because they were allowed to have more than one wife. We can find no evidence that the men discussed in the context (which goes back to Deuteronomy 24:1–4 for the specific passage of the Law) were divorcing their wives "for fornication" or because their wives had committed adultery. Since the Law called for the death penalty for adultery, this theory lacks credence (Leviticus 20:10).

Jesus, like all faithful Jews, was obedient to the Law. No one could accuse Jesus of changing the Law (before the cross) because He Himself promised, "Till heaven and earth pass, one jot or one tittle shall in no wise pass from the law, till all be fulfilled" (Matthew 5:18). In view of this, we see a serious error with the traditional teaching, attributed to Jesus, that a *divorced* person commits adultery if he marries. The problem, then, in understanding who has a right to marry, hinges on the meaning of *divorce*. Many of the newer Bible versions translate the Greek word *apoluo* as divorce, but the older and more reliable versions consistently translate *apoluo* as "put away" (or something similar).

Let us now note a couple of definitions from *Random House Dictionary* and make some observations:

Divorce:

1. Law. a judicial declaration dissolving a marriage in whole or in part, esp. one that released the husband and wife from all matrimonial obligations.

2. any formal separation of man and wife according to established custom, as among uncivilized tribes.
3. total separation; disunion: a divorce between thought and action.
4. to separate by divorce: The judge divorced the couple.
5. to break the marriage contract between oneself and [one's spouse] by divorce: She divorced her husband.

Judicial Separation

> Law. a decree of legal separation of husband and wife that does not dissolve the marriage bond. Also called limited divorce.

It is interesting that some contemporary writers use the phrase "put away person" when referring to a divorced person. This is misleading because "put away" is equal to being *separated*, not divorced—according to the Law of Moses. Even a *judicial separation* is not a divorce and does not end the marriage. While it is true that a divorce does separate a couple, it is also true that a couple can separate without divorcing. A married couple that separates might claim they are divorced but, in reality, they are still married. Those who teach that "putting away" a spouse (without a "bill of divorcement") constitutes a divorce are not only teaching error, but make Jesus a liar! If a "put away" person equals a "divorced" person, then Jesus broke his promise that the Law would not change until all was fulfilled (Matthew 5:18). When a woman who is "put away" (or separated) marries another, she obviously commits adultery. But it is important to understand that God gave a procedure for divorcing that would allow the divorced woman to marry another. Jesus could not possibly have contradicted Moses on this because to do so would have been transgression and would have given the Jews just cause to condemn Him. Interestingly, they did not charge Jesus with breaking the Law on this matter, yet people today (supposedly, his friends) contend that He did.

The apostle Paul spoke to the "unmarried" person in 1 Corinthians 7:8–9. The word *unmarried* means: single, unattached, free, not married, "not joined to another by marriage" [*Encarta Dictionary*]. To anyone who might not understand his universal divorce law, which freed the divorced, God gave a direct command:

"Let them marry." Unfortunately, a misunderstanding of Jesus's teaching has led many to ignore or try to explain away this command.

Many believe the only time God recognizes a divorce is when fornication has been committed, which they insist has to be the *cause* of the divorce, and it frees only the initiator of the divorce to marry. This is based on their conception of what Jesus was teaching in Matthew 19:9:

> And I say unto you, Whosoever shall put away his wife, except it be for fornication, and shall marry another, committeth adultery: and whoso marrieth her which is put away doth commit adultery.

The misunderstanding centers around two things: 1) the phrase "put away" and, 2) the definition of *fornication*. We have already discussed the meaning of *put away* so we will focus on the meaning of *fornication*. The word *fornication* is often believed to be a general term for any type of illicit sex. But consider the following quote:

> The Old Testament commandment that a bill of divorce be given to the woman assumes the legitimacy of divorce itself. It is this that Jesus denies. (Unless the marriage is unlawful): this 'exceptive clause,' as it is often called, occurs also in Matthew 19:9, where the Greek is slightly different. There are other sayings of Jesus about divorce that prohibit it absolutely (see Mark 10:11–12; Luke 16:18; cf 1 Corinthians 7:10, 11b), and most scholars agree that they represent the stand of Jesus. Matthew's 'exceptive clauses' are understood by some as a modification of the absolute prohibition. It seems, however, that the unlawfulness that Matthew gives as a reason why a marriage must be broken refers to a situation peculiar to his community: the violation of Mosaic Law forbidding marriage between persons of certain blood and/or legal relationship (Leviticus 18:6– 18). Marriages of that sort were regarded as *incest* (*porneia*), but some rabbis allowed Gentile converts to Judaism who had contracted such marriages to remain in them. Matthew's 'exceptive clause' is against such permissive-ness for Gentile

> converts to Christianity; cf the similar prohibition of *porneia* in Acts 15:20, 29. In this interpretation, the clause constitutes no exception to the absolute prohibition of divorce when the marriage is lawful.
>
> (www.usccb.org/nab/bible/matthew/matthew5.htm)

The word *fornication*, that Jesus uses in Matthew 19:9, refers to the violation of Mosaic Law forbidding marriage between persons of blood relationships. The only two examples of unlawful marriages, or fornication, that we have recorded in the New Testament are the man who "had his father's wife" (1 Corinthians 5:1) and Herod who married his brother's wife (apparently after divorce) while his brother still lived (Mark 6:18; Leviticus 20:21).

With this in mind, we offer the following paraphrase of Matthew 19:9:

> And I say unto you, whoever shall put away his wife without a certificate of divorcement, except for the cases of an illicit or illegal marriage, and shall marry another, committeth adultery: and whoso marrieth her that is put away without a certificate of divorcement doth commit adultery.

Three versions lend support to the accuracy of the above paraphrase: *The New Jerusalem Bible*, the *New American with Apocrypha*, and the *Holman Christian Standard Version*. These are quoted in chapter twelve.

The idea that Jesus was giving the grounds for a "scriptural" divorce and that only the one who initiated the divorce may marry another is not in harmony with the Bible. Such a doctrine has God not only punishing innocent persons, contrary to his nature, but also has Him contradicting Himself. When the apostle Paul (by inspiration) dealt with questions pertaining to marriage, he said to let men and women have a spouse so they can avoid fornication (1 Corinthians 7:1, 2). By teaching men to "love their wives" (Colossians 3:19) and women to "be in subjection" to their husbands (Ephesians 5:22), he teaches against separation and divorce; but obviously it happens. Yet only during the "present distress" were those who were separated commanded to remain "unmarried" or in the state they were in—as no command, example, or inference teaches that divorced persons must remain celibate. That idea is an assumption that is based on false premises.

In his answer to the brethren in Corinth, Paul makes it clear that people should marry, if necessary, to avoid fornication. He says to anyone who would object to the unmarried marrying: "Let them marry" and "if thou marry, thou hast not sinned." We therefore must accept that a legal divorce dissolves a marriage and that "unmarried" persons do not commit adultery when they marry. Paul's teaching in 1 Corinthians 7:1–2, 8, 9, and 27, 28 should leave no doubt in our minds that divorced persons may scripturally marry another. For a church to refuse to accept a couple because one person in the marriage has been divorced is to place an unnecessary burden on the couple and their children, which often results in their turning away from Christ. Thus, Paul's classifying "forbidding to marry" as "doctrines of devils" (1 Timothy 4:1–3) surely condemns the traditional teaching and practice of forbidding legally divorced persons to marry or continue in a legal marriage already contracted. Persons who are "unmarried," which includes those legally divorced, must be allowed to marry if the need is there, for they do not sin if they do. On the other hand, one who is guilty of "forbidding to marry" does indeed commit sin.

Conclusion

Acts 2 records the first gospel sermon being preached after the resurrection. Three thousand were baptized that Pentecost day and added to the church (Acts 2:41). In this chapter, we find no record of a discussion of divorce or of anyone's being questioned regarding his marital status. In only two places in the New Testament do we see a "marriage" questioned, and in both cases the problem was that the marriage was *incestuous* and *illegal*.

Yet the traditional practice today is to continually preach against "re"marriage (not even a scriptural term), question any who wish to be baptized or join local membership, reject any who marry after divorce, and mark and have no fellowship with any who oppose the traditional teaching. This practice profits only the devil, whose doctrines inspire such actions (1 Timothy 4:1–3). Jesus said that a woman who is *put away* commits adultery if she marries another. Many who think "put away" means divorce teach that the divorced may not marry and insist they live a celibate life. Those who teach this are usually seeking to do the right thing and want to please God regardless of the consequences; however, in trying to please God they are, in fact, displeasing him.

On a different matter, Jesus said, "If you had known what 'I want mercy and not sacrifice' means, you would not have condemned the innocent" (Matthew 12:7, ISV). Well, disciples across the land that have condemned the innocent to a life of celibacy would not have done so if they had known that "put away" does not mean divorce. Fortunately, slowly but surely, the truth is reaching those who are seeking it. Yet courageous religious leaders need to stand up not only for the truth but also for the "innocent" who are condemned to a life of celibacy. By teaching the principles set forth in this book, men will help evangelists in their efforts to convert souls, and at the same time, defeat one of the devil's most successful efforts to destroy us.

It is so important that we use good hermeneutics in our study of important subjects like divorce and the question of whether the divorced may marry. Good hermeneutics requires that we consider many things before drawing a conclusion. Unfortunately, many have drawn a conclusion simply because others have asserted it to be true (based upon one text) and are either too blind to see, too proud to change, or simply don't have the faith to deal with the earthly consequences of going against tradition.

> **The true follower of Christ will not ask, "If I embrace this truth, what will it cost me?" Rather he will say, "This is truth. God help me to walk in it, let come what may!"**
>
> A.W. Tozer

WORD STUDY

Divorcement

Hebrew:
Strong 8473H כּריתוּת
kerı ythûth ker-ee-thooth'
From H3772; a *cutting* (of the matrimonial bond), that is, *divorce*: -
- divorce (-ment) ו
Usage: 8473H כּריתוּת *kerı ythûth* Total kjv Occurrences: 4
divorcement, 3
Deuteronomy 24:1,
Deuteronomy 24:3, Isaiah 50:1 divorce, 1
Jeremiah 3:8

Greek: *apostasion*
King James Concordance
Total KJV Occurrences: 3 divorcement, 3
Matthew 5:31, Matthew 19:7, Mark 10:4

Thayer
G647 αποστασιον *apostasion*
1) divorce, repudiation
2) a bill of divorce

"Put Away"

Strong 1797H ׁחלש *shâlach shaw-lakh'*

A primitive root; to *send away*, for, or out (in a great variety of applications): --- X any wise, appoint, bring (on the way), cast (away, out), conduct, X earnestly, forsake, give (up), grow long, lay, leave, let depart (down, go, loose), push away, put (away, forth, in, out), reach forth, send (away, forth, out), set, shoot (forth, out), sow, spread, stretch forth (out).

Thayer

Greek: G630 απολύω (*apoluo*)

1) to set free
2) to let go, dismiss, (to detain no longer)
   2a) a petitioner to whom liberty to depart is given by a decisive answer
   2b) to bid depart, send away
3) to let go free, release
   3a) a captive, i.e. to loose his bonds and bid him depart, to give him liberty to depart
   3b) to acquit one accused of a crime and set him at liberty
   3c) indulgently to grant a prisoner leave to depart 3d) to release a debtor, i.e. not to press one's claim against him, to remit his debt
4) used of divorce, to dismiss from the house, to repudiate. The wife of a Greek or Roman may divorce her husband.
5) to send one's self away, to depart

King James Concordance

G630 απολύω (*apoluo*)

Total KJV Occurrences: 111

away 27; go 13; put 13; release 13; let 10; sent 7; send 6; released 4; at 2; depart 2; dismissed 2; liberty 2; loosed 2; set 2; departed 1; divorced 1; forgive 1; forgiven 1; lettest 1; putteth 1

If we had not been led to assume that *apoluo* (put away) means the same thing as "divorce" because of traditional teachings that go back even before the writing of the KJV, the teachings of Jesus in Matthew 19:9 would much more likely have been understood. Jesus did not use any words that were properly translated "divorce" or "bill of divorcement" except in the few places where it was apparent that "papers," to make it legal, are implied. The Greek word *apostasion* is translated "divorcement" and found three times in the KJV. All instances of the use of this word are in the Gospels and legal divorce is implied. These texts are Matthew 5:32 and 19:7 and Mark 10:4.

Shalach

Shalach is the corresponding word in the Old Testament for *apoluo* that is translated "put away" in the New Testament. Since, some, in defense of their belief that *separation* is *divorce* contend that *shalach* means divorce the following evidence. Copied from: http://studybible.info/strongs/G1544 is provided:

LSJ Gloss: ἐ κβάλλω

to throw

Dodson: ἐκβάλλω

I throw, cast, put out, banish, bring forth, produce

Strong's: ἐκβάλλω

to eject (literally or figuratively) Derivation: from G1537 and G906;

KJV Usage: bring forth, cast (forth, out), drive (out), expel, leave, pluck (pull, take, thrust) out, put forth (out), send away (forth, out). G1537 G906

Thayer:

1) to cast out, drive out, to send out 1a) with notion of violence

   1a1) to drive out (cast out) 1a2) to cast out

   1a2a) of the world, i.e. be deprived of the power and influence he exercises in the world

   1a2b) a thing: excrement from the belly into the sin

Vine's Expository Dictionary of New Testament Words

Bring, Bringing, Brought, Cast, Drive, Driven, Drave, Drove, Leave, left, Put, Send, Take, Thrust

Bound

It is important that we understand the meaning of this term because some are teaching that one can be *bound* to another even though not married. Others are saying one can be married to another but not bound. The latter would make sense in the case of an *illegal marriage*. The former makes no sense.

Thayer G1210 δέω deō

1) to bind tie, fasten

   1a) to bind, fasten with chains, to throw into chains 1b) metaphorically

   1b1) Satan is said to bind a woman bent together by means of a demon, as his messenger, taking possession of the woman and preventing her from standing upright 1b2) to bind, put under obligation, of the law, duty etc. 1b2a) to be bound to one, a wife, a husband

   1b3) to forbid, prohibit, declare to be illicit

Art thou bound unto a wife? seek not to be loosed.
Art thou loosed from a wife? seek not a wife.

1 Corinthians 7:27

Evidently one *bound* to a wife was *married*, legally.

Loosed

This term is very important because it is the Greek word that most closely pertains or applies to divorce, as we use the word.

Thayer G3080 λύσις lusis

1) a loosing, setting free

   1a) of a prisoner

   1b) of the bond of marriage, divorce

2) release, ransoming, deliverance 2a) of liquidating a debt

3) means or power of releasing or loosing

> For the woman which hath an husband is bound by the law to her husband so long as he liveth; but if the husband be dead, she is loosed from the law of her husband.
>
> Romans 7:2

It is evident that the woman whose husband died would no longer be under the law regarding him. What was the law? It was their *marriage*. (When two make a covenant it is essentially a law. Christ's law is called a *covenant* and a *marriage* is also involved; Galatians 6:2; Romans 11:27; Revelation 21:9.) Does the above passage teach that a woman would still be under the law (the bond of marriage) if her husband *divorced* her or if she divorced him? No. The passage does not say that, and to draw such a conclusion would be to take it out of its context.

> Art thou bound unto a wife? seek not to be loosed.
> Art thou loosed from a wife? seek not a wife.
>
> 1 Corinthians 7:27

The apostle Paul gave a command that was at least partly due to the "present distress." He commanded those *loosed* from a wife not to take a wife. I think most agree that *loosed* here means the couple got a *legal divorce*, resulting in freedom from responsibility toward the previous spouse. It might be argued that "loosed" is applicable only in the case of the death of the spouse; however, if in Romans 7:2, Paul intended to limit his words to the case of the spouse dying, why the admonition to "seek not to be loosed" in the letter to the

Corinthians? Did he mean "do not murder your spouse"? No, he obviously used the word in this instance to refer to *divorce*. Of course, he goes on to say that one "loosed" or "divorced" does not sin if he does marry.

Did the apostle contradict his own previous teaching by "forbidding to marry" when he said, "Seek not a wife" (1 Timothy 4:1–3)? Obviously, this was advice that was applicable because of the "present distress." He went on to say (verse 28) that a couple would not sin if they married. Thus, one "loosed," whether by death or legal divorce, would not sin if he married even if he went against Paul's advice. What does "loosed" mean? Does it mean the divorce must be "for fornication"? No. We find no indication of that. It simply means that the tie no longer exists, i.e., the bond (or binding) is removed or taken away. It evidently applies to persons who have not merely been "put away" but who have received a "bill of divorcement."

Depart

The meaning of the word *depart* is important in our study because of the importance of properly understanding 1 Corinthians 7:11.

> But and if she depart (chorizo), let her remain unmarried, or be reconciled to her husband: and let not the husband put away his wife.

Strong

[Grk. 5563] chorizo (kho-rid'-zo)

from 5561; to place room between, i.e. part; reflexively, to go away:—depart, put asunder, separate.

It is evident that *chorizo* does not mean divorce. First, it is not given in the definition. Second, the context (in the passage above) indicates that the woman is still married because the husband is exhorted not to put her away, which evidently is an exhortation to keep her in the house and remain a husband to her. Third, she is to "reconcile" with her husband rather than marry, which she would need to do if an actual divorce had taken place.

Adultery

(See chapter 13)

Fornication

This term is important because of its usage in the "exception clause," where it is often thought to refer to adultery in a marriage; however, as noted below, it can be "incest," which indicates the exception clause could be applicable to an illegal marriage, as some versions so translate.

The KJV New Testament Greek Lexicon:

> illicit sexual intercourse
> adultery, fornication, homosexuality, lesbianism, intercourse with animals, etc.
> sexual intercourse with close relatives; Leviticus 18 sexual intercourse with a divorced man or woman; Mark. 10:11,
> metaph. the worship of idols of the defilement of idolatry, as incurred by eating the sacrifices offered to idols

Treacherously

This term is important to our study because it describes the way Jewish men were treating their wives, which contributes to the reason for calling their action "adultery against her" (Mark 10:11).

Strong:

898H דגב

bâgad baw-gad'

A primitive root; to cover (with a garment); figuratively to *act covertly*; by implication to pillage: --- deal deceitfully (treacherously, unfaithfully), offend, transgress (-or), (depart), treacherous (dealer, -ly, man), unfaithful (-ly, man), X very.

King James Concordance:

Total KJV Occurrences: 48

treacherously, 23; transgressors, 8; treacherous, 6; deceitfully, 2; transgressor, 2; offend, 1; transgress, 1; transgressed, 1; transgresseth, 1; unfaithful, 1; unfaithfully, 1; very 1

A chapter by chapter study guide
is available at
http://www.totalhealth.bz

Or contact the author:
RobertWaters@yahoo.com

BIBLIOGRAPHY

Bowman, Henry A. *Marriage for Moderns*. McGraw-Hill, Book Company

Callison, Walter. *A Gift of God's Love*. Leathers Publishing, 2002.

Collins, Dyrel. Marriage Is God's Plan. South Bend, Texas, 2001.

Dawson, Samuel G. *Marriage, Divorce & Remarriage, The Uniform Teaching of Moses, Jesus & Paul.* Amarillo, Texas: Gospel Themes Press, 2002.

God's Kingdom Ministries, Jones, Dr. Stephen E. 03/14/2009, God's Laws on Sexual Sins—Part 5 (Law of Hammurabi) http://www.gkmnetsite.godskingdom.org/daily-weblogs/2009/03-2009/gods-laws-on-sexual-sins-part-5/

Gola, Stephen. *Divorce Hope*. Port Carbon, Pennslyvania. Hicks, Olan. *Divorce & Remarriage, The Issues Made Clear.* Searcy, Arkansas: Gospel Enterprises, 1990.

Joseph, Norma Baumel. *Jewish Women in Chains, Jewish Federation of Palm Springs* and Desert Area, Layfield, Lavelle.

Langfield, Weldon. *The Truth About Divorce and Remarriage.* Weldon Langfield Publications, Bakersfield, California.

When Marriages Bomb, There Is A Balm in Jesus Christ. Athens, Texas: LayMar Publishers, 2003.

Nobles, Sherman. *God Is a Divorcé Too! --- A Message of Hope, Healing, and Forgiveness*. Mustang, Oklahoma: Tate Publishing & Enterprises, LLC, 2004.

All the following may be found at www.TotalHealth.bz:

Smith/Waters Debate, J.T. Smith and Robert Waters.

Thrasher/Waters Debate, Dr. Thomas Thrasher and Robert Waters. *Thrasher Publications, 1705 Sandra Street S.W. Decatur, Alabama,* 35601–5457, 2007

Holt/Waters Debate, on Divorce and Remarriage, by Jack Holt and Robert Waters

Donahue/Waters Debate, on Divorce and Remarriage, by Pat Donahue and Robert Waters

Galloway/Waters Debate, on divorce and remarriage by Bryan Galloway and Robert Waters. The discussion is about whether Jesus taught new law.

Willis, Mike. *Truth Magazine*. Dayton, Ohio: April 3, 1980, XXIV: 14, pp. 227–230. Article about Deuteronomy 24:1, 2.

Other Publications:

Denham/Waters Debate

Divorce and Remarriage Thrasher/Waters Debate

Divorce and Remarriage Waters/Donahue Debate

Divorce and Remarriage Holt/Waters Debate

Divorce and Remarriage Galloway/Waters Debate

Divorce and Remarriage: Did Jesus Contradict the Law

Martin/Waters Debate: Deals with whether Schools and Foundations have a right to exist.

Bible Authority
51-page book on Bible authority. Sermons/class materials fully outlined.

The Ultimate Survivalist
What does it take to be the ultimate survivalist? Could it be YOU?

A Young Preacher's Dilemma
Written in the form of a play, this is a fictional account of a young preacher, Phillip, who is faced with a dilemma when he discovers that his friends, George and Angela, are, according to the traditional teaching on marriage, divorce, and remarriage, in an unscriptural marriage. How will Phillip react? Will he convince George and Angela that they need to divorce to get in a right relationship with God? What will he do if they refuse? 55 pages

Marriage and Divorce: A Clear and Intelligible Exposition (Tract)

The Security of the Believer

"Brother Waters has done excellent work in this booklet and it deserves to be read and studied by any sincere brethren. He denies all Calvinism but at the same time he advocates full assurance and confidence for the faith child of God." -- Leslie Diestelkamp

Continual Cleansing Verses Perfectionism (Tract)
"My thanks to you for sending me a copy of your excellent booklet, CONTINUAL CLEANSING VS PERFECTIONISM. It is a very forthright, effective and convincing presentation. I believe you to be right in each argument therein. I have preached this comforting doctrine for nearly sixty years. I never heard it questioned until recently. All scholarly men among us of every persuasion have taught it either directly or indirectly. -- Guy N. Woods

All the above can be downloaded for free at www.TotalHealth.bz

"Do you not know that in the Bible it is MARRIAGE FORBIDDING that is condemned and a component of apostasy, not marriage permitting?"

Olan Hicks

(1 Timothy 4:1-3)

If you are divorced you are in the category of the "loosed" and the apostle Paul clearly states, "If thou marry, thou hast not sinned" (1 Cor. 7:28). Being divorced puts one into the category of the "unmarried." Paul commands, "***Let them marry***" (1 Cor. 7:8, 9). **It is *truth* versus *tradition*. *Tradition* forbids marriage.**

www.TotalHeath.bz

Waters Publications
178 Madison 8657
Huntsville, AR 72740

Email: RobertWaters@yahoo.com
Website: www.TotalHealth.bz

Review Guide for "Put Away But Not Divorced."
http://tinyurl.com/y2285efu

www.ingramcontent.com/pod-product-compliance
Lightning Source LLC
Chambersburg PA
CBHW050654170426
43200CB00008B/1289
* 9 7 8 1 9 4 3 2 4 5 7 5 8 *